Roles of Wine
Japanese

I. Beginner

II. middle stages

III. where they are
now.

Daughters of the Moon

In the beginning, woman was the Sun...
Now she has become the Moon.

Motto of Seitō, 1911–1916

A publication of the
Institute of East Asian Studies
University of California
Berkeley, California 94720

The Japan Research Monograph series is one of several publications series spon-
sored by the Institute of East Asian Studies in conjunction with its constituent
units. The others include the China Research Monograph series, whose first title
appeared in 1967, the Korea Research Monograph series, the Indochina Research
Monograph series, and the Research Papers and Policy Studies series. The Institute sponsors also a Faculty Reprint series.

Correspondence may be sent to:
Ms. Joanne Sandstrom, Editor
Institute of East Asian Studies
University of California
Berkeley, California 94720

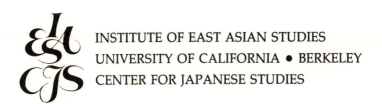

INSTITUTE OF EAST ASIAN STUDIES
UNIVERSITY OF CALIFORNIA • BERKELEY
CENTER FOR JAPANESE STUDIES

Daughters of the Moon

Wish, Will, and Social Constraint
in Fiction by Modern Japanese Women

VICTORIA V. VERNON

Although the Institute of East Asian Studies is responsible for the selection and acceptance of manuscripts in this series, responsibility for the opinions expressed and for the accuracy of statements rests with their authors.

Funding for research on this work was provided by a dissertation grant from the American Association of University Women and a postdoctoral fellowship from the Center for Japanese Studies at the University of California, Berkeley.

Yosano Akiko, "The Day When Mountains Move" (p. 1), Atsumi Ikuko, "Different Dimensions" (p. 33), and Nishi Junko, "Revolution" (p. 135) reprinted from Kenneth Rexroth and Ikuko Atsumi, editors, Women Poets of Japan. Copyright © 1977 by Kenneth Rexroth and Ikuko Atsumi. Reprinted by permission of New Directions Publishing Corporation.

"The Inn of the Dancing Snow," translation of Sata Ineko's "Yuki no mau yado," first appeared in Occident (Berkeley) (Winter 1981). Translated with author's permission. Reprinted by permission.

"The End of Summer" (Kurahashi Yumiko's "Natsu no owari") translated with author's permission.

Contents

I am obnoxious to each carping tongue
Who says my hand a needle better fits,
A poet's pen all scorn I should thus wrong,
For such despite they cast on female wits:
If what I do prove well, it won't advance,
They'll say it's stol'n, or else it was by chance.

Anne Bradstreet (?1612–1672)

A woman writing literature is truly culpable,
How bear the praising of the moon and singing of the wind!
Grinding down an inkslab is not my duty
Merit is achieved by wearing out the gold embroidery needle.

Chu Shu-chen (early twelfth century)

...But as the days and nights have gone by in monotonous succession, I have had occasion to read most of the old romances and I have found them masses of the rankest fabrication. Perhaps, I think to myself, the events of my own life, if I were to put them down in a journal might attract attention, and indeed those who have been misled by the romances might find in it a description of what the life of a well-placed lady is really like.

Michitsuna no haha (died ca. 950), *Kagerō nikki*

The day when mountains move has come.
Though I say this, nobody believes me.
Mountains sleep only for a little while
That once have been active in flames.
But even if you forgot it,
Just believe, people,
That all those women who have slept
Now awake and move.

Yosano Akiko, "The Day when Mountains Move"

BACKGROUND

CHAPTER ONE

Introduction

IN THE WEST, especially in England and the United States, the twentieth-century woman has become conscious that she has no story and no official history. Gerda Lerner, president of the Organization of American Historians in 1981–1982, captured this situation in the title of her work *The Majority Finds Its Past*,[1] in which she attempts to uncover some of the buried roots of the history of women in the United States. Half a century earlier, in England, Virginia Woolf spoke for writers when she lamented the lack of major woman authors in her nation's early literary history. In *A Room of One's Own* (1928), she posits the existence of a Judith Shakespeare, sister of William, whose genius was lost because her sex precluded her from the development and exercise of it. Summing up her tale, Woolf observes, "Any woman born with a great gift in the sixteenth century would certainly have gone crazed, shot herself, or ended her days in some lonely cottage outside the village, half witch, half wizard, feared and mocked at."[2] This may certainly be true of the England she describes, but we need not assume the universality of this situation. What, we might well ask, if there were a time and place when this had not been so? What if there were a culture in which the accomplishments of women writers had early been recognized and valued, in which the literature had been founded largely by women, thus affording the modern writer a past of which she might be proud, an example she might emulate? Such a situation need not be

---

[1] (Oxford: Oxford University Press, 1979).

[2] Virginia Woolf, *A Room of One's Own* (New York: Harcourt Brace Jovanovich, 1929), p. 51.

considered hypothetical; it is the situation of Japan's modern women writers.

The Western reader, fed, if at all, with an image of the Japanese woman as yielding and submissive, a delicate Madame Butterfly, might find this fact something of a surprise. And it is to this reader—who may already be aware that the single most monumental work of classical Japanese letters, *Genji monogatari* (The Tale of Genji, early eleventh century),[3] was written by a woman, Murasaki Shikibu—that the ensuing chapters will seek to introduce some of the modern inheritors of Japan's unique literary past. Twentieth-century Japan is, of course, not at all the same world that came to life in Murasaki's hand-written scrolls, but it is nevertheless true that today women are once again a vital force in Japanese literature. In contrast to the image of Madame Butterfly (distillation of a dream of the exotic that combines French and Italian fantasies in the encounter of a doll-like Japanese woman with the brash, unthinking American who destroys her), the works of Japanese women themselves present a different view. Their works are the product of experience as well as fantasy, and they challenge not only the Western view of the Japanese woman but also that presented in works by contemporary Japanese male writers.

The variety and power of modern-day literature by Japanese women defeats in advance any attempt at easy generalization. First of all, the Western critic must be sensitive to the fact that different paradigms have informed the literature of Japan from its early stages. Even feminist criticism in the West, with its recognition of the relationship between social context and literary production by women, must hesitate before the richness and difference of writing by Japanese women. As Westerners, we need to realize how much of what we perceive is the culturally conditioned product of a particular social past and to acknowledge how great a challenge to our views can be posed by the very different past of a Japanese culture in which literary expression was part of the birthright and the way of life of a distinct class of women writers. When we consider the historical background of Japanese literature, then, "Can women write?"

---

[3] I have given the English title only when a Japanese work is available in an English translation.

is not the same question as it has generally been in the West. Ability is not at issue there, for in Japan, more than in any other nation, that issue had been resolved before it was ever formally raised. As we shall see in more detail in the following chapter, in the Heian, or classical, period of Japanese literature (794–1185), women composed significant poetry and clearly dominated the field in prose. It appears that Japan once had a wealth of Judith Shakespeares who were not denied the opportunity to exercise their literary talents.

The unique situation in classical Japanese letters has, of course, led to much inquiry into the relationship between the literary text and the social context from which it arose. Even in the West, most historical studies of the period take cognizance of the crucial role that the woman writer played in the culture of the time. Ivan Morris, for example, in choosing to title his study of the Heian years between about 950 and 1050 *The World of the Shining Prince*,[4] underscores the fact that our present view of that age is indelibly colored by Murasaki's *Tale of Genji* and Sei Shōnagon's *Makura no sōshi* (Pillow Book) as well as by prose classics written by other women. It is the contention of the present work, however, that such an inquiry is of equal importance in understanding the literature of modern writers. They, after all, represent what might be called the "second wave" of women writers; for, strange as it may seem, the early magnificence of Heian women's writing was gradually to diminish with ensuing centuries, until the woman writer of prose had virtually disappeared from Japanese letters by the Tokugawa period (1603–1867). Since women had clearly demonstrated their ability to create literature of the highest quality in the early stages of Japanese literary history, factors other than innate capacity must have come into play. We must ask ourselves, then, why the progressive silencing of the woman writer occurred in the postclassical ages—the Kamakura (1182–1333), Muromachi (1338–1573), Momoyama (1573–1600), and the Tokugawa—and what were the historical and cultural conditions that favored the resurgence of writing by women in the modern age. As their widely fluctuating fortunes as writers in different ages suggests, Japanese women have been especially vulnerable to social and ideological constraints; thus, their literature offers a particularly

---

[4] (Oxford: Oxford University Press, 1964).

valuable record of the way in which such constraints can be both depicted and resisted in language. We must always remain conscious, however, that the experience of the Japanese woman writer has a particular historical context with its own pattern, a pattern not of progressive emergence from a silent past, but of an early glory followed by a gradual eclipse in the ensuing centuries.

Because the Heian prose writer was so successful as an artist, her manner of writing, her perceptual stance, and her aesthetic orientation, where they can fairly be generalized at all, have become naturalized in the tradition as its source and first mainstream. Thus, all Japanese writers, male or female, are to a great extent the inheritors of a common tradition that is often explicitly labeled "feminine." So it happens that imitation of the early prose models has not generally been regarded by the Japanese as a symbol of weakness or deviation but as evidence of faithfulness to a native tradition of refined taste. Male writers, then, acknowledging the Heian woman as the creator of the early prose art of the Japanese language, did not hesitate to adopt much of her style and approach. In fact, even before women writers had produced the greatest of their masterpieces, Ki no Tsurayuki, the renowned poet and aesthetician, assumed the guise of a woman diarist in composing his famous *Tosa nikki* (Tosa Diary, 935).[5] Other male writers in later centuries were frank in their admiration for the style and quality of literature by Heian women; Yoshida Kenkō, for example, held up Sei Shōnagon's *Pillow Book* as the model for his own *zuihitsu* (collection of miscellaneous notes or essays), *Tsurezuregusa* (Essays in Idleness, ca. 1330). More recently, Kawabata Yasunari, the winner of the 1968 Nobel Prize for Literature, could be (and has been, as we shall see) classified as among the most "feminine" of modern writers by virtue of his delicate sensitivity, allusive language, internalized point of view, and intuitive and associative narrative progression[6]—that is, if we were to accept uncriti-

---

[5] The Western reader cannot help but be struck by the difference between his motivation and that which lay behind the pen names selected by Mary Ann Evans (George Eliot), Amandine Aurore Lucie Dupin (Georges Sand), and Charlotte, Ann, and Emily Brontë (Currer, Acton, and Ellis Bell).

[6] For some of these qualities he was awarded the Nobel Prize as being particularly representative of "Japanese" sensibility. Kenneth Rexroth and Atsumi Ikuko point out in *Women Poets of Japan* (New York: New Directions, 1977) that Kawabata is perhaps

cally most popular definitions of "feminine" writing, whether originating in Japan or in the West.

Despite the high value placed upon the original prose models, however, we need to keep in mind that women's writing was subsequently to exert a very uneven influence upon the Japanese literary tradition. The actual history of women's participation in the prose production of the ages that followed the Heian reminds us that their efforts cannot be equated with the established continuum of Japanese letters. Changes in prevailing religious and political ideologies were to make clear just how dependent literary production by women can be upon particular moral, political, and economic sanctions. Moreover, the very strength of the classical literary heritage was to serve as an additional limitation for women of later generations; as long as the example of the past functioned as a single, fixed ideal for feminine writing, the weight of tradition was to impede the kind of experimentation with language necessary for the creation of works that are products of their own time. A focus, then, in the following chapter will be the investigation of significant ways in which the striking success of women in Heian letters was a distinctly time- and class-bound phenomenon, subject to revision as the society of which it was the expression vanished.

This is a reason why modern women writers of decidedly contrasting styles and literary persuasions are here grouped together. Although it is not the intention of this study to assert that there is no common ground in the writing of late nineteenth- and twentieth-century Japanese women, the ways in which changing historical and social configurations have provided new motivations and constraints for a variety of verbal acts require careful delineation. What women writers of the past century do share with one another is not simply the inheritance of a validated "feminine" aesthetic (a stylistic or perceptual biological set) but a specific contextual and conceptual social present, not simply language preferences or intuitive sensitivities, but the direct experience of social limitations as they affect the individual's potential field of action.

If modern writers in a shared Japanese context do not need to defend the same ground as that occupied by women writing in the

---

nearer to the sensitivities of the Heian period than is any other modern Japanese writer (p. 169).

West, that is only to be expected. Not systematically excluded from cultural enfranchisement by the weight of an overwhelmingly masculine tradition, as feminist critics would assert the nineteenth- and twentieth-century Western woman has been, the Japanese woman writer does not need to address, first of all, the questions of her own ability and right to write; she can and does channel her energy into a consideration of the social possibilities culturally viable for women. This is by no means the same thing. Her situation, then, is not that which Sandra M. Gilbert and Susan Gubar describe in *The Madwoman in the Attic: The Woman Writer and the Nineteenth-Century Literary Imagination:*

> Thus the loneliness of the female artist, her feelings of alienation from male predecessors coupled with her need for sisterly precursors and successors, her urgent sense of her need for a female audience together with her fear of the antagonism of male readers, her culturally conditioned timidity about self-dramatization, her dread of the patriarchal authority of art, her anxiety about the impropriety of female invention—all these phenomena of "inferiorization" mark the woman writer's struggle for artistic self-definition and differentiate her efforts at self-creation from those of her male counterpart.[7]

In fact, if such an account might be considered to be an accurate rendering of the situation in English letters, where women are seen as being "without a story," without a history, then it must be observed that very little in the description fits the Japanese experience.

In a literature marked on the whole by a preference for personal and internalized forms such as the "I" novel (*shishōsetsu*) and directly autobiographical fiction and the diary, it would be difficult to prove that writing by women is any less socially concerned or any more emotional and privatized than that by men; and a fair case could be made for the opposite position.[8] Women's literature in the

---

[7] (New Haven, London: Yale University Press, 1979), p. 50.

[8] Matsubara Shinichi, for example, in his essay "Joryū sakka ni okeru seiji ishiki" illustrates the point that although women writers present their protagonists in the context of everyday life, they are concerned with political problems in the larger society at least to the degree that male writers are. Yoshida Seiichi makes the same point in emphasizing the comparatively high number of women in the proletarian movement in "Kindai joryū bungaku" (Modern Women's Literature). Both essays appear in the issue of *Kaishaku to kanshō* (vol. 37, no. 3) devoted to women's literature. Added to these perspectives is the perception that women seem naturally more aware

West, however, has frequently been stigmatized for its lack of social relevance, political consciousness, philosophical and metaphysical depth, and such basic narrative strengths as scope and action.[9] Since very similar strictures have been applied to modern Japanese literature as a whole, we may be equally justified in challenging the basis for such discriminations whether we view the critical chauvinism involved as being "patriarchal" or *merely* cultural.

No area of social or political experience, with the obvious exception of the combat novel, seems to have been truly closed to the modern Japanese woman writer. True, social reality and political activism, war, defeat, and disillusion have all been explored from the perspective of protagonists whose social roles are those prescribed for the woman. The author's vision of the social world of these protagonists is no more constricted than that of her male counterparts. Moreover, she sees a different world from that of her great predecessors, and she captures the world she sees in language that is not theirs. Nevertheless, in her interaction with social reality and in her presentation of the life experience of women as defined and constrained by societal expectations and cultural ideology, she once more takes upon herself with confidence that same task of the transformation of world into word that occupied the Heian writer.

We need to put the reemergence of the woman writer in the twentieth century in the context of Japan's literary history in order to appreciate fully how much and for what reasons literature written by women in the past century differs from that of their predecessors. The following chapter, then, outlines the specific social forces that have exerted heavy pressure upon literary production by women from Heian times to the dawn of the modern age. Where text and context coexist extensively, as they do in the classical period, consideration is given to the relationship between them. Where texts are

---

of the special social, economic, and political constraints that directly affect their own lives. Since such constraints are considerable in Japanese culture, it might be observed that Japanese women writer's political and ethical sensitivities need to be broadly based.

[9] Rosalind Miles observes that writers who are seen as "feminine" in style, such as Virginia Woolf has been in the West, are made to stand for the qualities of all women, even though other writers, such as George Eliot, write of different concerns and in different styles. *The Fiction of Sex: Themes and Functions of Sex Difference in the Modern Novel* (London: Vision Press, 1974), p. 33.

largely lacking, as they are in Tokugawa (Edo)[10] literature, one term of the relationship is missing, and we can only indicate the lack, seeking to explore the elements in the ensuing Meiji (1868–1912), Taishō (1912–1926), and Shōwa (1926—) eras that have once again favored the production of works by women. In the three studies that form Part Two of this work, each of the writers considered has been handled in the literary and critical context most closely allied with her writing and times. Because the relationship between word (literature) and world (society) is both complex and subtle, however, these studies examine in some detail specific short stories selected from major literary movements in three periods crucial to the development of modern women writers—the late Meiji (turn of the century), early Shōwa (late 1920s) and postwar (to the present). Because the stories provide limited but complete formalizations, they permit relatively close textual analysis that can reveal how the aesthetic perceptions of three women, Higuchi Ichiyō (Meiji), Sata Ineko (Shōwa), and Kurahashi Yumiko (postwar), are marked by and, in turn, attempt to make their mark upon specific social and historical contexts. By thus confining the purview of these early chapters to the social and historical limitations that have been perceived and delineated by three particular writers, I am necessarily excluding certain vast and crucial areas also worthy of attention.[11] Nevertheless, because the stories selected for close reading have a direct connection to broad cultural, economic, and social issues, they can be seen as metaphors for the relationship between women and society. Each one is also a record of the verbal interaction between an author and her audience, being chosen, in fact, as an effective aesthetic model of a particular contemporary social process and because the models, in their differences from one another, indicate directions of social and literary change.

---

[10] I will be following the somewhat confusing general practice of identifying the historical/political period (1603–1867) as Tokugawa, the literary/cultural period as Edo. Thus, the historical and political focus identifies the ruling clan and the cultural focus the new capital and aesthetic center, Edo (now Tokyo).

[11] Most obviously, by selecting only five authors from an abundant number, I am precluding any comprehensive survey of material by women in modern Japanese. Moreover, I am not attempting a systematic or theoretical poetics of "women's writing," and the essential comparison of thematicization and aestheticization in works by male and female writers in chapter six is necessarily brief.

As different as the stories themselves may be from one another, the common ground for the readings lies in a modification of Western reader/response criticism allowing interpretation to reveal changing social and literary values and shifts in the relationship between author and reader. Moreover, the narrator/reader relationship can be extended metaphorically to that between a writer and her assumed public, and, in more general terms, to the individual and society. Each story utilizes particular technical and formal aspects arising from its own historical context, but the individual writer's development of a specific role for readers of her text also provides a vantage point from which the author's view of the function of literature can be evaluated.

Such an emphasis allows us to meet head-on one of the central problems of transcultural reading. If the "implied reader" of Wolfgang Iser's terminology is seen as one who shares the social context and cultural values of the "implied author,"[12] then Western readers of Japanese works, asked to share a historical and social context that cannot fully be their own, must always fall something short of the ideal. The studies that follow will seek to provide enough background for each story to indicate who its implied (or assumed) readers may once have been, but will regard the fullest description of such backgrounds as the task of the literary historian. From our perspective, a role more accessible to the interested reader of another culture would be that of what might be termed the "created" reader—the reader whose response is structured by the unfolding of textual mechanisms.[13] Of all the writers who will be considered in

---

[12] Wolfgang Iser discusses some implications of Wayne Booth's use of the term "implied author" in *The Rhetoric of Fiction* (Chicago: University of Chicago Press, 1961) in his own *The Implied Reader: Patterns of Communication in Prose from Bunyan to Beckett* (Baltimore: Johns Hopkins University Press, 1974), pp. 103, 114–115.

[13] Roman Ingarden, *Cognition of the Literary Work of Art*, trans. Ruth Ann Crowley and Kenneth R. Olson in Northwestern University Studies in Phenomenology and Existential Philosophy (Evanston: Northwestern University Press, 1973): "Literary scholarship should be concerned with the cognition of the literary work of art itself, whereas the concretizations of the literary work of art which are constituted in the aesthetic experience should be the domain of literary criticism, which should operate with different means of apprehension and presentation to bring the concretizations into view for the reader but which cannot claim the same objectivity and intersubjective accessibility and must thus be excluded from the realm of science" (p. 422). The readings that follow, then, would fall largely within the realm that Ingarden assigns to literary criticism.

the ensuing chapters, only the most recent, Kurahashi Yumiko, can be considered as potentially including the Western reader in her assumed audience. Each text, nevertheless, creates its own reader as a part of the communicative act, and to the extent that a work can convey its aesthetic values across the boundaries of time and place, its lasting functioning as verbal art is assured. The Higuchi Ichiyō chapter, "Between Two Worlds," for example, locates the author's work within the neoclassical movement of Meiji literature and focuses especially upon "Takekurabe" (1894), in which Ichiyō uses the syntax and some of the literary conventions of *waka* (the basic Japanese poetic form), Edo prose fiction, and the puppet theater to suggest a conflict between the demands of a traditional social world and individual aspirations. It examines the narrative balance that Ichiyō achieves between a pragmatic social world and a delicately suggested subjective world of human emotion and explores the subtle manner in which the narrative sets up an interplay between instruction and interpretation.

The Sata Ineko chapter, "Soundings in Time," uses the early "Kyarameru kōjō kara" (From the Caramel Factory, 1929) and the much later "Yuki no mau yado" (Inn of the Dancing Snow, 1972) to chart the author's growth as a writer/narrarator. The two separate narrative strata of "Kyarameru kōjō kara" demonstrate how personal experience can be used as the basis for the expression of the social concerns making proletarian writing a vital force in the literature of the Taishō and early Shōwa years and introducing a level of specifically political and economic criticism into the generally introspective world of Japanese letters. The mature craft of the later story evidences an extremely subtle artistry that conveys the impact of duration itself upon the experienced life of the individual. A demonstration model of the narrative process underlying much of the fiction of twentieth-century Japan, it, moreover, reveals the implicit ideology that shapes the experience of Japanese women to this day.

The third of the studies, "The Sibyl of Negation," bases its exploration of Kurahashi Yumiko's position in avant-garde literature upon "Natsu no owari" (The End of Summer), a story that supplies ample proof of a postwar concern with anomie. The loss of identification with cultural values and a concomitant concern with violence and eroticism are explored within the context of the studied cosmopolitanism that has affected Japan's postwar intelligentsia and of the structures through which the text creates its own individual narrative ideology.

The separate studies, pinpointing particular moments and literary movements in which the woman writer moved to the foreground of literature, may serve, in passing, to sketch in broad outline the evolution of modern Japanese literature; but they are particularly intended to illustrate the way in which each writer has translated the social values of her time into a specific aesthetic response. Chapter six, however, in seeking to identify patterns of self-depiction that have united women writers throughout the modern period, considers a number of works by two additional women, Hayashi Fumiko and Enchi Fumiko. In their works, both Enchi and Hayashi focus upon the social roles of Japanese women, and they could be considered more representative of Japan's "women writers" than Ichiyō, Sata, and Kurahashi, since they explicitly create "feminine" responses to the controlling social definitions of the woman's sphere. Although the roles they assign to the protagonists of their works are essentially the same (those codified by the Japanese culture), they approach these limits from complementary, maybe even opposite, viewpoints. Whereas Hayashi's protagonists are often marginal, sometimes "fallen" women, outside the boundaries of comfortable social acceptability, many of Enchi's central characters are "respectable" wives and mothers caught within the bounds of duty and obligation.

The thematization of these roles in the two women's work provides a marked contrast to the symbolic projection of the same roles in works by leading male contemporaries. Kawabata Yasunari and Tanizaki Jun'ichirō, the writers selected for comparison with Enchi and Hayashi in chapter seven, focus in many of their works upon the same "good" woman / "bad" woman dichotomy, but the dynamics of their presentation of it differ markedly. An awareness of this difference will make it possible to suggest how a "feminine consciousness" in works by women arises from exploration of the experiencing subject's perceptual stance rather than from the distance inherent in consideration of the woman as an aesthetic object.

We must ultimately move from the examination of what the conditions were under which Japanese women have emerged once more as a literary force in the modern period and of how their works

13

have responded to those conditions in specific instances—the separate studies—to a comparison of the depiction of women in works by male and female authors—a comparison of perceptual stances and of the process of symbolization. Only in this way may we adequately appreciate the dual nature (from our own culturally limited perspective) of the contribution that women have made to modern Japanese literature. The social and literary contexts of their times have informed the works of Ichiyō, Sata, and Kurahashi. But these writers share with Enchi and Hayashi an awareness of the pressures of strong social role patterning that occupies a central place in the works of the latter two writers. The contribution of individual women writers to a variety of literary movements in Japan demands acknowledgment, but so, too, does the particular perspective women writers provide on their nation's cultural inheritance. To say that women have been active participants in major literary movements of the twentieth century is not the same as saying that they have not provided Japanese literature with something uniquely their own. And to assume that one contribution would preclude the other reveals a peculiarly Western bias.

The final chapter of the present work, then, will attempt to place this issue in the broader comparative framework of transcultural perception, asking why the significant contribution of women to modern Japanese literature has been virtually ignored in the West until very recent years. The delayed and less than enthusiastic response of the Westerner is examined, in its turn, as evidence of unconscious cultural conditioning only now beginning to dissipate and of the preference for the reproduction of the symbols of the "exotic," so closely allied with the image of Japanese femininity in Western eyes (and so unlikely to appear in pure form in the writing of women themselves). Operative here, it would appear, is a kind of double estrangement, a compounding of sexual and cultural distance that makes the Japanese woman writer quite alien to a Western literary/critical academic world still largely masculine in perspective. The grounds for this double estrangement are worthy of consideration, not only in order to understand what is perceived as "other," but also to recognize the limits of our own occasionally naïve perceptions. For it seems to me that unless we identify our own blind spots, we can never be sure whether what we think we see is really there, or whether where we see nothing, the "nothing" that we see is not merely the reflection of our own blindness.

In a critical study intended as an introduction to a number of important women writers who have participated in shaping twentieth-century Japanese letters, it is crucial to recognize the difficulty inherent in transcultural literary criticism. The methods and terminology utilized hereafter will be Western in orientation, as the materials under investigation are intended for an audience largely unfamiliar with them in the original. Even students of Japanese literature in the West, however, may reasonably be assumed to be less familiar with women writers than are their counterparts in Japan. I have thus believed it to be particularly important to base the generalizations arising in chapters six, seven, and eight upon the extended examination of those literary texts presented in Part Two, so that my readers may have the opportunity to test these readings and generalizations against their own. In the same spirit, I would suggest that the two translations of stories examined in chapters four and five of Part Two should be read before reading the commentaries upon them.

It is the intention of this introduction, then, to invite the reader to participate in a preliminary investigation of a limited number of short texts that are examined in their own immediate contexts, before going on to the broader task of comparing the work of male and female authors in Japan and seeking to suggest differences on a culturewide basis. Only then, I believe, will we be in a position to understand how rich and how distinct the contribution of particular Japanese women has been to their nation's literature and how different their collective position has been from that of women writing in the West.

More than a thousand years ago, Michitsuna no haha (the mother of Michitsuna) took up her writing brush with an assumption of the fitness of that act in correcting the record of "old romances." A "well-placed lady," aware that her society endorsed her aptitude and right to describe what her life "is really like," she exuded a kind of confidence that is missing in other cultures. Neither the seventeenth-century Anglo-American Anne Bradstreet nor the twelfth-century Chinese Chu Shu-chen seems to have been able to view her own creative context with the same assurance. Although the Japanese literary context was also to change radically from that which favored the tenth-century Japanese woman, her writing was to become part of a past that could not be erased. When women began to write once more in Japan, they forgot neither the scope of the achievements of the classical woman writer nor the centuries of increasing silence that had intervened between her day and their own.

CHAPTER TWO

Revising the Legacy

IN JAPAN, as elsewhere, tradition and innovation cooperated in the formation of the national literature. The tradition showed remarkable tenacity; *waka*, for example, has remained a surprisingly consistent genre from the earliest poetry anthologies to the present, and other genres with origins in the Heian period still have their modern counterparts. The innovative, always based to some extent upon the forms and sensibilities of the past, nevertheless allows for the incorporation of new cultural norms adapted to the needs of a changing social and political reality. But in the premodern period the relationship of women writers to such innovative forms was as sporadic as their relationship to the traditional was persistent. The feminist poet Yosano Akiko (1878–1942) pictures the reemergence of the Japanese woman in the twentieth century in terms of the awakening of a dormant volcano, but the Westerner, when aware of the fluctuating nature of the Japanese woman writer's fortunes, may be tempted to compare her with Sleeping Beauty.[1] After a time of brilliant achievement in which she was favored by every gift of talent and success, she seemed to sleep for centuries. Like her fairytale counterpart, the writer was to be awakened at last. But instead of being brought back

---

[1] But our hypothetical Western reader would be wrong on a very fundamental level. The particular archetype in this story—the virginal girl who at the onset of maturity (symbolized by the blood of the pricked finger) is sexually frozen by sleep until the right man comes along to "waken" her—is less suitable for the Japanese context than the Western, as Sandra M. Gilbert and Susan Gubar's analysis of the related tale of "Snow White" demonstrates (*Madwoman in the Attic* [New Haven: Yale University Press, 1979], pp. 36ff.). I am merely using the metaphor for the silent centuries. Yosano, knowing the repressed force of the Japanese woman, uses a more powerful metaphor of inner fire and strength, which captures the way the Japanese writer sees and represents herself.

to life by a prince's kiss, she was jolted awake by the none-too-gentle embrace of the modern age. And she was no longer a princess; she had become a commoner—a townswoman, sometimes even a street waif or factory worker. Accordingly, the narrative thread with which she was to spin her texts reflected the needs and materials of a class far different from those of her Heian predecessor.

So it is that the two centuries of Japanese literary history during which women participated most actively in literary creation, those from 950 to 1050 and 1890 to the present are separated from one another by the better part of a millennium. The Heian world and its literature were aristocratic to their core, and although the classical model was maintained by a dwindling number of women throughout the intervening ages, the realities of that world had vanished. Only the radical social changes of the last one hundred years have once again freed the woman writer to a degree where she can create fictive models of the society around her. Paradoxically, this act of creation of new models for a new time brings her closer to the nature of the aesthetic act of the classical writers—describing what the life of the writer and other women of her times "is really like."

The history of premodern women's writing is connected only intermittently with the nation's literary history. Definite changes in the locus of the cultural ideal embodied in the literature of successive periods are the strongest indication of profound changes in the nature of the reading public, and there are at least two such breaks in Japanese literature. In general, the classical period had been an era in which the aristocracy of the imperial court had created a literature based upon such forms as *waka*, the *nikki* (personal diary), the *zuihitsu* (collection of miscellaneous notes or essays), and the *monogatari* (prose tale). This was the age when literary production by women was absolutely central. As the court became progressively more ornamental and ceremonial in function in the Kamakura and Muromachi eras, effective political control and economic power shifted to the major military clans, whose samurai code found its literary expression in warrior tales. Both men and women of the court continued to write *waka* and *nikki* during this time, but the former central role of women in literature, as creators as well as characters, underwent considerable erosion throughout the period.

Subsequently, women were to reappear in force in the role of significant characters long before they began to reemerge as writers, for a second major change affecting the forms of Japanese literature occurred in the Edo period, a time that may well have been the nadir in feminine literary production. At this time cultural values shifted from the warrior ethic of the preceding period to a townsmen's code, and this shift allowed for the development of a popular literature in which the depiction of women became central. The *gesaku* (popular "frivolous" prose fiction) and the *jōruri* (puppet theater plays) began to concentrate particularly upon the commercialized world of the licensed quarters and of the urban merchants (*chōnin*). The figure of the geisha, central in plays, prints, and fiction of this time, became a staple for writers until well into the twentieth century, thus constituting a new literary "tradition" for female representation.

In broadest outline one can trace a shift of the literary perspective that moved downward on the social scale from the court aristocracy to the warrior class, and then from the warrior class to the urban and merchant classes. Along with this shift came a change in focus from the highly aestheticized celebration of courtly tastes and emotional sensibilities to the validation of a samurai code of loyalty and bravery, and from this to the lively and pragmatic, sometimes ribald, sometimes sentimental, materialism of popular fiction in Edo Japan. Concurrent with these alterations were a continuing decrease in literary participation by women and a falling and rising of the significance of women as the subject matter of literature.

Of the two centuries of literary history in which women most actively participated as creators, however, the earlier is, of course, the purer sample. Ivan Morris observes of the years between 950 and 1050 that "almost every noteworthy author who wrote in Japanese was a woman." Calling this a time when "women had a virtual monopoly of famous names in prose and poetry," he declares in no uncertain terms, "This century was by far the most important in Heian literature, and in general the rise and the decline of this literature was closely associated with the role of women in it."[2] Accordingly, it is worth examining some of the specific factors within that

---

[2] Ivan Morris, *The World of the Shining Prince* (Oxford: Oxford University Press, 1964), p. 211.

historical period that fostered feminine participation in Japanese letters and controlled the nature of what women wrote.

One might classify the major factors thus involved in terms of lineage, language, and leisure. During this time every major writer was from the ranked aristocracy (although most were relatively low ranking), and all aristocrats, from the emperor on down, participated to some degree in literary activities. Because of the separation of the written language into *wabun* (Japanese- or "women's"-style writing) and *kambun* (Chinese- or "men's"-style writing), women were essentially in control of the prose usage of the purely Japanese language. Moreover, the social code and way of life of the woman in court circles provided her with the time and opportunity (almost to compulsion) for indulging in aesthetic pursuits.

Of the three factors, lineage had the greatest impact on subject matter. Heian writing depicts the social life of the upper class and for the most part of dwellers in Heian-Kyō (now Kyōto). Like the figures in their prose, all of the women writing, and all of their original readers, were from a small segment of the population comprising no more, perhaps, than one-tenth of one percent of the total population. Both the writer and her reader, then, were part of a singularly enclosed society in which aristocrats wrote for one another (as the only people with the necessary learning and cultivated sensibility) and in which women were identifiable as principal producers and consumers of fiction in the Japanese language. If the writer was not always a princess (though in fact she sometimes was), she was invariably of noble birth. Consequently, the social milieu of the nobility is reflected in Heian literature. It would be well, then, to touch upon some of the specifics of the well-born Heian woman's situation.

Within this restricted class, women still had a status and privilege higher than they were to have in the centuries that followed, although in all probability more restricted than that of preceding ages. The central significance in Japanese mythology of the Sun goddess, Amaterasu, the fact that early Chinese accounts of Japan name it the "Queen country," and the survival of matrilocal marriage traditions indicate that, in the period before recorded history, Japan very probably accorded to women a high degree of power and autonomy. If some of that power and autonomy had been lost, the Heian noblewoman nevertheless retained a measure of political importance, the possibility of economic independence, and some flexibility within accepted marriage customs.

At the very highest level of society, the system of "marriage politics" was to make female offspring a valued asset to importantly placed officials. The Fujiwara clan, especially its northern branch, had developed political control into a fine art by consistently marrying its daughters to princes in the line of succession, thereby achieving a virtual monopoly on the supply of imperial consorts, and thus, in due course, of mothers of future emperors. Daughters, then, were the means by which this clan could obtain power, making possible those frequent regencies exercised by Fujiwara grandfathers in the name of their imperial grandsons or sons-in-law.

On a broader level, the survival of the legal right of the Heian woman to inherit and bequeath property in her own name, even when married, gave the fortunate propertied few a substantial measure of economic independence. This was especially significant in a polygamous marriage system where a woman's officially recognized relationship to a man might be that of primary wife, secondary wife, or concubine. Beyond this, because Japanese marriage arrangements could be matrilocal or neolocal, but not patrilocal, a wife, even with young children, frequently remained under the protection of her own family and was, in any case, never subjected to the situation that became the fate of the wife in later ages of living as an outsider of low status within her husband's family.[3]

Although privileged in some ways beyond her female descendants for many centuries, the Heian woman's life was almost incredibly circumscribed physically. What was unique to her situation, however, was that in some measure the very constraints imposed upon her actually fostered literary activity. For the aristocracy of the times, truly civilized life was limited to the capital city of Heian-Kyō; for the aristocratic woman, contact with the outside world was even more restricted. Generally confined to the company of her serving women in her own quarters, the noblewoman, as custom dictated,

---

[3] For a vivid firsthand account in English see Ishimoto Shidzue's *Facing Both Ways: The Story of My Life* (New York: Farrar and Rhinehart, 1935). Ariyoshi Sawako depicts the daughter-in-law's struggle for place in her novel *The Doctor's Wife* (Tokyo, New York: Kōdansha, 1981).

was further shielded from the eyes of the world behind a screen of state. In theory, the only males whom custom permitted behind this screen were her husband or son. The numerous romantic intrigues around which the literature of the day is organized indicate that practice tended to contradict theory radically. Nevertheless, the day-to-day life of these writers was passed for the most part in a society of women, and both confinement and a lack of "privacy" (a peculiarly Western term) were fundamental conditions of their existence.

In addition to such physical constraints, an elaborate code of conduct, largely aesthetic in its discriminations, imposed what George Sansom calls "the rule of taste" upon the court society of the tenth and eleventh centuries.[4] Morris also distinguishes this society from other aristocratic societies by speaking of "the way in which refined standards of cultural appreciation and performance had become generally accepted values among members of the ruling class. Artistic insensitivity damned a gentleman of the Heian court as fatally as did a reputation for cowardice among the nobility of the West,"[5] and we can infer that it would stigmatize a court lady to an even greater degree. We must be careful in characterizing the Heian period in such terms, however, since such a view rests in large part upon an overwhelmingly literary presentation of the manners of the day. For, so successful were the women of the age in capturing a view of their enclosed social world and so durable were their writings, that the literary record that survived them has achieved a quasi-historical reality, and our impression of the age is inescapably marked by their perspective. As a result, because their own experience and interest were severely restricted to people of their own kind, little is known about the lives of the common people of the times. One might say, therefore, that the authors' lineage was largely responsible for the content of Heian literature.

In the case of style, however, language obviously plays the dominant role. The peculiar use of two written languages resulted in

---

[4] George Sansom, "The Rule of Taste," *A History of Japan to 1334* (Stanford: Stanford University Press, 1958), pp. 178–196, in which he discusses the aestheticized background of court life.

[5] Morris, *Shining Prince*, p. 183.

a situation wherein women were virtually the only ones consistently writing in Japanese. The vernacular Japanese language was unrelated to the Chinese language; but since the Japanese did not have a writing system of their own, they borrowed the Chinese writing system, progressively altering it to fit the demands of their own spoken language. It was not until the ninth century, through a process of experimentation with Chinese written forms, that the Japanese developed a system for representing the actual sounds of their language rather than merely adopting Chinese symbols for meaning or awkwardly using some Chinese symbols for meaning and others for sounds. Once Japanese words could be written by sound, the way was open for Heian literature.

By this time a distinct separation had developed between the writing of men and women, probably because of the high intellectual prestige invested in the ability to write Sino-Japanese. One could write in the symbols of Sino-Japanese (*kambun*), the language of official documents and of the formally learned, or one could make the choice of women and write directly in the sounds of their own language (*wabun*). Since instruction in the Chinese language was confined to men, they were the authors of *kambun* literature. The greatest classics of Japanese literature, however, were in *wabun*. Writers using the vernacular, while perhaps less impressive in the scholarly terms of the day, were able to forge the literature of their country in its own language, and, although both men and women wrote *waka* using *wabun*, women wrote most of the vernacular prose.

While lineage was a principal determinant of the content of Heian literature, and while linguistic circumstances go a long way toward explaining the predominance of women writers in the period, neither of these elements is sufficient to explain works on the scale of *monogatari* like Murasaki Shikibu's *Genji monogatari* (ca. 1002–1015), *zuihitsu* like Sei Shōnagon's *Makura no sōshi* (after 1000), and *nikki* like Michitsuna no haha's *Kagerō nikki* (972–976). Such lengthy productions demanded that third element which the Heian noblewoman had in abundance—leisure. Whereas social and political offices and responsibilities generally kept the aristocratic male moving about the city, the court lady's life was both stationary and leisurely.

Although physically confined and socially circumscribed, the court lady was encouraged to engage in aesthetic activities, and the prose forms of the day are an outgrowth of her way of life: they take days to read and years to write. She had such days and years. One of several wives of a husband who might be living elsewhere, the Heian woman could not expect a sustained marital relationship; she was dependent for diversion upon the company of her female attendants and upon her reading and writing. Although in the strictest interpretation of the religious and ethical precepts of the day, largely Buddhist in origin, fiction was theoretically frowned upon as untruthful and not morally improving, in practice it was justified as an interest that could occupy otherwise dangerously idle hours, especially for women. The writers themselves are quick to point this out. Michitsuna no haha's reference to the days and nights that had "gone by in monotonous succession" explains why she had first "occasion to read most of the old romances" and next the inspiration to write a journal that might contradict the "fabrications" she saw in them. Similarly, in one of the famous lists of things that play so prominent a part in *Makura no sōshi*, Sei Shōnagon cites *monogatari* as among those items that "relieve the tedium"; and, behind the fictional guise of the *Genji monogatari* itself, Murasaki incorporates a discussion in which its hero, Prince Genji, chides his ward for spending so much of her time reading and copying out *monogatari*, but then is forced to concede, "If it were not for such old stories, how could you fill the empty hours?"

The latter work has particular significance for our own discussion, for not only does it transmit Murasaki's views about the value of fiction and constitute a major source of latter-day impressions of the Heian world, but it is also the very emblem of the brilliance of the women's literature of the day. In addition, its fortune at the hands of critics in ensuing centuries is a valuable indicator of shifts in attitude toward literature in general and literature by women in particular. From the time of its composition, the *Genji monogatari* was acclaimed, but responses to the nature and content of the tale displayed a certain hardening of moralistic judgments as time went on. Works in ensuing centuries, especially those inspired by Buddhist thought, such as *Hōbutsu shū* (ca. 1179) and *Ima monogatari* (ca. 1243), depict Murasaki as having been damned for immoral writing.[6]

---

[6] Thomas Harper's dissertation, "Motoori Norinaga's Criticism of the *Genji Monogatari*" (University of Michigan, 1971), is an extremely valuable description of the

In spite of such reservations about what came to be seen as their lascivious content, the *Genji* and other Heian classics became the standard models for the education of women in later eras and served to conserve aristocratic values. At a time when such values were being relegated to the sidelines while the warrior code became the dominant national ideology, the defense of the *Genji's* worth by courtiers is understandable. Scholar-poets, such as the late Heian and early Kamakura Fujiwara Shunzei (1114–1204) and his son, Fujiwara Teika (1162–1241), sought to keep the spirit of the *Genji*, and with it, that of Heian letters, alive, and, in the rarified and isolated atmosphere of the court, succeeded to a degree in doing so. But at the very time that Teika was including poems inspired by the *Genji* in the imperial anthology, the *Shinchokusenshū*, such early warrior tales as the *Hōgen monogatari* and the *Heiji monogatari* had begun to circulate through a form of oral transmission that bears some resemblance to the bardic tradition of Western epic. Thus, when religious thought was altering moral evaluations of the work, rival forms espousing a new, more "masculine" ethic were gaining a hold upon Japanese literature.

By then, in the view of some, the court had become a small, lighted area of culture in a dark and chaotic world. George Sansom, for example, declares, "In an age of upheaval and disorder, when power was in the hands, often the blood-stained hands, of unlettered warriors, it was the sovereign and his nobles who kept the flame of learning alive."[7] The statement is too severe, since from the militant spirit of this new and dangerous age arose the great classic of warrior tales, the *Heike monogatari* (final form ca. 1375), an account of the fateful clash, almost two centuries earlier, between the Taira and Minamoto clans. Unquestionably, however, the literature of this new age had moved far from the social milieu and values of the *Genji*, and it must already have seemed as though the great outpouring of feminine writing in the tenth and eleventh centuries was destined to remain an isolated phenomenon. The prose classics of the past were

Genji monogatari's fate in the critical and moral evaluations of the centuries that followed its creation and culminated in Motoori Norinaga's masterful analysis of the work in the Tokugawa period.

[7] George Sansom, *History of Japan: 1334–1615* (Stanford: Standord University Press, 1961), p. 127.

not forgotten; indeed, Ichijō Kanera, a poet and scholar of the fifteenth century, could still proclaim in *Kachō yojō* (1472) that the *Genji* was Japan's greatest treasure, but the literature of his own age had elevated other ideals that obviously did not lend themselves readily to treatment by the woman writer, and even in court circles the cherished classical past had become the preserve of a class of masculine antiquarians.

Intermittent warfare between contending clans continued until the Tokugawa *bakufu* (shogunate) was established in the seventeenth century. Once Tokugawa rule was firmly entrenched, the second of the major shifts in literary values evolved. Almost none of the previous forms was to vanish completely, although the classical *monogatari* was produced in rather anemic imitations. To the *waka*, *nikki*, and *zuihitsu* of the Heian era had been added forms born in the centuries of warfare, such as warrior tales, Noh drama, and *renga* (linked verse). The Edo period was to develop forms of its own in addition to the traditional genres, notably *haikai*, drama, and new forms of prose fiction.

Although they were never entirely absent among poets, women had become rare indeed as fiction writers, and where they existed at all represented a survival of the classical women's literature and not participation in the prose trends of the time. For example, one of the few women writing prose fiction during this entire era, Arakida Reijo (1732–1806), composed romances in the classical style as well as *renga*, short tales, and a travel diary. Thus, especially in prose forms, the model for the occasional woman writer remained a model from the past even while *gesaku* had begun to develop new and popular forms.

Other, nonaesthetic aspects of Tokugawa culture were to play a role in shaping the consciousness and experience of the writers of the generations that followed. Principal among these was a new societal emphasis upon the importance of the *ie*, the extended family with a male head who was the figure of authority to family members and the public representative of his house as well as its spokesman in legal matters. Thus, the individual family's configuration was brought into conformance with the hierarchical structure of the shogunal state, and the woman's place became codified and subordinate. As

Joy Paulson states in her essay "Evolution of the Feminine Ideal," "According to Tokugawa feudalism, the male vassal was a juristic person with rights and privileges, while the female vassal has only duties and obligations. Women could not conduct ancestral rites, nor were they permitted to play a public role in society."[8]

From Paulson's description of the position of the married woman, we can see that in comparison with former centuries, women had suffered a general loss of status.

> A woman was unable to become the head of a household, to adopt or become guardian of her own child, own property, or make contracts in her own name. The family being all important, woman's function as "heir provider" in the context of Confucianism, feudalism and ancestor worship had rendered her, on the eve of the Meiji Restoration, virtually devoid of legal rights.[9]

The relative flexibility of the Heian structure had largely disappeared by Tokugawa times, and the concept of the woman's duty of complete submission to the family had become institutionalized. Both this and a rigid double standard inherent in the Neo-Confucian ideology of the Tokugawa period were, as we shall see in ensuing chapters, to survive as social configurations in women's literature even in the modern period. An essential social conservatism thus mirrors the aesthetic traditionalism of the Japanese. Just as the literary forms of the classical age had held sway over women's writing up through the Tokugawa centuries, so social structures articulated during those centuries were to survive and to make themselves felt (and sometimes opposed) in the twentieth century.

Perhaps the most influential work in defining and propagating a Confucian image of women during the Tokugawa itself was *Onna daigaku* (The Greater Learning for Women, 1672) by Kaibara Ekken. The work has become anathema to women of later ages, but in fact its author does not seem to have been bent upon composing an anti-feminist diatribe. Instead, his intention was more to provide a general handbook of conduct that would capture and transmit the actual ideological conception of the woman's proper position in a Confucian

---

[8] In Joyce Lebra, Joy Paulson, and Elizabeth Powers, eds., *Women in Changing Japan* (Stanford: Stanford University Press, 1976), p. 13.

[9] Ibid.

framework. Within this framework, marriage was viewed as a woman's only true role, and education was not to be overly encouraged. The only "greater learning" possible for her could be subsumed under the one word "submission," and the progress of her life was seen as the changing of masters, from father to husband to son.

Not too surprisingly, one handbook written by a woman in this time, *Onna chōhōki*,[10] while likewise enjoining its female readers to obedience and self-effacement, nevertheless contains a wistful reference to the former glories of the Japanese woman and mentions that Amaterasu, the mythical founder of the Japanese race, was a goddess. The author can only surmise that the present circumstances of the women in her society must be indicative of their moral degeneration as a sex since antiquity; nothing in the social context of her own day suggests that such power has remained in their hands.

In view of the special place classical letters played in the education of women, however, it would be unfair to characterize the Tokugawa as an era that completely denied women the pleasures of learning. Of course, to be justified, literature had to have a social and moral function; but the Japanese classics were deemed (with some reservations) appropriate to the needs of women. Exposure to the classics, especially for women of the samurai class, could have certain social benefits. As Ronald P. Dore explains in *Education in Tokugawa Japan*, which carefully documents advances in the general level of education during that age, it was considered that

> women should concentrate on *wafū no narai*—Japanese-style education in the poetry and novels of the Heian period as opposed to the more masculine rigors of a Chinese education. This would give them a knowledge of *ninjō*, of the workings of the human heart; it would encourage in them an appreciation of the beauties of nature, refine their feelings, sharpen their intuitions and give them the skill in literary expression in Japanese necessary for social intercourse.[11]

In the preceding pages we have examined some of the factors involved in the early feminization of Japanese letters. The separation

---

[10] The author is unknown, but the use of the feminine salutation *kashiko* indicates that the writer is a woman. The Seitō (Bluestocking Group) of the Taishō era refers to that same earlier glory in their motto, "In the beginning, woman was the Sun..."

[11] Ronald P. Dore, *Education in Tokugawa Japan* (Berkeley and Los Angeles: University of California Press, 1965), p. 66.

of literary language that had created the realms of *wabun* and *kambun* was, as Dore indicates, still in evidence in the eighteenth and nineteenth centuries, and the relationship of women to literature was still seen in terms of the Heian classics. Even on the eve of the modern age, then, the former success of women writers exercised a powerful influence upon the education and literary production of women. Whatever the relationship may have been between Heian women and the works they produced, the qualities with which their writing was imbued had clearly come to be identified as "feminine" by later ages. It should be remembered, nevertheless, that these works are as much aristocratic as they are feminine.

The popular literature of the Edo period, however, was no longer aristocratic; a new spirit of commercialism had entered the field of letters. Not only was there a division of taste between polite and popular literature, but there was also a change at this time in both subject matter and the motivation for writing. Many of the male writers who, especially in prose, had captured the mood of the times, were in the business of writing and shared the commercial interests of their largely merchant-class audience. The literature of the Tokugawa centuries had its high point in the Genroku era (1688–1704), a time when Ihara Saikaku was producing his lively stories about the life of the merchant class and the denizens of the licensed quarters and when the *bunraku* (puppet theater) dramas of Chikamatsu Monzaemon (1653–1724) were focusing upon that same world and were particularly successful in portraying domestic triangles ending in suicide. Both wrote for an audience of townsmen (and townswomen, for education was becoming widespread among the daughters of the urban merchant class), and they represent the innovative and urban side of Tokugawa literature, much as their famous contemporary, Matsuo Bashō (1644–1694), created a bridge between the aristocratic *renga* and the new, more plebeian form of *haikai*.

While women played virtually no part in the creation of this literature, in the commercialized atmosphere of the day they were gaining significance as commodities. Not only was the thriving commerce of the licensed pleasure quarters based upon the sale of the services of the geishas, courtesans, entertainers, and prostitutes, but the way of life of the beauties of the quarter inspired popular fiction and drama and became a favored subject for such early masters of the *ukiyo-e* (wood-block prints of the "floating world" of the pleasure quarters) as Moronobu, Jihei, and Ando.[12] The woman's role as aesthetic object became prominent as never before, and women formed a significant proportion of the audience for the arts of the time, even comprising, it appears, the bulk of the readership for one popular form—the *ninjōbon*, or sentimental romance.

As we shall see in the first of the three studies that follow, the Genroku period was to serve as an important source of inspiration for the most widely read writers of the Meiji period, those of the Ken'yūsha (Friends of the Inkstone). Among those who wrote under the influence of this school was the most prominent woman prose stylist of the age, Higuchi Ichiyō. Her unique perspective at once challenges the Genroku view of the pleasure quarters and testifies to the survival of some of the societal norms of the Tokugawa past. In her work the task of revising the legacy of the past is begun. Robert Lyons Danly emphasizes the way in which Ichiyō managed to combine Heian elegance with some of the best qualities of Edo fiction in his full-length study of her work, *In the Shade of Spring Leaves*. Referring to her discovery of Saikaku's works and their impact upon her own art, Danly remarks, "When Ichiyō happened on these works in the second half of her career, Saikaku's earthy approach to fiction liberated her from her classical prejudices, and in fact made it possible for her to return to the classical tradition and draw from it what had made the poets and the Heian women writers truly great: passion and frankness and honesty."[13]

Ichiyō then became the first major figure to mark the emergence of the woman writer from the constraints of tradition. Although relieved of her "classical prejudices," she retained much of the sensitivity of the Heian writer while completely transforming the nature of the content of feminine literature. Using her knowledge of the fringe world of the Yoshiwara pleasure quarters (the experience of which she shared with Saikaku), she created some of the most memorable fiction of the Meiji period.

---

[12] Later *ukiyo-e* masters such as Utamaro et al. are more famous, but the earlier artists are the contemporaries of the Genroku writers.

[13] Robert Lyons Danly, *In the Shade of Spring Leaves: The Life and Writings of Higuchi Ichiyō* (New Haven: Yale University Press, 1982), pp. 110–111.

With Ichiyō, we turn to the second of the two centuries in which women's writers directly interpreted (and reinterpreted) the material of past and present. Just as the Heian age is read through the metaphoric representations of its great practitioners, each of whom possesses a distinctive tone, so the selection of particular works by specific authors from the second major period of women writer's literary production will necessarily affect the construct we make. Although the three writers whose works we shall examine in ensuing chapters are related to the broader literary history of the modern age—Ichiyō, the Meiji era's foremost woman fiction writer; Sata, one of the major writers springing from the proletarian ranks; and Kurahashi, prominent in the avant-garde of the present day—a second reason for their selection is their responses to the world and the way in which those responses illuminate a changing range of possibilities for the woman writer.

Ichiyō, the most obvious of the choices, being, in the view of some, the most significant creator of short fiction of the day, could be seen as opposing the modernizing spirit of the Meiji era because of her use of traditional materials and classical language (*bungo*). Yet her fiction captures a part of what was an inescapable contemporary reality—the survival of the influence and forms of the past in the lives of women. Despite such idealistic advocates as Fukuzawa Yukichi, who championed equal treatment of women and attacked the ideology inherent in *Onna daigaku*, the actual liberation of women from the constraints of tradition fell far short of the ideals of the progressive intellectuals of the day. And Ichiyō's fiction in part is a testimony to that fact.

Sata, only one of the many women proletarian writers whose ranks also include Hirabayashi Taiko and Miyamoto Yuriko, shares their theoretical grounding in social realism, especially in her early fiction. More particularly, however, her persistent concern with the importance of human relationships and her depiction in art of the process by which the past is redeemed and given meaning by present consciousness adds complexity and temporal ambiguity to her work. In her fiction, moreover, the interplay of resistance to and compliance with social mores demands consideration and indicates the dilemma of the writer who numbers among her very real concerns a recognition that even among progressive thinkers there seems to be a separate set of rules for women.

Resistance to social pressures rather than compliance is most abundantly clear in the work of Kurahashi, who shares with other avant-garde writers a stance of defiance toward conventional social and sexual mores. Pushing against the limits of realistic representation, she shows a frank intellectualism which can be seen as a deliberate extension of the prerogatives of the woman writer. Thus, although Ichiyō's fiction remains largely in the familiar aesthetic realm considered traditional for women, Sata's political concerns exemplify a growing confrontation between the woman writer and the political and historical realities of her context, and Kurahashi extends her verbal opposition to social dictates beyond the economic and political to the intellectual and literary.

What is it? Something sought by everyone?
Suddenly it splits me in two.

I feel free to walk anywhere,
at least for now. I stride over the distant past.

Some time ago, in a silence stronger
than soy beans popping in the pan.

Hope? Waiting for footsteps?
Perhaps to become a Heian court lady

surrounded by a screen of illusions
waiting for some prince?

Or is it the prayer of a wife in war-time,
anxious for her man in the field?

Don't say it rises like a spinning wheel
without hitting all the rungs.

Is it resolution? The blazing blue flame
of mothers secretly resisting their patriarchs?

But I can't get by on that alone.
Why not simply break out?

I have only to get the rhythm down
to fly through the day to day.

Like a pilot, astronaut
I too am in a capsule, though.

Atsumi Ikuko, "Different Dimensions"

TEXTS AND CONTEXTS

CHAPTER THREE

Between Two Worlds: Higuchi Ichiyō's "Takekurabe"

T HE MEIJI PERIOD is regarded by many literary critics as the beginning of modern literature in Japan,[1] but some care must be exercised in isolating specific moments within what was a time of great but uneven change. In the unstable literary world of Meiji a decade often had centennial force, and it is a generally accepted truism that the opening of Japan to the West had a powerful catalytic effect upon Japanese letters. Although this view is true in the main, it requires, like most generalizations, a great deal of tucking and trimming before it can comfortably fit the contours of even a single work; furthermore, it tends to gloss over an important neoclassical reaction to Western influence, especially noticeable during the 1880s and 1890s.[2] Moreover, one has an uneasy sense that whatever may be said of the times as a whole (times that span the development from feudal to "modern" Japan) must be applied with particular caution to the work of the woman writer. For Higuchi Ichiyō, unquestionably

---

[1] Donald Keene, for example, in bringing us his two-volume anthology of Japanese literature, begins the second, *Modern Japanese Literature* (New York: Grove Press, 1956), with selections from the Meiji period. Some Japanese critics, however, have come to differentiate a "modern" (*kindai*) period, which begins with the Meiji, from a "contemporary" (*gendai*) period, which encompasses only Taishō and Shōwa literature.

[2] The Ken'yūsha represented the formal position for writers of this neoclassical bent. In *A History of Japanese Literature*, vol. 3: *The Modern Years*, trans. Don Sanderson (Kōdansha: Tokyo, 1983), Shuichi Kato points out that the work of Ken'yūsha writers attests to "the continuity in literature after the Restoration. This both demonstrates their own close relationship with literary tradition and also indicates by its quality the shallowness of the influence of Western literature on the work of many writers, whatever they may have claimed" (p. 125).

the Meiji period's foremost woman writer, does not comfortably fit into the scheme outlined above, and the fact that Ichiyō chose to write in a deliberately conservative style and utilized traditional prose forms emphasizes the intricate connections between inherited tradition and the social realities faced by women in this period. Most crucially, we dare not lose sight of the years (1892–1896) during which Ichiyō's prose was written, nor of the specific circumstances that informed her view of the world.

Born May 2, 1872, four years after the Meiji Restoration, Higuchi Natsu (Ichiyō was a pen name) was the second of three daughters of Higuchi Noriyoshi and his wife, Taki. Both parents came from farm families of some standing in Koshu, but in 1857 they migrated to Tokyo, where Noriyoshi was later to become a minor functionary in the Meiji government. Toward the end of his life, he invested money in an unsuccessful attempt to operate a transportation company, and after his death and the death of his eldest surviving son, Natsu, along with her mother and her younger sister Kuni, was forced to earn a living for herself. Among the means of gaining a livelihood that they attempted with only minimal success were taking in sewing and laundry and operating a confection and sundries shop. Only in the final years of Ichiyō's life could she devote herself entirely to writing.

Since she died in 1896 at the age of twenty-four, her career as a writer was not a long one, but the fiction published before her death nevertheless shows considerable evolution.[3] A review of Ichiyō's educational career is instructive in arriving at some understanding of her mature prose style. Her formal education ended in 1884 when, at her mother's insistence, she was taken from school to devote her time to the development of housewifely arts. Early attempts by her parents to arrange a marriage for her ended in failure,

---

[3] Discussing this evolution, Shioda Ryōhei divides it into three periods (*Meiji joryū sakka ron* [Tokyo: Nara Shobō, 1966], pp. 137–138). The first, which he terms *kotenteki* (classical), includes the works from "Yamizakura" to "Samidare," composed under the guidance of Nakarai Tōsui. The second, in Shioda's terms *katateki* (transitional), exhibits some influence from Kōda Rohan in works from "Umoregi" to "Yamiyo." The third period, which Shioda calls *gendaiteki* (contemporary), includes some of her best known works, from "Otsugomori" to "Takekurabe." He considers this to be the period when she had achieved a distinct personal style.

however, and her father, recognizing his daughter's love of learning and aptitude for letters, persuaded his wife to allow Natsu to study the techniques of *waka* poetry by enrolling in the Hagi-no-ya, Nakajima Utako's well-known school for young women interested in that traditional literary art.

Encouraged by a schoolmate's success in publishing a short story, Ichiyō turned her attention to writing prose. Her first advisor in this effort was Nakarai Tōsui (1860–1926), a journalist and *gesaku*-style writer for whom she formed a romantic attachment that has been of considerable interest to her biographers. Eventually, the association with Tōsui ended, and Ichiyō began to develop her craft under the influence of other writers, such as Kōda Rohan and Ozaki Kōyō.[4] In common with these writers, Ichiyō emulated the literary style and form of the Genroku period literature, which was in considerable vogue at the time. But her years of training in poetic techniques left an evident mark upon her prose style, and her distinctive use of Japan's long literary tradition is pronounced.

Ichiyō's relationship to traditional literature provoked considerable discussion even during her lifetime, and has continued to engage critics to the present day.[5] For our purposes, it is crucial that we explore this relationship, not only within the context of literary history as a whole, but also in terms of the moment when Ichiyō wrote. Her social and economic background and the limitations and opportunities that her personal experience provided were instrumental in determining the content of her work and forming her finished style, and unless we specifically delineate these elements, we may be tempted to indulge in half-truths of generalization—admiring her for the wrong things or criticizing her for her particular strengths. For Ichiyō's work represents, I think, a broad and generalized feminine experience constrained by the particularities of an actual and limiting

---

4 Ozaki Kōyō was a spokesman for this return to the spirit of the *genroku* period. Rejecting the need to go outside the Japanese culture for narrative models, he suggested that Ihara Saikaku's work was a sufficient model for aspiring writers.

5 See especially Matsusaka Toshio's detailing of her sources in *Higuchi Ichiyō kenkyū* (Tokyo: Kyōiku Shuppan Sentā, 1971). Seki Ryōichi's *Higuchi Ichiyo kōshō to shiron*, (Tokyo: Yūseidō, 1971) analyzes traditional dramatic techniques evident at points in "Takekurabe" (pp. 310–317.) Yoshida Seiichi's essay "Ichiyō shōsetsu to koten" in vol. 3 of *Kindai bungaku kanshō kōza* (Tokyo: Kadokawa Shoten, 1959) also touches upon this issue.

context, and from the tension between the two developed a literature of unique power and sensitivity which evades easy classification.

In coming to a balanced understanding of her work, we cannot ignore the fact that Ichiyō was a young woman shaped in traditional mold, a mold far more pervasive in the lives of her countrywomen than the Western veneer of the times would indicate. Although "Westernization" had a profound impact upon Japan throughout the Meiji period, the actual effect of Western ideals upon the condition of women in general is a complex issue.[6] In literature by male writers of the time, such as Futabatei Shimei's *Ukigumo* (1887–1889), we find depictions of the "modern girl," educated in accordance with the new Western ideas; but although such portraits tell us something of the situation of the "new" woman, as seen from the perspective of the progressive male intellectual (and something of the perplexity with which he viewed this modern hybrid creature), they do not address the more widespread circumstances of the traditional woman.

A few women of wealthy and upper-class families received the mixed blessing of a Western education at Christian schools set up for that purpose, but women such as Ichiyō—whose social opportunities and privileges were quite restricted—had to face the survival of feudal attitudes more directly. That the relative influence of social and economic status and the changes taking place rapidly throughout the Meiji period are crucial in appreciating the full significance and quality of Ichiyō's literary production is far clearer when we see Ichiyō through the eyes of a progressive feminist thinker, Hiratsuka Raicho (1878–1971), founder of Seitō.[7] Raicho does not give full weight to

---

[6] As is clearly pointed in Joy Paulson's introductory chapter in *Women in Changing Japan* (Joyce Lebra, Joy Paulson, and Elizabeth Powers, eds. [Stanford: Stanford University Press, 1976), the Meiji Restoration represented only a relative loosening of restrictions on women. Although it did permit women to obtain divorces, a right previously denied them, the revised Meiji Civil Code of 1898 "rather than improving the status of women simply codified existing custom, providing additional sanctions to the family system." The national universities were closed to women until 1913, when a few were admitted to the least prestigious. In reaction to an incipient movement for the social and political equality of women, Article Five of the Peace Preservation Law of 1889 "prohibited women from joining political associations and from sponsoring or attending political meetings." And, of course, it was not until December of 1945 that the Japanese woman obtained the right to vote (see pp. 14–16).

[7] Seitō was both the name of the group and the name of the magazine it published from 1911 to 1916.

either Ichiyō's own origins or the constraints of her special literary moment. In his article "Naze josei kaiho no undo na no ka?" Haga Noboru quotes Raicho.

Indeed, the basic thoughts and feelings flowing through all of Ichiyō's brief life and the more than twenty volumes of her personal record can be condensed in a single line from one of the diaries: "I am only a woman, so although I may wish for certain things, how can they possibly come to pass?"...I understand that Ichiyō's works are all the more attractive to men now. That is not surprising, for in addition to the appeal of a "feminine" writer, sincerely and intimately depicting the private emotions of women, each additional rendering in this manner of some weak woman's sad fate fits into the concept men have of women—or rather the concept itself assuages an egotistical need, inciting masculine pity by awakening in men the pleasant sensation of awareness of their own strength.[8]

As cited in Haga's article,[9] Raicho severely criticizes Ichiyō for lacking creativity and the power to address social issues and states further that she does not think for herself. In contrast, Raicho praises the work of Yosano Akiko because her poetry does exhibit a strong feminist consciousness. Haga, however, sounds a necessary note of caution concerning the aptness of Raicho's critique, especially as it seems to equate literary value with the assertion of a kind of feminism still largely the possession of a particular class. "In other words one cannot help wondering whether the women's liberation of people with Raicho's privileged background and upper-class standing was not superficial, and, moreover, did not have a certain prefabricated quality because it had been absorbed from Western culture."[10]

In these terms liberation was a concept affordable by only a privileged few among the millions of Japanese women of the day. After all, Ichiyō and her mother and sister had found themselves caught in the contradictions of a particular social and historical moment. Raised to depend financially upon the male, they had no male

---

[8] The article appears in a special issue of *Rekishi Dokuhon*'s biographical series, *Meiji-Taishō o ikita gojūnin no onnatachi*, no. 15 (Summer 1980). The quotation from Raicho appears on p. 54.

[9] Haga's alteration of the order of Raicho's argument in her original essay, "Higuchi Ichiyō onna toshite" has the effect of subtly altering her emphasis.

[10] Haga, "Naze josei kaiho no undo na no ka," p. 55.

family members upon whom to depend and had to reconcile the traditional concept of the woman's role with a social reality in which their adherence to that role could not protect them from the economic upheavals of a new age. Additionally, we should not lose sight of the fact that in the period of more than fifteen years between Ichiyō's death and the publication of Raicho's article (1913), societal changes had altered the literary context to a marked degree. Added to the differences in their educational and social backgrounds, then, is the fact that the author and her critic cannot really be seen as women of the same time. Although born only six years earlier, Ichiyō did not survive the nineteenth century, whereas Raicho established herself as a force in the liberation movement of the early twentieth century and understandably opposed attitudes in the immediate past that she saw as standing in the way of change.

If we are to appreciate Ichiyō's contribution to Japanese letters, then, we must seek to relocate her in the context of her own time, to understand how her work actually transforms the traditional forms of the past into a vision of the present, and to uncover the connection between her personal experience and the view of her own historical moment that emerges from her work. To do this, it is quite possible to start from the same place that Raicho does and yet arrive at an entirely different evaluation. Although Ichiyō was in no position to challenge established tradition directly, she is far from merely pandering to a male sense of superiority by supplying male readers with poignant stories about weak women. Instead, her fiction uses a context in which the full weight of traditional values is brought to bear upon the individual's personal aspirations. The lasting impact of her mature fiction, in fact, arises from just this fictional combination of individual desires and public constraints, for Ichiyō's works, while fully in the received tradition of Edo and earlier fiction—in being almost illustrated literary histories in fictional form, rich in the polysemous intertextuality that has always been a hallmark of Japanese letters[11]—are yet thoroughly accessible to a more modern (and Western?) concern with the conflict between the individual and the environment. In many of her works (here "Takekurabe" is

---

[11] In "The Boundless Text," chapter three of *To the Distant Observer* (Berkeley and Los Angeles: University of California Press, 1979), Noël Burch discusses the implications of the polysemous and intertextual character of Japanese literature. Discussing

perhaps the best example), she combines the multifaceted social scene of Saikakuesque prose—which Western critics sometimes label "realistic"—with the image-centered lyricism that has come to be identified with the traditional Japanese poetic "sensibility," thus offering to the Western reader something of the bipolarity between objective reality and subjective experience generally associated with successful fiction. Because of this, her works at once escape the criticisms of lacking a true center of identification and narrative coherence levelled against Edo prose fiction in general and the equally severe criticism of the perceived timid solipsism of the *shishōsetsu* of the later Meiji and Taishō eras. Her fiction evinces the imprint of the social and literary realities of both times and yet combines some of the most traditional elements of Japanese fiction and poetry with a perspective that is strangely more modern and even, in a sense, more "Western" than that of her contemporaries. Ichiyō's fiction contains both "classical" lyricism and "realistic" objectivity within language; and especially in the story generally considered to be her finest, "Takekurabe," she achieves a balance between the two that tempts one to say that she gives the dictum of the *Shinkokinshū* poets, "*kotoba furuku, kokoro atarashi*" (old words with a new spirit), its extension in prose.

Admittedly, critics have long noted Saikakuesque elements in her prose style[12]—an Ichiyō sentence does frequently have the syntactic appearance and grammatical constructions of the Saikaku sentence—and the resemblance in the surfaces of their fictional worlds is indeed striking. Substantial differences in tone and focus

---

polysemy, he suggests that this tendency shows "the extent to which the 'Japanese mind' rejects linearity and 'the transparence of the signifier,' which had dominated both Western thought and art since the eighteenth century." In Burch's view, the intertextuality of Japanese literature is equally challenging to Western presuppositions for it is "a practice which in various ways totally contests the myth of the closed text and the concomitant notion of originality" (p. 47).

[11] According to Shioda Ryōhei (*Meiji joryū sakka ron*, p. 141), the comparison to Saikaku was publicly suggested in the Osaka Asahi as early as the publication of "Yamizakura." In *Nihon no kindai shōsetsu* (Tokyo: Iwanami Shoten, 1974), Nakamura Mitsuo points out that the resemblance is largely formal, and in his *Gendai Nihon bungakushi* (Tokyo: Chikuma Shobō, 1964), p. 32, Yoshida Seiichi states that she clothes what might be termed romantic emotions in a Saikakuesque style. Danly's discussion of the influence of Saikaku is a valuable one; see *In the Shade of Spring Leaves*, pp. 109–115.

indicate, however, that the fiction of each author is the product of the consciousness of a particular time, and that those times are not the same. What had been general practice among the writers of Saikaku's age had become a deliberately conservative approach by Ichiyō's time, nearly two centuries later.

Saikaku's world was one wherein the bustling vitality of the *chōnin* was evidence of an era of economic change, new social mobility, and altered values. By the time Ichiyō writes, however, that world of *chōnin* (merchant class) and pleasure quarters (a setting crucial in both "Takekurabe" and "Nigorie," two of her most famous stories) had become a fixed literary tradition and an Old Japan in its turn. Published almost ten years earlier, Futabatei Shimei's *Ukigumo* had attempted to develop and implement a new and more modern style of written language and to depict the currents of social change and the turn to the West for literary and philosophical values that distinguish the Meiji era from the past. These concerns do not seem to have touched the world of Ichiyō, a situation Raicho deplores and one that may have prompted Donald Keene to observe that her work "in a sense represents the last flowering of Tokugawa literature."[12]

Yet however traditional the society she depicts, and however conservative her prose style may seem, Ichiyō's work is no anachronism. She was a woman of far more vision, courage, and artistry than even her canonization in the Japanese literary tradition suggests. Her determination to make a living by writing, although a woman, her focus upon the psychological lives of her characters, and the conflict depicted in her works between traditional values and individual aspirations are unmistakable evidence of the consciousness of the Meiji era. Nor is there a simple equation on the formal level between Ichiyō's work and earlier models. Saikaku's fiction has a far more rapidly shifting perspective and episodic structure than does Ichiyō's. The focus of her later stories is comparatively steady, developing

---

[12] Keene, p. 70. The collection contains the translation by Edward Seidensticker of "Takekurabe" entitled "Growing Up." Robert Lyons Danly includes the full text of the story, entitled "Child's Play," among the translations appended to his critical study, *In the Shade of Spring Leaves: The Life and Writings of Higuchi Ichiyō* (New Haven: Yale University Press, 1982), but since I wish to pay particular attention to some sequences of phrases as they appear in the Japanese original, the translations in this chapter are my own.

with a careful, restrained subjectivity that offsets their vivid sense of scene and incident, and her controlled use of language serves to implicate the reader in the confrontation between the specific socioeconomic realities of her chosen context and the more universalized emotional needs of her protagonists.

Since the vitality of the writing arises in large part from a confrontation so recognizable in Western fiction, it is deceptively easy for the Westerner to identify with the apparent universality of her themes. The smoothly integrated surface of the text and the "universal" emotions depicted in many of the later works tend to lull the Western reader, especially, into a facile acceptance of a product deftly finished and fully refined. However genuine our appreciation may be at this level, it neither recognizes the craft of the writing as the culmination of a process of discipleship, experimentation, and adaptation nor acknowledges the crucial role that particularity of scene, linguistic multivalence, and the historic moment play in the articulation of the specific text.

To be sure, the first privilege of the reader, and by extension the critic, is a simple response to artistry. Yet despite the emotional validity of such a reaction, there is much to be said for the conscious and conscientious reconsideration of the grounds from which response itself arises. The question becomes, then, not "How does the text make me feel?" but "How does the text make me feel what I feel?" In that case, we as critics reconstruct neither ourselves nor the text but the process by which the text becomes what it is for us. Recognizing that the apparent human truths of the literature of another tradition are also the product of its distinct historical and social formations, we can then move beyond the universal or the general to the particulars from which they arise. The work of art is a historical fact, an event that must be delineated in its verbal unfolding, and only the discipline of the actual language and structures of individual texts can serve to keep criticism (and generalization) honest.

Nowhere, perhaps, can direct textual analysis yield more than in the cases of those works that do not fit theoretical constructs—of genre, of period, or, for example, of the kind of polemical ideal that Raicho has proposed—those texts that slip between the interstices of that tidy classification once so dear to Western critics and so inadequate for the textual reality of Japanese literature. And nowhere is this more evident than in "Takekurabe." In the opening pages, a virtual panorama of Japanese literature (classical sensibility and imagistic compression coexist with Tokugawa vitality and commercialism from the initial sentence), the text begins to build its own implicit framework from the language and sensibilities of the past. Beneath the glitter of image and the flash of event lies the syntax of plot.

> Mawareba Ōmon no mikaeri yanagi ito nagakeredo, Ohaguro-dobu ni tomoshibi utsuru sangai no sawagi mo te ni toru gotoku. (p. 402)[13]

> If you go around to the great gate of the quarter, the way is long as the trailing branches of the willow of the backward glance, but the lights gleaming in the Ohaguro ditch and the revelry in the third-floor rooms of the pleasure houses which they reflect seem close enough to touch.

In the opening phrases, the appearance of the concessive form (*nagakeredo*) provides some hint that this is a world in which superficial judgments are not always reliable and marks the first sounding of a linguistic motif that verbally signals an almost regular alternation between an initial impression and a corrective reality. What may seem far at first is synesthetically transformed into images of sight and sound close enough to touch. The reader's locus is instantly pinpointed spatially, but the temporal perspective is more fluid. The great gate of the Yoshiwara, the willow of the backward glance, and the Ohaguro ditch are at once landmarks and symbols of a world familiar to the reader from Edo plays, tales, and prints. It is the famed "floating world" into which the reader is about to be drawn, and the initial phrases evoke it whole. Although Raicho might object to the established traditions that the use of a world so familiar from the literature of the past calls to mind ("one more depiction of the sad fate of a weak woman"), a less polemical perspective should permit the text to suggest another reading of that world, as the language of the passage subtly begins to build a particular structure of desire and defeat.

Almost photographically realistic detail combines with striking images and carefully controlled language to delineate a social context

---

[13] The page citations from "Takekurabe" are from Shioda Ryōhei, Wada Yoshie, and Higuchi Etsu, eds., *Higuchi Ichiyō zenshū* [Collected Works of Higuchi Ichiyō], (Tokyo: Chikuma Shobō, 1966), vol. 1.

that limits and alters expectation, not only for the characters, but for the reader as well. Although none of the characters of this world has yet appeared, the traces of human action are everywhere ("*Mawareba,*" "*mikaeri,*" "*sawagi,*" "*te ni toru*"), for the context of the quarter is a surpassingly human one. The very name "*Ohaguro,*" by invoking the image of blackened teeth, indicates the presence of the quarter's women and serves the function of poetic compression by superimposing this image on that of the lights gleaming in the dark water. Yet for all the rich intertextuality of this beginning, it has particular reference to a specific commercial reality—a social world built upon a saleable product—these women of the Yoshiwara. Their customers, too, themselves the lifeblood of the quarter, are merely suggested in the ceaseless going and coming of the carriages: "And one divined immeasurable prosperity in the ceaseless to and fro of the carriages" ("akekurenashi no kuruma no yukiki ni hakari shirarenu zensei o uranaite," p. 402).

In the next clause another concessive reversal creates an awareness of the paradox that a place whose name has the very odor of sanctity is situated in the area of the pleasure quarters: "*Although* the name of the Daionjimae area smacks of the holy image of Buddha, *even so* the people who live here say it's a lively place," ("'Daionjimae to na wa hotoke-kusakeredo, saritowa yōki no machi to sumitaru hito no mōshiki," p. 402). Obviously, the inhabitants' values have little to do with Buddhist goals. The first people to appear in the narrative are those whose lives are devoted to the ends of the quarter. And despite the prosperity that the traffic of carriages suggests, we, as readers, encounter only a very particular group of people—those who live merely on the fringes of the quarter and do not share in the financial success it holds out to some.

Accordingly, with another turn—"Once you turn at the corner of the Mishima Shrine" ("Mishimasama no kado o magarite yori")—we are in an area where the dwellings become jumbled together and prosperity is a ceaselessly pursued chimera, "a place where a decent living cannot be made at all" ("akinai wa katsufutsu kikanu tokoro," p. 402). Before going on to single out some typical figures from among the crowds of this neighborhood, in each of whose lives might be seen a history of the area, Ichiyō makes an almost casual generalization about this community that makes explicit the discrepancy between its ambitions and its actuality.

"Please Ōtori Daimyojin, if you will vouchsafe great riches to our customers, then we will make many times the profit on our goods!" was something everyone seems to have been saying, *but* ... (pp. 402–403)

Namu'ya Ōtori Daimyojin, kau hito ni sae daifuku o ataetamaeba seizōmoto no warera manbai no rieki o to hitogoto ni iumeredo

For all the obvious pragmatism of this prayer, it is the expression of the most heartfelt desire of the people here—qualified immediately, however, by the imposition of reality: "Well, that was something beyond the realm of possibility; around here one did not hear rumors of wealthy men" ("Saritowa omoi no hoka naru mono, kono atari ni daichōja no uwasa mo kikazariki," p. 403). Ichiyō poses human aspiration against social limitation, the world wished for against the world that is. With a light flick of irony, she restores a fuller sense of the surroundings.

The syntactic reversals of the passage, while not obtrusive, nevertheless make the implicit demand that the reader be constantly willing to modify expectations, and this linguistic undercutting prefigures a dynamic that will be reinforced in characterization and in imagery, ultimately becoming the thematic ground of the story. Thus, Ichiyō's controlled language sounds a first note of caution, although our consciousness of this connotation of the phrasing is blocked by the lively and shifting detail of the scene. In "Takekurabe" surface events are not the whole tale; rather, our sense of being drawn into the life of the quarter will be integrated with a movement into the lives of its people. We pass through the turning streets toward a perspective that runs ever deeper beneath the surface. In contrast to Saikaku, who chooses to remain on the surface of this world and to move his tales rapidly through the episodes that make up the lives of his protagonists, Ichiyō creates a sharp sense of conflicting interiority, usually by concentrating upon a brief but crucial episode in her protagonists' lives.

The incredible density of the opening description, then, subtly illustrates the process Frank Kermode describes in *The Sense of an Ending:* "All plots have something in common with prophecy, for they must appear to deduce from the prime matter the form of a future."[14] The prime matter in this case is a particularly constraining

---

[14] Frank Kermode, *The Sense of an Ending: Studies in the Theory of Fiction* (New

and constricted social reality, and the form of an inevitable future is already latent in this early passage, in the reversals we have examined and in the series of vignettes that follow and that trace the evolution of individuals within the patterns of the quarter. As the first section draws to a close by focusing on those characters whose experience will be our most particular concern—the children—one cannot escape the particularity of the setting.

It is a mark of Ichiyō's discernment as a writer that she chooses not just children, but these children living in the shadow of the licensed quarter, who are surely a challenge to the concept of childlike innocence. They have, moreover, already reached that moment in life when the future presses heavily upon them. They are adolescents between the ages of twelve and fifteen, specific children at the moment of transition from a relatively carefree world in which they merely imitate the outward forms of adulthood (its fashions and its language) to the actual world of the adults of the quarter—one that has its darkness as well as its brash lights.

Soon necessity will impose its harsher rules on what is yet for them a game, and their vivid present will become an immutable future. The forms are waiting to be filled. Nobuyuki,[15] the story's central male character, already has the air of the priest he will become, and young Shōtarō is even now going about the business of collection which he will inherit from his moneylending grandmother. Midori, too, has a partial sense of what is to come, for she is a constant observer of her older sister, Ōmaki, a geisha whose profession has become the foundation of her whole family's comparative prosperity and whose present is Midori's future.

Ichiyō has selected precisely that time in their lives, however, that allows a kind of innocence fundamentally at odds with the limitations of the outside world. For if the children are thoroughly at home on the fringes of the Yoshiwara, they are as yet unaware that some human aspirations and emotions must be denied root in such

---

York: Oxford University Press, 1967), p. 83.

[15] The reading given the characters of this name is not uniform. The initial reference includes the surname and is given as Fujimoto Nobuyuki. Thereafter the character is referred to variously as Nobuyuki, Nobu, Fujimoto, and Shin'nyo, the last reading having more specifically Buddhist overtones. In the translation I have confined myself to the use of Nobuyuki and its shortened form, but the reading given in the *Zenshū* is retained in the romanized text.

an environment. As the story progresses, we find that, whereas minor characters like Chōkichi and Sangorō have essentially come to terms with their situations, Nobuyuki, Shōtarō, and Midori are all developing signs of a sensitivity in conflict with the mores of the quarter. Since Midori's maturation is so close to the story's central significance, we will be considering it at some length later on, but Shōtarō and Nobuyuki indicate in their thoughts, words, and actions how they, at this particular time, have developed an introspective separation from what had until now been their normal context.

Shōtarō, for example, has not yet gained the detachment that will be necessary for him if he is successfully to assume his grandmother's role in the quarter. He is too easily moved to tears, he confesses to Midori.

> I wonder if I have a weak spirit. Sometimes I will be thinking about one thing and another, you know. Just now it's still all right, but on moonlit winter nights when I go around collecting interest in the Tama-chi area and come to the embankment, many times I start crying. Not that I would cry because of the cold, and I don't even know myself why it is that I cry. It's just that I start thinking about various things. (p. 417)[16]

This is hardly the sensibility of a moneylender. Yet even though his statement here is remarkably frank, there is an obvious separation between emotion and understanding.

Nobuyuki, in his turn, is quite aware of the distance between himself and his family, of whom he actually disapproves, but the definite nature of his feelings does not seem to make it any easier for him than for Shōtarō to translate feelings into outright opposition. He may be uncomfortable with the ways of the quarter, but his father could be called the ideal priest for this place, so much in harmony is he with the prevailing neighborhood materialism. "Invocations to the Buddha in the morning—the accounts at night" ("Asa nembutsu ni yū kanjō," p. 428), sums up his approach to life. Much to Nobu's disgust, his father encourages his mother to sell wares at the frequent festivals and sets up his sister in a shop where her

---

[16] *Zenshū*, p. 417. In this and other longer passages where I am concerned not so much with an examination of the linguistic technique as with the operation of longer narrative units within the story, the romanized version of the text is omitted.

charms are as much on display as the tea she sells. From the crass commercialism of his family only Nobu stands back. Yet, for all of his objections to his family's conduct, he remains silent: "In the society of his friends he was considered to have the perverse nature of the obstinate, but, in fact, underneath, he was weak-willed" ("tomohōbai wa henkutsumono no ijiwaru to mezasedomo onozukara shizumi iru kokoro no soko no yowaki koto," p. 428).

The same overdeveloped sensitivity to appearances and the same contradiction between a harsh exterior and internal weakness are evident in his relationship with Midori. What had earlier been the friendly association between two schoolmates rapidly begins to break down for him under the pressure of teasing from others. Nobu withdraws from Midori without her being aware of any reason for the withdrawal and without his understanding the complex nature of his feelings toward her. Thus, what had formerly been an unself-conscious relationship is now subjected to that peculiarly painful introspective scrutiny of which adolescents are often capable.

In presenting the contrast between the world as the young protagonists wish it might be and the realities that surround them, Ichiyō maintains a subtly differentiated role as mediator. When it comes to sketching in the quarter's background, she clearly functions as the reader's guide. This position is taken from the opening passage, where the *"Mawareba"* (if you turn) and *"magarite yori"* (once you turn) are linguistic signs of her directing hand. The emphasis upon the specifics of the particular locale, which echoes in phrases like *"kono atari ni"* (in this neighborhood) indicates how strong a determinant she feels the social setting is. The reader becomes her initiate, then, and all the detail provided becomes a means of instruction. Therefore, when she wishes to explain the reasons for Midori's precocious assurance, she carefully describes the value placed upon the young girl in the neighborhoods surrounding the quarter as to those to whom this world is in large measure alien: "It is difficult to explain just why it should be so, but honor is accorded here to the courtesan that those who live far from the quarter have no way of comprehending" ("doko ga yoi tomo mōshigata-keredo oiranshū tote koko nite no uyamai, tachi-hanarete wa shiru ni yoshi nashi," p. 423).

This is the world that must be made clear to the reader, but there is another world that seems to open up for a time for the main characters, a private realm of feelings and emotions for which the quarter has no vocabulary. Face to face with a new dimension in their lives, the young people lose their cheerful glibness—for this new world is best described by silence and most clearly illuminated by the image. It is in dealing with this other reality, peculiar to the last days of childhood, that Ichiyō's lyric powers come into full play. She serves as an instructor and guide in the objective rendering of setting, and when she deals with this psychological and emotional aspect, she apparently maintains the same objective distance. At the same time, however, she allows the protagonists' actions and silences to speak for themselves in a second, minor key, and the significance of this inner life is built upon through a series of brief images that carry the brunt of a meaning the characters themselves do not fully understand. It is almost as if the reader and the characters make a journey to the same border between a public world and a private realm of feelings from opposing directions. Readers must be initiated into those realities that are the background of the story and that are familiar ground for the characters. Then they in turn must take on the role of interpreter of that private realm which is new and inexplicable for the children. Although the children continue their accustomed activities for a while, changes in each one of them and in his or her psychological relationship to the others and to their world are already beginning to take place, and it is through the use of imagery that Ichiyō marks this divergence. In the scenes of the battle at the stationer's, the encounter at Midori's gate, and the final festival and in the closing passage, her use of an image as the unexplicated symbol of the inner world becomes increasingly clear.

Perhaps the functioning of such an image is most muted in the battle between the main-street and back-street gangs, but that may well be because, at this point in the story's development, action still seems to have the major claim upon the reader's attention. The children of the main street are gathered at their "place," the stationer's shop, preparing for the evening's entertainment. Shōtarō sends his underling, Sangorō, to fetch Midori, and then he, in turn, is called away by his grandmother. In planning his attack, the swaggering Chōkichi, leader of the opposition, had envisioned it as a final showdown battle between himself backed by Nobu (as the emblem of back-street "respectability") and Shōtarō, the male leader of the main-street gang. Once again expectations are not fulfilled. Shōtarō has gone, and Nobu is prevented by an errand from joining with the invading back-street forces, so what in fact takes place, along with the beating of Sangorō, is a bitter clash between Chōkichi and Midori.

In more ways than one, the incident makes its most indelible mark upon Midori, who has approached the evening as the lady princess of the main-street gang. While poor Sangorō loiters outside her house, Midori is prepared for a triumphal entry by her doting mother.

> Midori might be her own child, but she thought her beautiful, and repeatedly stood back to look and knelt down to apply finishing touches. There at the neckline, for example, the powder was not yet heavy enough. The unlined kimono Midori wore was of a cool-looking pale blue silk, bound round by a rather narrow straw-colored obi embroidered with golden thread. (pp. 412–413)

This carefully constructed image will receive a final touch quite out of keeping with the meticulous preparation pictured here. For when Midori does finally arrive at the paper shop, she meets not Shōtarō, but the invading gang from the back street, and in the quarrel that she has with Chōkichi as she seeks to protect Sangorō, she is muddled in fact and by words.

> "What's this prostitute's sass for? You beggar trailing after your sister! This is the answer you deserve." From behind the crowd, Chōkichi took off his muddy sandal and threw it, hitting her squarely on her forehead where it left a dirty mark. (p. 414)

A less visible injury is also inflicted on Midori at the same time, for Chōkichi then shouts to the crowd that Nobu is on their side, and Chōkichi's insult and Nobu's betrayal become tied together in Midori's mind. Although she seems to pass off the incident without taking it too seriously, at this point a separation takes place between her childish words of defiance and the adolescent wound they conceal. For some time previously Nobu had been cold to her for fear of being teased by others, but the night of the battle at the stationer's marks an open break.

> Stretched between them somehow was a great river on which boats

and rafts were forbidden and each of them walked apart along its opposing banks.

Midori may have completely stopped going to school on the very day
after the festival because, needless to say, she could not erase the feelings of humiliation that tormented her as easily as she had washed the
mud from her forehead. (pp. 420–421)

Here it is obvious that Ichiyō is using the images of the river and the
mud as metaphors to capture emotional states and that these images
are a more trustworthy indication of Midori's feelings than her own
words would be. Just as Chōkichi's insults were connected with her
sister's profession, so Midori bases her defiant response on a different
sense of position as Ōmaki's sister, and she makes a brave-sounding
argument from this: "Her sister was Ōmaki of the Daikokuya, and
although she herself was just someone who kept an eye on things
when no one else was around, there was no reason why she had to
give way to that Chōkichi or to endure the persecution of young
master priest Nobu at the Ryugeji" (p. 421). The mark on her forehead, coupled with references to her sister, would seem to indicate a
sense of shame about Ōmaki's occupation that Midori nowhere ad-
mits; and her abuse of Chōkichi, and, especially, Nobu, with its stur-
dy assertion of her own worth, is belied by the fact that from the
very next day she refuses to go to school any longer.

Midori's words are now an unreliable indicator of her feelings,
a fact that becomes increasingly evident as the story progresses. This
is not because she is lying, but because she herself does not understand what is happening to her. Midori's delight in the world of the
quarter had lasted longer than had Nobuyuki's or Shōtarō's, but it is
already clear that there is a certain hollowness in her proud defiance.
The resonance of the images of the river and the mud is not obtrusive in the above passage; but, as the words of the characters become less reliable or, in fact, are absent altogether, the reader learns
to rely more heavily upon what their actions and the images suggest
when considered together. Here, Ichiyō herself seems to offer no
help, appearing to profess a studied ignorance of what is going on
and to maintain carefully the same distance from her characters that
had been hers from the beginning. Readers are, nevertheless, guided
in constructing their own meaning for the text on more subtle levels.
The pace of the action is one guide; the silence of the characters and
the vividness of the imagery are others.

All of these elements are evident in the two-part sequence that takes place by Midori's gate. There, the reader can sense a new reality that contradicts expectations one more time. Once the characters have been deprived of speech as the mode of accurate expression of feelings, imagery comes into its own as an emblem of emotion. Seki Ryōichi[17] feels that the influence of *jōruri* and *kabuki*, which in his opinion is a generally important element in Ichiyō's writing, is especially clear in the construction of these sections. The dramatic tension of the narrated scene combined with the almost stylized postures of the silent characters does give, as he suggests, a strong impression of dramatic pantomime. Two full sections are required to encompass what is essentially about five minutes of the story's action, the first beginning *in medias res*. Nobu is already caught in the predicament in which he will be frozen for a good part of the passage. He is immobilized outside the gate of the house where Midori lives by difficulties in managing a package for his sister and a recalcitrant umbrella. To make matters worse, the thong of his sandal has snapped.

Midori, seeing someone by her gate who is having difficulties with a sandal, snatches up a strip of cloth that might serve for makeshift repairs and hurries out with it. When she comes close enough to see who it is, however, the scene begins to take on a slow-motion intensity. The moment hangs in an agonizing seesaw of adolescent self-consciousness. Action, inaction, and gesture take the place of words.

> Her face turned crimson, and as if this were a momentously important meeting, her heart beat faster and she looked about to see if anyone was watching; as she was timidly drawing closer to the gate, Nobu, too, suddenly glanced behind him, and seeing who it was, broke into a cold sweat, mutely wishing that he could dash off barefoot as he was. (pp. 435–436)

That the strong reactions of the two seem out of proportion to the apparently trivial nature of the incident is an indication that something quite outside their normal experience is happening within them. What they do not understand cannot be put into words; only motion betrays emotion.

---

[17] Seki, *Higuchi Ichiyō kōshō to shiron*, pp. 274–276, 315, 316.

Ichiyō underlines the significance of this behavior by going on to contrast it with the vocal behavior one would have expected from the Midori of yesterday, the Midori we are used to, *"tsune no Midori."*

> If this had been the usual Midori, she would have pointed at him saying, "Look, look! Look at the helpless thing." Laughing uncontrollably, she would have abused him roundly, saying, 'You did a good job of spoiling our fun on festival night—trying to get revenge on Shōta. You had them beat up poor harmless Sangorō. You were behind it, telling them what to do and then leaving them to do it. Aren't you going to apologize or say you're sorry? Who do you think you are? I never asked you for anything at all. I have my father and mother. I have the master of the Daikokuya and my sister, and I don't need any favors from a two-faced priest like you. Be good enough to stop calling me a prostitute. If you have something to say, stop snickering in the shadows and come here and say it. You'll see I'm ready to take you on any time. Well, then, how about that?" (p. 436)[18]

In fact, the extraordinary thing about this passage, as narrative, is that Ichiyō spends so much time in composing a denunciation that is never uttered. She chooses to maintain an ostensibly uncomprehending attitude toward her character and emphasizes this by continuing to speak in the quarter's terms when the protagonist herself begins to move away from that perspective and toward a more introspective consciousness. Given the manner in which Midori has been presented to this point, everything in the imaginary speech sounds completely natural, but this is the language of yesterday's Midori, rich in the abuse that is almost second nature to the combative children of the quarter, and it no longer rises to her lips. She is not even thinking in these terms now: "Without saying anything, she shrank into the shadow of the gate; even her hesitating there, unable to go away, with her heart beating wildly, was not the behavior of the usual Midori" ("mono iwazu kōshi no kage ni kogakurete, sari-tote tachisaru demo nashi ni tada ujiuji to mune todorokasu wa tsune no Midori no sama nite wa nakariki," p. 436).

---

[18] *Zenshū*, p. 436. The passage both begins and ends with the phrase "tsune no Midori," a device that emphasizes the content.

By contrasting Midori as she was and as she now is and what Midori ought to do and say but does not, Ichiyō accomplishes two things. She clearly shifts the burden of interpretation of the actions of this new, changed Midori to the reader, maintaining what seems a uniform aesthetic distance. From this point to the end of the story, the focus of the reader's attention, however, will be moving ever further into the private realm of the characters' emotions. In the scene under consideration, some of the conditions of this inward turn are made clear. The narrator will no longer attempt fully to explain the character's motivation to us, but instead will describe actions and keep us mindful of the social context. From now on, then, just as we become aware that the characters' own words are no longer reliable guides to their inner worlds, so we also seem to have lost the guiding hand of the narrator. The desertion is only apparent, though, for, through the use of imagery, Ichiyō suggests what she does not explain.

Perhaps the clearest example of the way in which an object becomes transformed from a passing image into the symbol of an emotional construct occurs precisely at this point where the narrator professes such bewilderment. For the scene we are examining contains an image that will signify all those things that the characters and narrator do not seem to understand.

The image of a scrap of cloth is casually introduced in the scene's first section and gradually developed throughout the second. The opening of the second section indicates a shift in emphasis; rather than explaining Midori's puzzling behavior, which had occupied the narrator's attention at the close of the first section, Ichiyō retraces her own narrative and brings Nobu back to approach the gate once more. As the two are once again brought to the point where they are hovering, each on his or her own side of the gate, in an eternity of hesitation broken only by the voice of Midori's mother calling from inside the house, Midori finally breaks into action. She tosses the strip of cloth she is holding through the gate, only to have it ignored by the silent Nobu. Indignant and feeling once again rebuffed, she turns and stalks back into the house, but the strip of cloth lying abandoned on the ground becomes the focus of suggested emotion as the passage continues.

Once Midori is gone, Ichiyō turns her narrator's eye upon the unfortunate Nobu, stranded not only in the rain but also in hesitation between his inner wishes and his inability to act upon them. At this point the bit of cloth that Midori had offered him begins to grow in significance—first in Nobu's eyes and then in the reader's own. The gesture of friendship and concern had indeed been rejected, but the text suggests how unwilling that rejection is. As Midori's footsteps fade away, Nobu's public role of stern indifference slips: "And as Nobu looked back in desolation, there it was, with the elegance of its design of maple leaves and its scarlet silk, drenched by the rain and lying close by his feet where it had fallen. Unaccountably, despite the appeal it held for him, he could not bring himself to pick it up, but stared helplessly at it in bitter distress" ("Shin'nyo wa ima zo sa-bishū mikaereba beniiri yūzen no ame ni nurete momiji no kata no uruwashiki ga wa ga ashi chikaku chiriboitaru, sozoro ni yukashiki omoi wa aredomo, te ni toriaguru koto o mo sezu, munashū nagamete ukiomoi ari," p. 438).

What had been referred to in passing, when Midori first snatched it up, as a scrap of silk left over from sewing, becomes much more explicitly described from Nobu's perspective, even to the color and pattern on the remnant, and endowed with both beauty and emotional significance. Even as Nobu stubbornly moves away from the gate, the strip of cloth exerts a power upon his emotions: "The silken maple leaves lingered in his mind's eye, and as he looked back regretfully, finding it hard to leave it abandoned there..." ("yūzen no momiji me ni nokorite, sutete suguru ni shino-bigataku kokoronokori shite mikaereba," p. 438).

For Nobu, the cloth represents at one and the same time Midori's action in extending it, a gesture toward reconciliation—and therein lies much of its appeal—and his own action of rejecting it, not in distaste but through a debilitating combination of pride and weakness. As he looks back at it this second time, Chōkichi appears, and the cloth becomes doubly out of Nobu's reach since he accepts the loan of the other's sandals. The residual image of the scene, and its last, is of the scrap of cloth lying abandoned in the rain: "Containing such regrets, the scarlet silk rested its forlorn form in vain outside the gate" ("omoi no todomaru beniiri no yūzen wa ijirashiki sugata o munashiku kōshimon no soto ni to todomenu," p. 439).

Now there is no one to see it but the narrator and the reader. Yet the strip of cloth, a mere object when Midori picked it up, has become the subject not only of the clause, but of the emotion contained in the episode. Lying unclaimed in the rain outside the gate, it is symbolic of the relationship between the two young protagonists, with its hesitations, silences, and failed reconciliation.

Whereas Nobu's hesitation seems to be totally in character, arising as it does from self-conscious pride and passive weakness rather than the harsh rejection that Midori sees in it, Midori's silence is definitely evidence of a profound shift in her consciousness. The Midori who, on an evening just prior to this scene, was totally unperturbed when the woman at the stationer's shop teased Shōta about wanting to marry her, is here mute, hesitant, and vulnerable.

That change, first manifested in this intensely private scene between the two, is registered on a public level in the next section, for Ichiyō never allows us to lose sight of the specifics of this social setting. The progression of time has been marked throughout the story by references to the public festivals and events of the quarter, and the Otori festival in November becomes the occasion for describing the point of greatest divergence between the social world of the quarter and the subjective responses of adolescence.

On Otori day, an alteration in Midori's appearance evokes a strong negative psychological and emotional reaction in her, confounding the expectations of her family and friends. Midori's hair has been fixed for the occasion in the Shimada style. Her new hairdo, a traditional geisha style, is an announcement that Midori is now to be considered a woman. Accordingly, her first public appearance as a grownup makes a visible statement of her value in terms that the quarter well understands. As Ton'ma, one of the hangers-on of the main-street gang, puts it, "That's great, isn't it? If she does become a courtesan, then next year I'll start selling seasonal goods and make some money, you know, so that I can go and buy her services" ("Ii jaa nai ka? Oiran ni nareba, ore wa rainen kara kiyamonoya ni natte okane o koshiraeru ga ne, sore o motte, kai ni yuku no da," p. 440).

The life of a young and attractive girl in the Yoshiwara area, which before held no terrors for Midori, now seems much closer and much less appealing, and she resents the Shimada hairstyle that is the outward sign of her new adult status. Because Midori has the strongest personality of all of the young protagonists and because she is the only girl among them, it is her confrontation with the quarter's mores that is most clearly marked and that allows Ichiyō to suggest her own perspective concerning the position of women in a world still controlled by the standards of the traditional mentality. Here, if anywhere in "Takekurabe," is Ichiyō's acknowledgment of the special economic constraints upon women on which the quarter is built. It is for Midori to adjust to the only real future that her world can offer, for Ichiyō has implied from the beginning that individual sensitivities cannot long survive the commercial pressures of this environment. But the sharp contrast between the lively child and the brooding young woman indicates how high at times the personal cost must be.

The section dealing with this event is handled skillfully, for the perspective Ichiyō selects for it is for the most part Shōta's, and his helpless bewilderment in dealing with Midori's reaction once again emphasizes the contrast between childhood and adulthood and between expectation and reality. Prior to the festival Midori had promised to accompany Shōta to it. While he is searching for her, he encounters those who have already seen her in her new role. Although he reacts to Ton'ma's remark with indignation, he does not understand Midori's behavior when he does find her. For he, too, is impressed by the change in her appearance, seeing her as a veritable Kyōto doll in her new finery.

Midori, however, resents her new outwardly adult status and is ashamed to be seen on the street where she had previously been so at home: "As she was sunk in a mood of heavy embarrassment and bashfulness, people's praise sounded like insults to her, and when people turned to look in admiration at the Shimada hairstyle, she imagined that they looked at her in scorn" ("Ukuhazukashi [ku, tsutsumashi] ki koto mi ni areba hito no homeru wa azakeri to kikinasarete, shimada no mage no natsukashisa ni furikaeri miru hitotachi o ba ware o sagesumu metsuki to torarete," p. 441). Her alienation from her environment is made complete when she insists on retreating in sulky silence to her home.

Shōta is thoroughly confused, and all his attempts to comfort her are rebuffed. He follows her home, attempting to coax her out of this strange mood, but Midori wants no more of words and sends him away: "Go away, Shōta, for heaven's sake, go away. I'll die if you stay any longer. Talking makes my head hurt, and listening makes me dizzy. I don't want anyone here at all, so will you please just go away" ("Kaette okure Shōtasan [gosho dakara] kaette okure, omae ga iru to watachi wa shinde shimau de arō, mono o iwareru to zutsu ga suru, kuchi o kiku to me ga mawaru, tare mo tare mo watashi no tokoro e kite wa iya nareba, omae mo dozo kaette," p. 443).

Shōta is a perfect foil for Midori here, for he still possesses the childishness to which Midori is bidding a painful farewell. The pain he feels at Midori's dismissal echoes that which Midori herself so resented when Nobu seemed to spurn her own friendly overtures. The line between them now is the line between childhood and adolescence, and once it is crossed, understanding is ruptured, and there can be no going back. As Midori puts it in her thoughts: "Ah, it's awful, it's awful, growing up is an awful thing. Why did I have to get old like this? I wish I could go back to seven months, ten months or a year ago" ("Ee iya iya, otona ni naru wa iya na koto, naze kono yō ni toshi o ba toru, mo nanatsuki, totsuki, ichinen mo moto e kaeritai ni," p. 443). Still insulated in the world of childhood, Shōta could not possibly understand her feelings, and Midori cannot bear to listen to him.

Midori's recent experience has been filled with painful emotions, which, although she cannot explain them, or perhaps because she cannot explain them, are nevertheless quite strong. The final section of "Takekurabe" becomes a measure of the acknowledgment of change, not just for Midori, but for the whole world of her childhood. She is no longer to be found among the children and gives her friends only vague promises when they invite her to join them. The wounded Shōta can no longer be heard singing cheerfully in the neighborhood, and everything now seems different on the main street: "The main street seemed rather desolate as though a light had gone out" ("omotemachi wa niwaka ni hi no kieshiyō sabishiku narite," p. 446).

The closing paragraph itself becomes a subdued envoi to childhood and its relationships. Still maintaining what seems objective distance from her characters, Ichiyō juxtaposes a series of clauses that suggest through the association of seemingly objective statement and nuance-laden image much more than what is explicit. Having lost touch with her friends, Midori has not heard the rumor that Nobu is entering a seminary, but while she is absorbed in her new self-consciousness, a small incident takes place: "On a certain frosty morning there was someone who tucked an artificial narcissus through the latticed gate from the outside" ("Aru shimo no asa suisen no tsukuribana o kōshimon no soto yori sashiireokishi mono no arikeri," p. 446). Ichiyō does not attribute this action to anyone in particular; in fact, she insists, "there was no way of knowing who had done it" ("Tare no shiwaza to shiru yoshi nakeredo"). Nevertheless, the flower appears to have a singular significance to Midori, and here Ichiyō again qualifies: "for some reason or other" ("nani yue to naku"). Midori, "with a wistful feeling" ("natsukashiki omoi nite"), "placed the flower by itself in a vase on the shelf and gazed fondly at its lonely and pure form" ("chigai dana no ichirin-zashi ni irete sabishiku kiyoki sugata o medekeru"). As was the case with the strip of cloth, the flower becomes the embodiment of emotions only by implication those of the character. And with a casual and removed statement, the story closes: "Without having herself inquired, she heard it said somewhere that the following day was the very day on which Nobu had changed to a priest's black robes in a certain seminary" ("Kiku tomo nashi ni tsutaekiku sono ake no hi wa Shin'nyo ga nanigashi no gakurin ni sode no iro kaenubeki tōjitsu narishi to zo," p. 446).

The connection between Nobu and the flower is nowhere made explicit. Only the juxtaposition of clauses suggests that the flower may have been a farewell gesture. In fact, this meaning of the association is up to the readers' discretion, for theirs has been the responsibility of interpreting the silences and the images that suggest the private realm of the protagonists' feelings. The effectiveness of this combination of a clearly delineated and fully explained outer social reality and a delicately suggested counterreality of implied emotion lies in the use of the proper narrative modes, which express two coexistent forms of experience and which place the reader in the position of mediator between them.

"Takekurabe," then, succeeds in simultaneously evoking two worlds, with aesthetic traditions of their own. The first, the surface reality, clearly formed by its Edo past, has indeed become "close enough to touch" for the reader. Taking the world of Saikaku and Chikamatsu and using a style resembling theirs, Ichiyō transforms it into one of the two poles of fictional experience. The sights and sounds, the festivals and occasions, the ins and outs of the winding streets, and the standards of conduct in the pragmatic and commercial setting of the pleasure quarter are clearly etched; but this environment no longer suggests a context of infinite possibility for variety and change. Instead, the life on the fringes of the quarter is a life grown old. Patterns have become entrenched, and social change and personal aspiration are possible only outside its sphere. Ichiyō herself had learned a hard economic lesson when she unsuccessfully attempted to operate a shop in this same neighborhood, and it is with a sense of its very restrictions that she turns to this environment for her story.

No full picture of the Meiji era in literature could emerge if we were not kept aware that in the midst of the sweeping changes instituted by the government, and in the midst of a literary context that explored the dilemma of modern "Westernized" Japanese seeking to find themselves in an increasingly industrialized society, the forms of an older Japan remained, offering a stubborn resistance to the new ideas. In the 1890s in Japan the older traditions still constrained the experience of most women. Thus, as a contrast to *Ukigumo's* Osei—caught between her advanced "Western" education, with the freedom it appeared to offer to women, and the time-honored necessity of establishing herself as someone's wife—there is Midori, whose options are even more severely limited.

The roles that the three major characters in "Takekurabe" are destined to play as geisha, priest, and moneylender take their definition from the past, and Ichiyō has been our guide and theirs to the acceptance of the inevitabilities inherent in such fixed patterns. The way in which the story develops seems naturally to "deduce from the prime matter" of the opening section the "form of a future" shaped by Yoshiwara realities. Where explanation is necessary to build up a sense of this world, Ichiyō is capable of description as colorful as Saikaku's. Where dramatic techniques will heighten our sense of the significant, as in the scene by the gate, she employs a tone reminiscent of that of Chikamatsu's *jōruri* (puppet theater) narrator. In addition, some of the rich texture of her prose comes from what may be termed contemporary intertextuality, for there are frequent allusions to songs that were then popular in the quarter and familiar to the reader of her own time.

The smooth integration of all of these literary strands from past and present is matched by a deft handling of narrative perspective. Although the story's focus upon the experience of the child/adolescent within the quarter never falters once it is established, skillful shifts in perspective accomplish a great deal in reinforcing the reader's role as interpreter. Midori's emergence into the adult world lies at the heart of the tale's significance, but Ichiyō avoids a sustained immersion in Midori's own point of view. Instead, she suggests a great deal more by using Nobu's perspective for the second of the two sections at Midori's gate and Shōta's point of view for the presentation of Midori's crisis on Otori day.

Ichiyō's intention is not to describe the world of subjectivity from a subjective standpoint, but much of the story's power lies in its evocation of the subjective world. The emotive action, after all, takes place in the abyss perceived when the world of childhood gives way to the world of adult realities. Ichiyō's success in manipulating point of view is reinforced as she renders the subjectivity of this experience in an objective manner through her skillful presentation of images. In doing so she can rely upon a tradition even more venerable than those of Edo fiction—that of classical *waka* poetry. For Ichiyō owes more than the title of her work and an occasional *engo* (word association) or *kakekotoba* (pivot-word) to the traditions of classical Japanese poetry. Her early training in *waka* techniques was to prove invaluable to her, for, in the long tradition of Japanese poetry, modes for the objectification of emotion had been thoroughly explored. Especially in the aesthetics of the *Shinkokinshū* poets, the use of images to suggest apparently agentless emotion had been developed to a fine art. Robert Brower and Earl Miner term this "descriptive symbolism," an effect arising from noun/image-laden poetry in which "the associations of the images convey the significance of the scene for human experience."[19] Ichiyō's use of imagery is strongly reminiscent

---

[19] Robert H. Brower and Earl Miner, *Japanese Court Poetry* (Stanford: Stanford University Press, 1961), p. 275.

of this technique, her treatment of the scrap of cloth and the flower illustrating how emotion seems at times to reside in the object itself rather than in the characters.

With an objective narrative pole firmly established in the detailed social setting of the Yoshiwara fringe world, Ichiyō presents subjective experience which gains depth by being posed against its inflexible reality. The images of a muddied forehead, a strip of cloth lying in the rain, a young girl's hairdo, and a single flower standing alone in a vase call upon the reader's power of association and memory or understanding of the uncertainty and pain of adolescence, and create the effect of universalized experience that transcends one time and place. Images become the transmitters of unarticulated emotions, attaining their full symbolic value only by the delicate operation of suggestion. We can, after all, be taught the realities of the quarter, but we must know implicitly the realities of the heart. Neither kind of reality can be understood in its fullest dimension, however, at least in Ichiyō's fictional world, without the opposite and equal presence of the other.

Ichiyō herself keeps the narrative lines flowing continually between the two poles of her fictional world. When we examine the nature of the images she uses, it is clear that they are not as classical as they might seem. Could anything be more apparently traditional than red maple leaves or a single flower? Yet, in fact, these are not natural maple leaves, nor is this a living flower. Instead, the images from nature are found in manufactured goods, and the artificiality of the quarter enters into what might be seen as the most purely lyric moments of the story. It requires only a small extension of the imagination to realize that Midori herself faces the future as what could be termed one of the primary "products" of Yoshiwara commerce.

So, although the conflict between the experiencing self and a limiting objective world forms the dynamic of "Takekurabe" and strikes a sympathetic chord in even the Western reader (who is accustomed to dealing with the individual character as one who defines himself against society), there is nothing Western in Ichiyō's approach. She has, however, made herself difficult to classify for Japanese critics because of the bipolarity of her world. The facile generalization that Western critics are often tempted to make about the overwhelmingly lyric and subjective nature of Japanese literature tends to skip rather lightly by the lively objectivity of Saikaku and the *gesaku* writers who followed him. Ichiyō's particular ability to synthesize the objective and realistic tradition with other more poetic elements in her country's past indicates that it is not inevitable that one pole be sacrificed to the other and that, even though the introduction of the Western novel had tremendous impact upon the development of modern Japanese fiction, the native tradition has a greater flexibility than is frequently accorded it, for Ichiyō was able to construct a literary edifice—comprehensible to and beautiful in Western eyes—from purely native materials.

Mori Ōgai called Ichiyō "a true poet," recognizing her place in a continuing classical tradition. She was also termed "a female Saikaku" and "Chikamatsu's daughter." A close reading of "Takekurabe" confirms that there is justice in all of these observations. Ichiyō did make full use of the literary tradition; and the vitality of her work suggests that, at the very time when other, more "modern" and experimental writers were turning to models outside their culture for a new spirit to revitalize the depleted fictional forms of the immediate past, Ichiyō and other neoclassicists managed to realize an alternative possibility. That she was able to do so serves as a reminder that, although for many Japanese writers—and this includes even those Westernized writers of her time—subjectivity may be the natural and easy mode in which to express the individual's response to the world, it is not the only potential the language and the literature have. Remembering this, we may not fall back too soon upon the comforting assurances of classification. "Objectivity" was not any more the gift of the West to Japanese literature than it was the inheritance of the Edo past; and even the "subjectivity" of Japanese writers, which we are quick to acknowledge, eludes its fullest definition in Western terms. The terms and the dichotomy perceived between them are themselves Western.

Unless the abstract operation of a generalized (and imported) terminology is confronted by the verbal processes of the specific text, we might remain complacent in our assessment of Japanese literature. Overlooking the existence of the Ken'yūsha and the works of writers related to it, we envision the field of Meiji literature as one more area in which the cultural hegemony of the West can clearly be demonstrated. To the extent that we remain receptive to the discourse of a

more conservative literary tradition that flourished still in this particular social and literary context, we shall not sacrifice the rich complexity of the functioning and still vital work to the comfort of a
unified "overview."

Furthermore, the close examination of "Takekurabe" permits us
to consider the justice of observations like Hiratsuka Raicho's in a
more purely literary context. Whereas her position on the life and
works of Ichiyō may be justified from Raicho's own polemical perspective, a careful balance should be struck in our own response to it.
It is after all true that Ichiyō's works do not directly challenge established literary and social conventions in their depictions of the
woman's role. In "Jūsan'ya" and "Nigorie" (both works in the mature style of "Takekurabe"), the confrontation between individual
desire and social reality results in the same thwarting of the
character's wishes observable in "Takekurabe." The young wife of
"Jūsan'ya" remains within an unhappy and unequal marriage because of the benefits the relationship has afforded her own parents
and brother, thus reinforcing the claims of the *ie* upon the individual.
And in "Nigorie," Ichiyō reveals more of the squalid underside of the
life of the Yoshiwara fringe area as she somberly recounts the life
and death of the geisha O-Riki, thus approaching more nearly a realistic assessment of the desperation awaiting Midori.

In "Takekurabe," Ichiyō has presented an extremely atypical
situation by depicting the young Ōmaki as having been accompanied
to Tokyo by her family as she entered the world of the licensed quarters. In fact, the daughters of the rural poor were sold into prostitution and essentially abandoned there by families to whom they were
still obligated to send financial support. In his chapter on "Poverty
and Prostitution" from *Peasants, Rebels and Outcasts*,[20] Mikiso Hane
details the more general economic and social conditions with which
the young women of the Yoshiwara and other "pleasure" quarters
were faced and reminds us of the scale of this economic enterprise of
licensing prostitution. In Tokyo alone there were six licensed quarters. In one, the Yoshiwara, at the time when Ichiyō was writing,
there were between five thousand and seven thousand prostitutes.

---

[20] Mikiso Hane, *Peasants, Rebels and Outcasts: The Underside of Modern Japan* (New
York: Pantheon Books, 1982), p. 208.

And perhaps because she thus softened the fate of Ōmaki and the projected fate of Midori and placed even the unhappy O-Riki within the traditional tragic literary triangle of geisha-patron-wife, it is possible to see why Raicho condemned Ichiyō for having failed to challenge the conventional view of the floating world first articulated in Genroku fiction.

Nevertheless, we have seen from our reading of "Takekurabe" that Ichiyō's works do not passively transmit the past forms and ideals, but rather give them a new configuration. Ichiyō does draw fully upon traditional literary sensibilities in suggesting the reality of equally traditional culturally validated norms of behavior. But by focusing on the traditions themselves as one of two contending poles, Ichiyō shifts their role as social underpinnings and makes them visible. Her process here is perhaps analogous to that which Wolfgang Iser outlines for the Western tradition in *The Implied Reader:*

> Norms are social regulations, and when they are transposed into the novel they are automatically deprived of their pragmatic nature. They are set in a new context which changes their function, insofar as they no longer act as social regulations, but as the subject of a discussion which, more often than not, ends in a questioning rather than a confirmation of their validity.[21]

The care with which Ichiyō outlines the specific norms of the Yoshiwara fringe world and their opposition to the personal desires of the protagonists suggests that her acceptance of their validity is far from unquestioning. Ichiyō's own circumstances were not such as to suggest that societal forms could easily be overturned. More than did the progressive intellectual feminists who were to appear on the scene shortly after her death, Ichiyō had personally to contend with the very limited choices available to most of the women of her time.

The average woman of the mid and late Meiji period was in fact subject to powerful pressures to submit to the still transcendant authority of the family and of convention and possessed very few social options. While new ideas about the rights of the individual and the social equality of women were current in intellectual circles, they were *ideas* for the most part, existing as yet in theory rather than in

---

[21] Wolfgang Iser, *The Implied Reader* (Baltimore: Johns Hopkins University Press, 1978), p. xii.

practice. The brief success and notoriety that Raicho's own Seitō school was to achieve depended upon social conditions that had not yet matured when Ichiyō was writing.

Ichiyō's work can be judged by the standards that Raicho set forth in 1913 only with a certain nonchalance toward the questions of historical change and the relative impact of social class and educational background upon literary production and human potential. Ultimately, Raicho's essay says less of critical importance about Ichiyō as a writer than it suggests about an ideological shift taking place in the last years of the Meiji era. What might be called Raicho's "hard line" toward Ichiyō in 1913 was understandably the initial strong reaction of a social pioneer to a literary figure in the immediate past whom she saw as reactionary and all the more dangerous because of the acknowledged appeal of her fiction.

Direct challenge to the inherited social system in Japan was to grow as the stuff of literary discourse in the early decades of the twentieth century. The author whose works we will consider in the next chapter, Sata Ineko, was one of the leading writers in a proletarian movement constituting the principal literary and political opposition to established authority in those years. Nevertheless, Sata, who, in 1986, received the Yomiuri Bungaku prize for her study of Ichiyō, "Tsuki no en," takes a position opposed to Raicho's. Even into her eighties, then, she has maintained an interest in the Meiji writer that goes back for many decades. As her introduction to an anthology of Ichiyō's stories issued in 1953 illustrates, Sata compels us to address more directly the issue of the relationship in literary production between polemics and personal experience. It might be fitting, then, to close our discussion of Ichiyō's work with Sata's assessment. With a social and economic background more akin to Ichiyō's than Raicho's, Sata is inclined to minimize neither Ichiyō's own compassion for the people she depicts in her works nor the limitations imposed by the world in which both the author and the children of her imagination were enmeshed.

> The special characteristic of Ichiyō's fiction is that it clearly yet subtly reflects the constrictions of the society of her time along with the aspirations of human beings. The six works selected for inclusion in this edition are already established as masterpieces, but each of them is a song played upon human sorrows which cannot be controlled. The

feelings of sorrow in which she herself was trapped to a point which might be termed despair create a unity of tone in six stories whose manner of representation differs according to the various characters that are depicted in them. The tone of Ichiyō's fiction is dyed by the resignation to which she herself was forced, in other words is connected with her own life, but the deepest impression left on us by those works is not resignation, but on the contrary, is connected with the surpassing aspirations of the human spirit, and arises from Ichiyō's inner being.[22]

As we shall see in the ensuing chapters, Sata, too, strove to combine a vision of her society with the exploration of the emotional needs of the individual. This keeps her early proletarian literature from having an overwhelmingly polemical tone just as her political commitment prevents her largely autobiographical oeuvre from seeming self-indulgent. And perhaps it is their mutual concern with both poles of human experience (as well as a greater objectivity conferred by time) that enables the later writer to recognize that Ichiyō's fiction does indeed reflect "the constrictions of the society of her time" as well as "the surpassing aspirations of the human spirit."

---

[22] Sata Ineko, *Sata Ineko zenshū* [Complete Works of Sata Ineko], (Tokyo: Kōdansha, January 1978–June 1980), vol. 17, p. 112.

CHAPTER FOUR

Soundings in Time: From Sata Ineko's "Kyarameru kōjō kara" to "Yuki no mau yado"

M ORE THAN THIRTY YEARS after the death of Higuchi Ichiyō, Sata Ineko published her first short story, "Kyarameru kōjō kara" ("From the Caramel Factory) (1929).[1] In spite of some superficial resemblances in their early experiences, the literary careers of the women are in sharp contrast. The brevity of Ichiyō's life colors the view of many of her critics and interpreters with an aura of poignant romanticism not unlike that which tends to surround the poetry of Keats in the English tradition. Conversely, the extreme length of Sata's career as a writer (lasting more than fifty years into the present) is a crucially important factor in the evaluation of her overall contribution to Japanese letters. The eighteen volumes of her collected works[2] force the critic in their reading, as they undoubtedly forced the writer in their original production, to undertake a continual reevaluation of the nature of human consciousness as it accrues in time and of the social forces that act upon the evolution of the individual in the various circumstances and stages of life.

Time can be metaphorically seen as an instant in Ichiyō's work—the moment between childhood and adulthood in "Takekurabe"—or her work may be seen as the product of a

---

[1] First published in *Puroretaria geijutsu* [Proletarian Art]. At the time of its publication, Sata was married to Kubokawa Tsurujirō, a leading Marxist, and her early fiction is published under her married name. Following their divorce in 1945, however, she resumed use of her maiden name.

[2] Sata Ineko, *Sata Ineko zenshū* [Complete Works of Sata Ineko], (Tokyo: Kōdansha, January 1978–June 1980). "Kyarameru kōjō kara" appears in vol. 1, pp. 21–31, and "Yuki no mau yado" in vol. 14, pp. 314–325. My translation of "Yuki no mau yado" as "The Inn of the Dancing Snow," which is appended, appeared in *Occident* (Berkeley) (Winter 1981), pp. 4–8.

moment—a "last flowering" of Tokugawa literature. That Sata's work bears a different relationship to time becomes more evident as her career progresses, until duration and survival underlie much of her later work as a persistent motif. For, if with Ichiyō we must isolate a particular moment of transition in order to perceive clearly the interaction of her literature and the society that gave rise to it, with Sata and her works we must pass through virtually all the history of twentieth-century Japan. Many of the changes set in motion in the Meiji era, but not yet mirrored in Ichiyō's fiction, have become inescapable by Sata's time.

The development of the writer's social consciousness and commitment was to come into a focus so sharp as to make it one of the most pressing literary questions of the 1920s and 1930s. We might appropriately turn, then, to the consideration of another aspect of the activities of those women of the Seitō group, who, with Hiratsuka Raicho, were prominent discussants of the position of the "new woman" in Japan's rapidly changing society midway between the time of Ichiyō's death and the commencement of Sata's career as an author. Seitō's condemnation of the past and its traditional restraints upon women presented a challenge to contemporary established authority. Predictably, conservative elements in Japanese society responded by attacking the Seitō ideas and way of life. If the members of Seitō could see Ichiyō as an apologist for tradition, however arguable that stand might be, they themselves were in the dangerous position of being far in advance of the social consciousness of their own day. Thus, the Seitō experience was to have important implications for the future as well. Both the weaknesses and inconsistencies in the program of reform they espoused and the reaction of the government to their "radical" notions are indicative of a pattern that would reappear in later movements based upon the ideals of political freedom and social reform. And in time, the criticisms leveled against Seitō by conservatives were matched in fervor by attacks from leftist feminists because of what they saw as the elitism of the group and an "individualistic radicalism" that resulted in a "lack of rational measures for fundamentally changing society."[3]

---

[3] Noriko Mizuta Lippit's summation of the position taken by such feminists as Yamakawa Kikue in "Seitō and the Literary Roots of Japanese Feminism," *International Journal of Women's Studies* 2:2 (March/April 1979): 161.

Such issues were to remain crucial in the approaching period of confrontation between established authority, now embarking upon a government policy of increasing nationalism and imperialistic adventurism, and a growing organized left, which sought a transference of the base of power in Japanese society. Long after Seitō had ceased publication, the question of the progressive intellectuals' responsibility for social change and for opening a dialogue with the working class whose cause they espoused was to absorb much of the energy of left-wing theoreticians. From the Meiji period onward, the nation's rapid industrialization had given rise to an expanding working class, and, just as the townsmen and merchant class had been an emerging literary and cultural force during the Tokugawa, so in the Taishō and early Shōwa eras the industrial laboring class began to seek its place in the nation's consciousness. The increasingly militaristic and oppressive government of the early Shōwa years, however, could hardly be expected to lend a sympathetic ear to the voice of the disenfranchised worker.

The process by which this class formulated its literature, that "proletarian" literature which ultimately came into being, was a complex one; its roots can be seen, however, in early socialist writings, which began appearing shortly after Ichiyō's death and which would fight a long battle against government censorship and repression. A work as popular as Kinoshita Naoe's *Hi no hashira* (1904), for example, along with expressing the opposition felt by many socialists to the Russo-Japanese war, showed how the government used censorship and imprisonment as weapons against opposition thought, and his *Ryojin no jihaku* added to these concerns an explicit exposé of the near slave-labor conditions imposed upon farm women whose families virtually sold them off to the silk mills.

In a very real sense, however, early socialist writers like Kinoshita were intellectuals whose own experience was substantially outside the locus of the economic realignment and struggle that were the fundamental issues of the times. At this point the literature produced by intellectuals was cut off to a degree from the experiential truths later to be so highly valued in the proletarian movement. The ideologues had the intellectual and theoretical resources but not the practical experience needed to address the pressing economic and political realities of the time; and the workers themselves, whose experience of these realities was all too intimate, were in no condition to do more than survive. As George Shea observes in *Left-Wing Literature in Japan*, "Far from possessing socialist thought, the workers were so completely suppressed by the Emperor system that it was virtually impossible for them to rise against it successfully let alone acquire the theory of a movement."[4] By extension, workers were even less likely to have the leisure, the energy, or the encouragement to create a literature of protest, a situation that was soon to be a major topic for discussion in Marxist circles.

Since women represented a particularly crucial segment of the labor force, literary works focusing upon them gradually began to appear. As *Ryojin no jihaku* had indicated, even in the early days of industrialization, a time when Ichiyō was chronicling the life of the fading pleasure quarter, the position of women elsewhere in the work force was stark indeed. At first, they were most extensively employed in the textile industry—making up more than 50 percent of its workers by 1900. Jon Halliday describes the situation in these terms in his *A Political History of Japanese Capitalism*: "Much of the textile industry was located in rural areas, and most of the labour was recruited from villages. The majority of the workers were women who were simply sold off to labour bosses and forced to send most of their wages back to their families. This constellation of factors contributed to the preservation of 'family' relations in industry."[5] In effect, the female factory worker of this time was in much the same position as those young farm girls traditionally sold into prostitution to provide money for their impoverished families. The expendability of the daughters remained the same; only the economic laws of supply and demand were altered to permit a new use for the girls themselves. And even while the mills demanded their service as cheap labor, the trade in prostitution continued to absorb enormous numbers. Given the ever-increasing emphasis placed upon industrial expansion in the Taishō and Shōwa periods, it was not to be won-

---

[4] George Shea, *Left-Wing Literature in Japan* (Tokyo: Hosei University Press, 1964), p. 31.

[5] Jon Halliday, *A Political History of Japanese Capitalism* (New York and London: Monthly Review Press, 1975), p. 45.

dered at that by the 1920s the situation of the young girls who had been pressed into the service of industrialization began to attract notice. A young male factory worker, Hosoi Wakizō, was in fact so concerned about the dimensions of their exploitation and suffering that he published a voluminous work entitled *Joko aishi* (The Pathetic History of Female Factory Workers) documenting the inhumane conditions in which women found themselves in Japanese factories of the day.

Obviously, any comprehensive attempt to examine the problems of the working class had to take seriously the situation of its women, and literature that sought to address such issues ought, in theory, to have arisen from the ranks of the women writers themselves. In fact, the proletarian movement did provide an especially sympathetic forum for the woman writer; many of the leading women writers in prewar years had some connection with this school.[6] Yet although left-wing women writers such as Miyamoto Yuriko were concerned with the role of the working-class woman in Japan, they were not themselves members of the proletariat, but rather intellectuals originally from middle-class backgrounds. And although male members of the working class like Hayama Yoshio in his short "Imbaifu" (1925) and "Semento-daru no naka no tegami" (1926) had dealt compassionately with women at the mercy of an inhuman economic system, Sata herself represents the realization of a polemical ideal. She, after all, was a woman with a working-class background who wrote proletarian literature, and her first short story was written at the urging of Nakano Shigeharu, a leftist theoretician who had long advocated the active participation of the workers themselves in proletarian literature. Indeed, the elation with which Nakano was soon to greet the worker-writer Tokunaga Sunao's *Taiyō no nai machi* would have been equally appropriate in Sata's case: "The bride has come. The remarkably beautiful proletarian bride has

---

[6] Along with Sata, Hirabayashi Taiko and Miyamoto Yuriko are perhaps the most famous of the true proletarian writers, but such writers as Hayashi Fumiko were associated with the movement, and even previously established women writers such as Nogami Yaeko wrote works in sympathy with proletarian social realism.

come. The bride we have waited and waited for has now come to us."[7]

In the face of the events of the next decade, however, this remarkably beautiful proletarian bride embarked upon a perilous new life. At a time when leftist writers' sense of mission was accompanied by a sharp realization of the dangers of suppression by governmental authorities, the act of writing was invested with an obvious political significance, and the worker-writer, on the basis of personal experience, felt especially responsible for exposing the economic injustice upon which Japan was erecting its new system. Sata, having made so early an alliance with the proletariat, was insured against criticism such as that which Raicho leveled at Ichiyō, but her plainly political orientation was to expose her to government pressures that Ichiyō never faced.

Despite the differences in the political and economic conditions of their respective eras, there are certain shared elements in the work of the two women, as Sata's previously cited sympathetic commentary on Ichiyō's work suggests. If not strikingly evident, such similarities have prompted at least one critic, Hasegawa Hiroshi, to suggest in his brief essay, "An Inheritance from the Literature of Ichiyō,"[8] that Sata's focus upon the lives of the ordinary or insignificant, those who have restricted lives ("Chiisana seikatsu no hitobito"), indicates a certain similarity in the perspective of the two writers. Their concern with the "little people" after all rests upon identification with them, for both women had had personal experience of urban poverty. Like Ichiyō, Sata was taken from school at an early age to serve the family, and she, too, began her literary career by writing poetry.

A full sense of the genuine differences between them in social and literary concerns, however, can be attained if we compare "Kyarameru kōjō kara" with "Takekurabe." Undoubtedly it is unfair to compare an initial effort by one writer (Sata) with the generally acknowledged masterpiece of another (Ichiyō). Yet such a comparison, while it cannot suggest Sata's technical skill at its peak, still en-

---

[7] Cited and translated from Nakano's private correspondence in Shea, *Left-Wing Literature*, pp. 281–282.

[8] Hasegawa Hiroshi makes this comparison in his essay "An Inheritance from the Literature of Ichiyō," which was included in the publisher's insert in vol. 7 of *Sata Ineko zenshū*, p. 4.

ables us to consider how the special social and literary contexts of a particular time may act as both constraint and opportunity. Moreover, the works themselves demonstrate how substantially both literary and social values had changed in the thirty-year period separating the stories.

The language and setting of the initial sentence in "Kyarameru kōjō kara" signal such changes. To be sure, the first sentence of "Takekurabe" is an almost elusive construct in Western terms, since there is no periodic break in the flow of phrases during the entire opening section of that story. In contrast, not only does "Kyarameru kōjō kara" begin with a brief sentence—"Hiroko, as usual, folded back the futon on which her brother was sleeping so that she could make a space in which to eat her breakfast" (p. 21)[9]—but its syntax and linguistic forms are those of contemporary Japanese. The resonances, which in the opening phrases of "Takekurabe" create a deep awareness of a whole tradition and an entire fictional world (the aestheticized Edo of the wood-block prints and of Saikaku and the *gesaku* writers), are totally absent in Sata's story. Absent too as yet is any reference to the kind of detailed setting that opens the earlier story. Whereas Ichiyō only gradually narrows the focus of her work to that of three characters, among whom Midori is most prominent, the first word in "Kyameru kōjō kara" is the name of the protagonist, Hiroko. And, although Ichiyō only slowly develops the reader's awareness of limitation and of constraining social patterns, from the beginning of Sata's story we are confronted with limitation and deprivation in the most graphic terms. The crowded living quarters of Hiroko's family, indicated by the fact that she must fold back the corner of her brother's bedding to make space to eat, are explained and clarified in the story's development, but our initial impressions are those of physical discomfort (crowding, hunger, darkness, cold).

Sata opens, then, by plunging us directly into one of Hiroko's normal working days, and she keeps the focus of the story almost unswervingly upon the figure of the lone protagonist. The broad outlines of the two stories do, however, have strong resemblances. The protagonists are both young adolescents confronting the expecta-

---

[9] I have translated directly from *Sata Ineko zenshū*, vol. 1; the page numbers refer to the text in Japanese.

tions of the adult world, wishing that they might in some way alter the future they see stretched out before them, but realizing that they cannot. Yet the verbal recording of the limitations of the world "as it is" (and as they wish it were not) supplies the principal measure of difference between the two stories. Ichiyō starts from a world that seems broad in scope, a scene peopled by lively and energetic children whose clashes add adventure to their lives, but the frequent appearance of the concessive conditions us to accept a dynamic wholly in keeping with the concept of traditional restraints. Whereas tradition and convention obviously imply limitations, they are limitations deemed necessary to the protection of accepted values. Thus, the whole structure of an established social world serves in Ichiyō's depiction to limit the scope for individual desires, and, even though Ichiyō portrays a society that is itself a fringe world, she presents it as having its own complete network of patterns and expectations.

Limitation is more immediate, more unconditional, and more material in the world articulated in "Kyarameru kōjō kara." Hiroko wishes for more than one bowl of rice in the morning, but is constrained to forgo this by the inflexible schedule of the factory where she is employed. Hers is not a world in which play has any part; it is definitively a world of work. In "Takekurabe" money is always a consideration for the people of the Yoshiwara border area, but it retains a certain magical ability to incite fantasy. The people there can (and do) dream of getting rich. Although the setting is geographically the same, in "Kyarameru kōjō kara" this is no longer a half-legendary Edo being described, but a lower-class Tokyo where money is a grim practical necessity and such hopes are vain. Hiroko cannot, no matter how she tries, rise above the level of filling two and one-half containers of caramels a day. The inflexible rules of time and production constitute the material base of the limitations placed upon Hiroko's life. And in describing this starkly defined and completely constricted world, Sata's linguistic preference is for a straight, declarative prose style—a style in keeping with the accepted doctrine of "social realism" but not devoid of an emotional coloration ("Her dark little face was poorly colored and still swollen with sleep. . . . The chill of the grey dawn pierced [the old woman's] body although she was chafing her hands to keep warm," p. 21), or of a certain metaphoric dimension ("Hiroko, who had finished breakfast while her grandmother scolded, buried her head in her scarf, and was walking along feeling as if she were off to battle. Outside the glint of dawn was like a newly honed knife. It was gratingly cold," p. 22).

Much of the overall effect of "Takekurabe" depends upon the reader's awareness of the separation of Midori's consciousness from her previously comfortable context, her loss of communality with the standards of the neighborhood, and the failure of the language of her childhood to articulate a new, but tenuous, perception of her relationship to others. In Hiroko's case, the isolation is initial. Young as she apparently is, and we are told in the story's second sentence that she is both young and small, she is nevertheless hurrying off to work at the beginning of the story. Not until the second of the eight sections will the reader be told specifically that she is thirteen and had been permitted only some five years of schooling. For Hiroko, that very different world of childhood, which she embodies in the idealized "school," had already been taken away, and she must function in a particularly harsh adult world. Since the protagonist will remain the only major character whom the narrator names (all other names, and those only of extremely minor characters, come up in conversations among the factory workers), Hiroko is both spotlighted and isolated from the story's first word. The other members of her family are simply described in terms of their relationship to her, with the exception of her uncle who is termed "the invalid." Even from Hiroko's own perspective, her closest co-workers are identified not by name but by feature or relationship (for example, as "the girl with the runny eyes" and "the forewoman's sister").

One effect of such a specific focus upon the protagonist is to increase our sense of the helplessness of the individual (named) personality when confronted by the demands of formalized social relationships (from "her father," "her grandmother") and of more organized and impersonal economic pressures (from "the forewoman," "the owner's wife," "the management"). By creating so strong an initial impression of the unequal combat of a lone child's strength with adult responsibilities, Sata early indicates the nearly inevitable direction of the story's unfolding and gives her protagonist symbolic importance. On the streetcar in the morning, "Hiroko wedged herself between the legs of the grownups. She, too, was a worker just the same as they—so small and weak a worker that she might have been eaten by a horse like a single blade of grass" (p. 22).

The discrepancy between the task imposed upon her and her child's strength is, if anything, made more pronounced by the interaction between the protagonist's perspective and that of the narrator, by what may be interpreted as the dual function of the story, and by the initial grounds for its creation. Sata was originally urged to write the story by Nakano and her husband largely because they saw her as someone who could depict the conditions of the female factory worker from personal experience. Accordingly, as a finished piece of prose, "Kyarameru kōjō kara" serves complex aims; the story is at the same time autobiographical fiction and a representative work of proletarian social realism, combining personal recollection with the public stance of ideological commitment. Although the story draws directly upon the author's life, Sata's concern with social conditions and their effect upon the individual testifies to a consciousness of broader class interests.

The confrontation with socioeconomic reality gives Hiroko's story its ideological impact. Moreover, although the narrative of "Kyarameru kōjō kara" is handled smoothly on the whole, traces still remain of a dual symbolic/autobiographical intent. From the standpoint of her mentor, Nakano Shigeharu, the story's autobiographical base gave validity to what he saw as its central social and literary value as "the perfect representation of the working-class child." Certainly, there is truth in his observation to the extent that, in Sata's presentation, Hiroko's role sometimes has overtones implying that it has as much communal as personal significance. That Sata had something of the same vision of her protagonist is evident in the somewhat sentimentalized image contained in the clause "so small and weak a worker that she might have been eaten by a horse like a single blade of grass," an impression strengthened the more by the response of the adult workers in the car. A short conversational exchange translates the everyday detail of Hiroko's life into terms made universal for the worker.

"Good for you, little girl. Are you going far?" The man who said this had made a place for her. "What does your father do?"
"He doesn't have a job," Hiroko was ashamed to admit.
"That's ridiculous! What a loafer." Saying this, he assumed a friendly expression. Compassionately, the people around them avoided staring at her. For them, the situation resembled theirs; she was the image of their own children, and her presence touched them directly. (p. 22)

Brief as the exchange is, a sense of community is created among the passengers, all on their way to work in the early morning hours. A child—but a child who is "a worker just the same as they"—appears among them, and for a moment their consciousness of their own lives expands to include her. This sense of solidarity, unrecognized by the embarrassed Hiroko, is underlined by the committed narrator.

This snatch of conversation typifies the way in which Sata employs dialogue as a medium of social exchange and the means by which the nature of the subtle relationships between people may be gauged. She rarely uses long expository passages, unbroken by dialogue. Although there are many resemblances between Sata's style and that of her friend and contemporary, Kawabata Yasunari—the simplicity of language, the sharpness of imagery, and the treatment of time in small, discrete, but ever-shifting units to name only a few—of the two, Sata uses conversation in a more positive, communicative sense, generally conveying through it, not the separation between people, but their interconnectedness. In "Kyarameru kōjō kara," then, it is significant that the positive exchanges in which Hiroko participates are with fellow workers, here on the streetcar and at the factory with "the girl with the runny eyes" whom she considers a friend. To be sure, the dialogue is not invariably positive; exchanges with her grandmother merely allow Hiroko to vent her complaints, while those with her father deflate her confidence because he scolds her, bullies her, or horrifies her by his impractical indifference to her struggles and his almost casual exercise of control over her life.

In her later works Sata exhibits an extremely delicate but sure touch for the way in which a code of verbal/nonverbal exchange operates among the Japanese. This kind of communication, rather than transmitting "facts" or opinions, registers attitudes and establishes some sort of relationship between the parties in the exchange. Even in this first story, the man who speaks to Hiroko operates by such a code, addressing her as "Neechan," a word meaning the older sister of the family, but frequently used as an informal but cordial address to young girls. The atmosphere in the streetcar following these few phrases becomes deepened by a sense of the connection between one life and the human situation we all for a moment are aware of sharing.

But what might be termed "worker solidarity" is indicated in the first story only through brief glimpses of this kind. "Kyarameru kōjō kara" clearly falls into the classification of descriptive rather than prescriptive proletarian literature. Here Sata is more concerned with depicting the reality of the workers' plight as she had actually known it than she is with advocating direct action, which played no part in the original events she reports. Certainly, however, the poor working conditions of the proletariat are more poignant in the case of a child, and the shared moment in the streetcar emphasizes the symbolic role invested in Hiroko. The fact that she is the only named character serves to increase our sense of Hiroko's isolation, just as her physical frailty increases our understanding of the weight of the workers' burden. Moreover, by distancing narrator and protagonist somewhat, Sata suggests a contrast between the naïve child, caught up in circumstances she can neither control nor fully understand, and a more knowledgeable narrator—a contrast paralleled in life by Sata's past and present.

For Hiroko, the thirteen-year-old factory worker, had her real-life predecessor in the author. Born in Nagasaki on June 1, 1904, the first child of a young couple, then unmarried, Sata Ineko was officially registered as the daughter of her great-uncle but spent her early years with her parents and grandmother. When Sata was seven, her mother died. Her father subsequently remarried, but this second marriage ended in divorce, and the family moved to Tokyo soon after. There they were to find life increasingly difficult, and her father's almost chronic unemployment was responsible for her withdrawal from school in the fifth year, at which time she was sent to work in a caramel factory and from which point the action narrated in "Kyarameru kōjō kara" takes up.

Hiroko, as the protagonist of the story, represents the early, politically unsophisticated Ineko, the thirteen-year-old sent off to work even though she longed to continue her schooling. Behind the character's point of view, however, can be seen the point of view of an older narrator, whose perspective is politically informed. While this second perspective is nowhere obtrusive, its presence is enough to ensure a proletarian tone for the story. Although Sata eschews the more obvious kinds of didacticism, some of the rhetoric of the left-wing intellectual does appear at points. Thus, in describing Hiroko's father, she uses the pejorative term *"puchi-buru"* (petit bourgeois) to characterize his vain pretensions to respectability. She depends generally, however, upon detailed description of the actual working conditions in the factory to establish the concrete nature of the oppression of the women working there. The very fact that the wages Hiroko received for a day's work were scarcely enough to cover the streetcar fare to get her to the factory and back indicates how totally inadequate the wage scale was; the cold, poorly lit workroom needs only to be described to indicate the employers' lack of concern for the welfare of their employees.

Perhaps the use of Hiroko's perspective (with the narrator's controlling hand behind it) is one of the elements that keep the story relatively free from obvious polemic. Far from establishing a rigid, black and white, capitalist and worker separation between good and bad, Sata is careful to indicate that, in Hiroko's case, the initial source of exploitation comes from within the family circle. While Hiroko reacts to her father's demands with verbal complaints but physical obedience, the narrator's tone is almost scornful when, after detailing the trip her father takes with Hiroko to obtain the factory job, he exposes his irresponsibility.

> "Well, it seems a little bit far, but try commuting and see what happens. As for school and things like that, somehow or other it may work out."
>
> In fact, the trip to the factory alone took forty minutes by streetcar. Even worse, when the carfare was subtracted from a day's wage, the effort was not worthwhile. Female factory workers all took jobs in places they could reach on foot. If they couldn't find such a job, then they ended up in large factories that had dormitories. However, Hiroko's father didn't think about things like that. Since he had heard the name of this factory mentioned somewhere, he simply decided on it.
>
> From the following day, Hiroko commuted bleary-eyed. (p. 24)

Hiroko's essentially passive compliance is tempered by a narrator who is aware of general conditions and practices in the work world and accordingly can make evaluations that are beyond the capacity of the protagonist.

Characteristically, Hiroko makes no explicit judgment about the unfairness of her own situation as far as society is concerned, but Sata allows such judgments to arise in the reader from a combination of Hiroko's naïveté and surviving fantasies (being able to excel as a worker, being the breadwinner, somehow being able to make the money that will enable her to return to school), and the objective third-person description of actual conditions. The gap between the world "as it is" and the world she wishes for becomes quite clear, but Hiroko does not make the significance of such discrepancies explicit even to herself. Thus, when she sees the well-dressed women beginning to appear in her morning streetcar merely as an omen of her own disastrous lateness, the reader is aware of other terms on which this might be interpreted. The early morning cold and dark in which the factory workers (whose presence would reassure Hiroko) make their way to work has given way to that later, brighter, and warmer world possessed by the well-groomed middle class. In that world Hiroko has no place.

Accordingly, she regards her failure to arrive in time to be locked behind the factory gates at 7:00 A.M. as a simple economic calamity and attempts to adjust to her new life in terms of old values. Almost unaware (as the narrator manifestly is not) of the fundamental injustice of the conditions at the factory, Hiroko simply wishes to recapture the experience of excellence that she remembers from her schooldays. When the lists of the best workers and the worst workers are posted, she is covered with shame by the knowledge that inevitably her name will appear among those of the worst workers.

> Hiroko remembered the way things had been at school. There, too, her name was always being posted. But the difference was that at school it was never the poor performers who were singled out for notice.
> Hiroko wanted somehow to quickly become skillful at the job. While the other women had already filled five containers, she had not yet completed two and a half. Even at times when she thought she was doing better than usual, in the end her production was still only two and a half.
> She was anxious somehow or other to get off the list of those who were worst.
> All of them went on working furiously. The competition was like that here. Aiming at being posted high, the factory girls drove their fragile bodies with all their might. (pp. 25–26)

While Hiroko simply desires to increase her skills, to become better at her job, the narrator suggests in the final paragraph something of the enormous physical cost expended in the workers' efforts to meet the standards set by management. The next section of the story (section four) is all the narrator's own, comprising as it does a vivid description of the workplace and detailing the physical deprivation that is the lot of workers there. In this section, the workers are viewed as a group—aware of the discomfort, but essentially unable to bring about any significant improvement.

> Then it became completely dark in the room. Since at this time of year the wind blew every day, all day long, the window panes rattled, and the wind would whistle through a hole in one of them. Although they had repeatedly asked that this hole be repaired, it remained just as it was.
> The women worked all day, standing and walking about on the hard wooden floor. Until they became inured to this, their legs would get as stiff as boards, their throats would constrict, and they would be seized by spells of dizziness. By the time evening came, some of them would be overcome by severe stomach cramps from the cold. Around their waists and under their smocks, they all wore their fathers' cast off underwear, which they had cut down to fit. (p. 26)

In all this detailed factual background, and even in the following section (five), in which there is a direct encounter between the management and the workers, the narrator does not move into explicit condemnation of the employers' callousness. Sata has only, after all, to allow the circumstances themselves to suggest their own moral. The reader cannot help but register the contrast between the well and warmly dressed owner's wife, who stands in the middle of the room with her attending maid, and this room full of poorly dressed women and girls whose bodies are continually twisting in a mechanical pivot from counter to carton. Hiroko confines her criticism to thinking the woman conceited. Her reaction comes from the former schoolchild's code in which someone addressed as "Osukan" (Ma'am) would show a friendly interest in the factory girls. But, as her neighbor with the runny eyes realizes, "Hiroko still did not understand the realities of this place very well." To her employers, Hiroko is not a little girl, but just a worker, one of many production units. The owner's wife, for example,

> stood there gloating, with a complacent smile: The women had always worked docilely, and yet in spite of that the management had ordered some of the workers to search the sleeves, pockets, and lunchboxes of

each one of them at the gate at quitting time. All those who waited behind in the line had to stand in the bone-chilling wind until it was their turn to be searched. (p. 28)

The indifference and greed of the capitalist and the indignities visited upon the worker are clear. But it is the narrator who places the present scene of the women at work in a chronological relationship to the daily search that takes place at quitting time.

Hiroko's essentially passive suffering can be interpreted as a statement of the hopelessness of the worker in the early decades of Japan's industrialization. Certainly this is intensified by her youth and unworldliness. And although there are seeds of a labor/ management conflict in the women's demands for warm water in which to wash the bottles and in the supervisor's uneasy response to the demand, it is mainly through the narrator's descriptions that a consciousness of the possibility of class conflict is suggested.

In stories published later the same year, such as "Joten'in to su-toraiki," Sata was to depict strikes and union activities, but in this first story, she remains content with exposing the working conditions she had encountered as a child. Nevertheless, we gain a broader understanding of the worker's helplessness through the depiction of the child-worker's desperation, and Sata's adult reflection upon her past experience enables us to perceive a resistance possible beyond the reactions of the protagonist herself.

The story's temporal perspective is far from uncomplicated, for, although the plotting is quite straightforward, the shifts from Hiroko's perspective to the narrator's provide variation. Even the protagonist's present experience must be considered in relation to a remembered past and an implied future. The simple action of the story begins four or five days after the first time Hiroko had been late to work at the caramel factory and continues through her stay there to a slightly later point when she is already living at her second place of employment, a *soba* (noodle) shop. The last scene of the story, in fact, provides a transition to a second story in which Hiroko figures as protagonist, "Omemietoku" (Working on Probation, 1928), and which deals with Sata's again autobiographical experience at the *soba* shop. Beyond the story's elapsed time, however, there is another temporal dimension—a kind of psychological or emotional time—that runs beneath occurring events.

For Hiroko, this second, longer span of time has a definite negative progression. The past, which throughout the story has been connected with wistfully remembered school days, had had a sort of golden promise that Hiroko longs to recapture. The final scene of "Kyarameru kōjō kara" has the effect of depriving her of that promise. The receipt of a letter from a former teacher is the source of the deep depression into which Hiroko, who had been cherishing the hope that one day she would be able to resume her schooling, is plunged at the conclusion of the story. By telling her that "going back to school isn't that difficult. At least you should graduate from elementary school" (p. 31), the teacher seems to be minimizing obstacles that Hiroko has gradually come to recognize as insurmountable. At one stroke, the young girl's past has been robbed of value and her future of hope. Here there is an echo of the narrative comment upon Hiroko's father and his aspirations: "He did not seem to recognize that for people like him there was no hope of getting ahead no matter what they did" (p. 23). Crouching in a dark and no doubt pungent toilet, Hiroko is reduced to helpless tears. She has come face to face with the recognition that her father has avoided. For the worker of the day, there is little opportunity to change the depressing conditions of her life; the future promises only the continuation of present distress. Her realization of the irrevocable loss of the past serves much the same function as did Midori's experience on Otori day. Just as Midori's new hairdo symbolized the future she wanted to avoid, so Hiroko's letter symbolizes her loss of hope.

The interaction of past, present, and future adds a note of finality to Hiroko's story. Because she is so young, the hopelessness of the future seems an especially poignant note on which to end, and no doubt that is why Sata chooses to conclude "Kyarameru kōjō kara" as she does. Paradoxically, of course, Sata's life has proceeded in direct opposition to the downward curve on which Sata ends the autobiographical story. For by virtue of being drawn from the author's own life, the remembered experience, which achieves so bleak a completion in the story, has obviously been resurrected as the basis for another mode of existence, becoming the material upon which the author has based her literary career (a feature it shares with the popular *shishōsetsu* of the time). Even Sata's presence as narrator within the story indicates that the author had already transcended Hiroko's consciousness.

Despite some shortcomings, "Kyarameru kōjō kara" does suggest the outline of the form of Sata's future as an author. Elements that will endure as an integral part of her craft are already present in this early story. Dialogue is employed as a significant plot mechanism as it will continue to be. The use of autobiographical material, tempered by mature recollection and interpretation, will remain the basic format for much of her later fiction. And, although represented here on a relatively uncomplicated level, Sata's use of the flow of time will continue to develop the sense, already implied here, that life is experienced in the context of a multidimensional temporality. Beyond this, the reader can already perceive a certain complexity in the author's view of society, a complexity that does not suggest a single ideological explanation for the individual's ills.

The capitalists pictured in "Kyarameru kōjō kara," while they clearly enforce social inequities, nevertheless do not loom on the scene as the embodiments of all evil. To be sure, there is no stinting of the detail establishing the inhumanity of their treatment of the workers, but Sata does not lose sight of the more immediately personal basis for Hiroko's misfortune. Largely as a result of her father's selfish indifference, Hiroko is abandoned to the demands of an exploitative and impersonal economic machinery. The individual has always to function in a world in which personal desires and necessities must be accommodated to a social and political system in which they are not valued. If this is implied in "Takekurabe" and in Ichiyō's work in general, it becomes an explicit issue in the works Sata was to write in the decade following the appearance of this first story.

That was a decade in which Sata and her fellow proletarian writers were to experience increasing persecution from the government and in which hard personal decisions were to be exacted from the writers themselves as they sought to reconcile the conflicting demands of survival, integrity, and art. Proletarian literature was already at its peak when Sata's first story was published, and her works from that time are a fictionalized record of the delicate interplay of experience, recollection, and judgment within what can only be termed a time of crisis.

In the month after the publication of "Kyarameru kōjō kara," a series of events took place. The first was the March 13, 1928, inaugural meeting of an organization intended as the combining of various left-wing literary coteries into a united front in the Japan Federation of Left-Wing Artists. Two days later a nationwide, coordinated roundup of communists and radicals by the Tanaka government, among other things, nipped the new organization in the bud. Ten days after that, however, a new organization for left-wing writers, the NAPF (Zen Nihon Musansha Geijutsu Remmei [All Japan Federation of Proletarian Arts]), was formed. Nakano Shigeharu, Sata's mentor, was one of the members of the executive committee of this new, strongly Marxist-Leninist organization. Sata's second published story, "Joten'in to sutoraiki," appeared in *Senki* (Battle Flag), the official organ of this group, in July of the same year.

The existence of the proletarian school, while nearly unchallenged on the literary scene, was nevertheless constantly threatened politically as Japan's government intensified surveillance and harassment of potential opponents. The political and international concerns of the NAPF, its close ties to the Comintern and its policies, and its potential danger as an avenue of protest for the laboring class provoked increasing government interference in the activities of the organization, and its future was constantly in jeopardy. In April 1929 there was a second wave of nationwide arrests of communists, and police harassment of those remaining at liberty intensified. The Manchurian Incident in September 1931 signaled the Japanese government's increasing commitment to a course that would eventually lead to its involvement in the Pacific theater of World War II, and the position of those belonging to organizations opposed to its policies became nearly untenable.

Two months later the NAPF was reorganized into the KOPF (Nihon Puroretaria Bunka Remmei [Japan Proletarian Culture Federation]), an organization whose policy called for the decentralization of membership and activities, an action that had been recommended at the Moscow Profintern of 1930 in the case of those countries in which the Communist Party was illegal. From that period on, police surveillance and government censorship became sources of continual threat to writers like Sata who were affiliated with the KOPF. In the period between early 1932 and mid-1933, police actions against the left were ceaseless and widening in scope. Nakano was arrested for the third time in 1932 and held in custody for two years until a *tenkō* (statement of conversion or renunciation) could be extracted from him, and Kubokawa Tsurujirō (Sata's husband) was caught in the same cycle of arrest, detention, and forced conversion. In February 1934 perhaps the most shocking of the police incidents took place when Kobayashi Takiji[10] was taken into custody and killed. In 1935 Sata herself, after having been arrested on several occasions, was jailed for some two months, an experience she details in the novel *Kurenai*.

The intensification of the police campaign against the left virtually broke the back of the proletarian movement. Those who had been active in it previously reacted to the new severity in a number of different ways. Kobayashi was of course the martyr of the movement, but an additional small number of the former leaders, among them Miyamoto Kenji and Kurahara Korehito, refused to make any statement of even conditional renunciation or conversion. They spent long years in police custody. Even those who had some measure of freedom, like Nakano and Miyamoto Yuriko, were for a time absolutely prohibited from writing. Within such a context, however, a new kind of literature began to take shape, the so-called conversion literature. Some former proletarian writers did an abrupt and complete about-face, eschewing political discussion in any form; but a number of them, including Nakano, Kubokawa, and Sata, managed to produce a literature that used various methods of keeping alive the spirit of the earlier movement. Sata was able to use autobiographical fiction to present her experience of arrest, detention, and persecution in terms that accorded in many respects with the descriptive social realism of her earlier works but did not advocate actions that would provoke government censorship or reprisal. One of her best known works from the period when she was under government suspicion is the novel *Kurenai*, which attempts to explore the complexities of conflicting loyalties—political and personal—that have a claim on the progressive woman writer who is simultaneously a wife and mother.

---

[10] Probably the best known of the proletarian writers. Kobayashi's *Kani kosen* (The Crab-canning Ship) is considered one of the classic works of proletarian fiction.

Although she was to return to the material from the period of persecution in works written at later stages of her life, it did not seem to have required as painful an effort of reexamination as did her experience as a war-time correspondent mobilized by the government. Many of her works of the late 1940s and early 1950s involve her in just such a return to moments in the past when she succumbed to personal weakness and what she sees as opportunism, and "Onna Sakusha" (1946),*Watakushi no Tokyo chizu* (1947), "Kyogi" (1948), and "Homatsu no Koroko" (1948) are attempts to use the failures and bleak moments of the past as the basis for an exploration of the possibility of personal "human growth" based upon the scrutiny and perhaps redemption of the past.

Although in such works as *Kikai no naku no seishun* (1954), she returns to the theme of social realism, the issue of self-determination appears to have become central to her following her divorce from Kubokawa in 1945, for from that time she wrote a number of works (such as *Karada no naka o kaze ga fuku,* 1956) about the problems of working women with children to support, and in "Kodomo no me" (1953) she used the perspective of a young child from a broken home to explore the area of personal domestic tragedy. Even in the works like this last, which is not clearly autobiographical, her personal experience and perspective has continued to inform her literary works. And, in the series of twelve linked stories entitled *Toki ni tatsu* (Standing in Time), which received the Kawabata Yasunari Prize for 1976, she once more drew upon the sources of her own life and the times through which she has lived.

From such an abundance of literary material, then, the task of selecting one brief piece that would do justice to the evolution of Sata's authorial perspective is difficult, and one is tempted to use a portion of one of the late works like *Toki ni tatsu* as a basis for allowing Sata herself to pull all of the temporal and contextual strands of her life together. In fact, it is undoubtedly a risky business to attempt to suggest the scope and subtlety of a fifty-year career from the evidence of two short works, no matter how carefully selected. Nevertheless, the early "Kyarameru kōjō kara" has been hailed as representative proletarian fiction; and the translation appended to this study, that of "Yuki no mau yado," while only one among many short stories and novels that she wrote during her late sixties, demonstrates Sata's increasing narrative complexity.

Almost as much can be inferred from the similarities in these two stories as from the differences. The differences, on the one hand, have something to suggest about the personal development of one writer, about changes in literary fashion, and about the degree to which Japan as a nation has changed in fifty years. On the other hand, the similarities have something even more fascinating to suggest about the human personality and about its linguistic extension—"style."

What remains constant through the shifts in emphasis and through the years is testimony to the persistence of the linguistic, perceptual, and conceptual patterns separating this writer from other writers. It makes her, if not instantly, then at least ultimately, recognizable only as herself. In the spirit of the fingerprint and the voice print, these constant elements comprise what might be termed the author's "print print." And in fact, I believe that a comparison of two stories that differ greatly in many other respects will enable us to isolate clearly the consistent stylistic elements in Sata's work.

Yet, however important it may be to establish the idiosyncratic literary qualities of any given writer, the satisfaction that arises from such an activity has a limited value for understanding the significance of her works as a whole. An analogy to detective fiction might help here; such an identification goes far in establishing "who done it" but does little to clarify those aspects clustering around the concept of "motivation." In critical terms, concentration upon those qualities that may be termed "stylistic," pushed too far, will isolate the works themselves from that fuller literary context in which their significance can be evaluated most properly; we become more aware of the verbal habits of an individual than of what may be considered the intention of the implied author who may be sensed in the works.

Sata's own works are instructive at this point in our discussion, for she attempted in a long and distinguished career to relate personal experience to broad political and social issues. In her case, the result is the development of that distinctly moral consciousness that many Western critics have considered generally absent in Japanese literature. Her emphasis upon personal experience and the subtle nuances of human relationships precludes the use of that single-minded didacticism that could mar the writings of the most earnest of early proletarian writers upon occasion. But the recognition of the social, political, and economic conditions that affect the personal experience prevents even the most clearly autobiographical of her works from the frequently expressed criticism of the *shishōsetsu* form as self-indulgent.

Even the clearest understanding of both the personal and public (proletarian, and, later, left-wing) aspects of her literary stance, however, cannot tell us much about her work as art. That is where both "style" and the conscious craft of the experienced writer come into play, and that is why I have selected "Yuki no mau yado" as the companion piece to "Kyarameru kōjō kara." Ultimately, the combination of the four elements of social relevance, personal experience, style, and an increasing mastery of literary techniques must all receive recognition in any adequate treatment of Sata's work. Although the two stories represent the merest fraction of her impressive literary production, they do provide a sufficient basis for examining all four of these components of her art and suggest Sata's use of fiction as a metaphor of social process and of the process of fictionalization itself.

"Kyarameru kōjō kara" supplies an early, if somewhat simplified, pattern of the form that is to remain the mainstay of Sata's craft. Unlike many better known *shishōsetsu*, it demonstrates how autobiographical fiction may effectively emphasize those elements of personal experience that have communal rather than simply individualistic significance. On the other hand, part of the value "Yuki no mau yado" has for the discussion of Sata's work lies precisely in the fact that it is not specifically autobiographical. More important, however, than the lack of direct material from the author's life is that the story itself can be seen as the verbal replication of Sata's own creative process of turning experience into narrative, projected against an almost symbolic setting. There, I think its fictionality saves it from the Morton's Salt syndrome of a writer writing about a writer writing about a writer's life, so that the narrative becomes not simply the mechanics through which one creates a representation of one's own past, but rather focuses upon the function that the present serves in the reconstruction of the past. Moreover, in "Yuki no mau yado" the inclusion of the listener (audience, reader) within the field of narrative provides an opportunity for the exploration of multiple points of view, the sum of which is infinitely more subtle and complex than the dual perspective of "Kyarameru kōjō kara." The story provides a working model, then, of the process that gives rise to autobiographical modes like the *shishōsetsu*, as its three protagonists in turn resurrect the events of their own pasts.

The story is simply plotted—three women come away from their Tokyo lives to spend a few days at an inn in the snow country, each telling a story that the others comment upon. Each speaker re-creates in this way the process that authors of forms like the *shishōsetsu* use in making the printed page a structured extension of past into present consciousness. Behind the narratives of the protagonists and the reported interaction of speaker and listeners in each case is the dimly perceived presence of the narrator of the whole. In addition to the complexity of its structural craft, the story's controlled setting increases its special atmosphere.

Nothing could seem further from the depiction of a poor little factory girl, working for a pittance in the midst of harsh conditions, than this portrait of three comfortably situated, middle-aged women on vacation. The strong impression we receive from "Kyarameru kōjō kara" of "social realism" is precluded in this narrative by the almost fantasy-like beauty of the snowy inn, but a great deal of power undoubtedly comes from the way setting is used to provoke a kind of reflection on the part of all three. As the snow piles up, covering the outlines of the landscape and transforming its everyday features into the vision they have set forth to find, each of the women goes beneath the surface of her daily life to detail an incident from the past emblematic of an emotional life previously unsuspected by the other two. And the progressive discovery of these "other" lives adds to our understanding of the way in which truth contradicts appearance and the life the individual has come to think of as private in fact represents a kind of human commonality.

As in Ichiyō's "Takekurabe," a contradiction between actuality and expectation arises from the beginning. Initial impression will receive a necessary correction through the separate testimonies. One of the women, Haruko, has been to this place before, but the other two suspect nothing of the turmoil of her first visit. Shigeko, apparently the most happily married and placid of them all, has had a complex and difficult experience of her husband's infidelity, which caused her to question the basic trust upon which the marriage was built. Aki-ye, perhaps the most unconventional of the three because of her circumstances as a widow who has raised three children by herself, has a story that also alters the impression the other two have of her. In short, here are three childhood friends whose deepest personal experiences in their postschoolgirl years have remained concealed from the others. The story's dynamic is built upon the way in which this long-term relationship shifts and changes to accommodate the maturer perspectives each has come to have.

A fourth presence makes its belated appearance. That presence is the snow, which will play its role as at once concealer and revealer. By obscuring the outside world and creating a reflective space within which the women are enclosed, it brings about their revelations. But its late arrival upon the scene allows for the setting up of an initial dynamic that must be overcome—each of the women is struggling against an image of herself that, out of respect for appearances, she has allowed the others to form.

For Haruko, the snow is a remembered old friend (*kyūchi*), to which, along with the tiny mountain train, she has often referred in conversations with Shigeko and Akiye. In spite of her high hopes, however, neither of these "old friends" is present in the initial scene. In the opening pages, Haruko seems to be the major protagonist of the story. She is revisiting the site she has remembered for so long, and her disappointment at the changes that have taken place at the hot spring underscores her role as guide to the other two.

Most of the presumptions upon which the trip has been built will be challenged in the opening pages. Even the initial motivation for this small journey is shown to have been misguided to a certain extent. Shigeko and Haruko have planned the visit to the inn as a consolation trip for Akiye, who must, they assume, be feeling lonely now that her only son, the first of her three children to set up an independent life, has gotten married and moved from her household. Upon their arrival at the inn, Akiye is quick to correct the conventional impression the others have.

This first movement toward reflection depends upon the arrival of snow, however. Shigeko unwittingly sets in motion the confrontation with the actualities of one another's lives that will sustain the action of the story.

"Well, after all, we did spend nearly seven hours coming all this way because you wanted to see the snow. That certainly was a natural wish on your part; however, you must have felt that way because you are in a special mood right now."

"What do you mean by 'special'?" Akiye laughed self-consciously.

"Well, don't people say that a son's marriage makes his mother feel deserted?" Shigeko had to phrase it this way, since she herself was childless.

Akiye turned back to the *kotatsu*, smiling slightly at this. "Yes, people are always saying that. Still, I don't feel that way at all. Because everyone talks that way, though, I sometimes wonder if I'm cold-hearted. However, I know how much I care about my children, so I don't really think I'm callous. It's just that when my son got married I wasn't at all sad. Instead I felt that my responsibilities were lighter now that there is someone else to look after him." (p. 218)[11]

This conversation becomes the first hint that, as well as the women may feel they know one another, they nevertheless make evaluations of one another's feelings and experiences based simply on what "people say," and without understanding the reality of the other's life. Here, Shigeko's own lack of children makes her ready to believe in a parental mystique closed to the uninitiated. Akiye's insistence on saying no more than the truth, even at the fairly casual level of this early exchange, sets the tone for the ensuing conversations. The passage also establishes the familiar mode of conversation among the old friends and supplies some of the background of the lives of two of them, Shigeko and Akiye. But omnipresent in the conversation is the pattern of the expectations, not merely of the narrative, but of the culture.

Soon we become quite aware of the direct role of the snow in evoking a sense of reexamined lives, for the initially conventional responses to the beauty of the snowy night give way to a special atmosphere of genuine communal understanding.

The powdery snow was still falling when the evening meal was brought to their room shortly thereafter. As they looked out into the darkness, the swirling snow had spread a whiteness abroad, and when blown about by the wind, it looked almost like the wild dance of living

---

[11] The page citations refer to the appended translation, "The Inn of the Dancing Snow."

things. Inspired by that dance, Akiye exclaimed, "My, it's really falling down; it seems to welcome us—we who have come here to pay a call on the snow"

"I'm so glad," said Haruko and held out the sake bottle. "'Well then, shall I pour? For Akiye first..."

Offering her cup, Akiye said, "How wonderful here at this snowy inn to feel the happiness of being alive."

"Yes, indeed," Shigeko put in quietly, sensing the complex feelings in Akiye's words. She realized that for Akiye even "the happiness of being alive" meant cherishing the memory of her late husband. (p. 219)

This time Shigeko's interpretation is based not upon conventional folk wisdom but rather upon a sensitivity to Akiye's tone and mood. The first differentiations are beginning to appear among the women. Shigeko takes on the role of the sensitive listener. Quite soon it will be she who asks the leading question, "Something had happened?" which generates the first of the recitals. From this point on the individual tales become counterpointed in their telling by the conversations between the women and the various contexts for the series of stories. Once Haruko has explained that the actuality behind her first visit had involved her flight from an unfaithful husband, we see all these levels of discourse in operation. The tales themselves are told for the most part in third-person narration of represented rather than direct speech, while the commentary upon the tales is generally cast in the form of dialogue.

In making this narrative choice, Sata places a heavy emphasis upon the interrelationship between past and present experience. The remembered past, as the indirect discourse of the third person indicates, is the stuff of personal history, the "closed material" which must be given form. The experienced present, wherein the interpretive function upon the inert material of past events is performed, is cast in the open form of dialogue, a form that suits the changing and contingent nature of interpretation. Nowhere is the relationship between the two modes of expressed temporality clearer within the framework of the narrative than it is at the close of the first tale. Detailing the manner of her discovery of an affair her husband had been involved in for some time, Haruko's narrative is presented at one remove. The narrator describes what Haruko is relating: we do not hear her own words. Haruko and her husband, it is reported, had been on a visit to her family during which they had carefully concealed the crisis in their marriage. "Then, upon their return, she declared that she was going off alone to the hot spring. Awestruck and uneasy at his wife's behavior, Kawada finally went along with her" (p. 221). Only when her story draws near its conclusion does the present context intrude. The narrative has been the reported discourse of the tales themselves, but there is a break here between it and directly recorded dialogue. Haruko's listeners and the reader are still firmly contained within the context of the narrated story when the first break occurs.

> When the story reached this point the two listeners caught their breath and Akiye broke into the narrative. "You knew all along that your husband would come with you, didn't you?"
>
> "I wasn't so confident as that. But if he hadn't come, I would have killed myself out of spite. I hated him. It wasn't a matter of love, but rather of pride."
>
> "But doesn't that mean that you loved him?"
>
> "Well, I don't know. In any case, at that time I simply could not behave like a dutiful wife, enduring it all silently." (p. 221)

Again we understand the difference between the traditional concept of what one ought to feel and what one actually does feel in the specific circumstances being underlined. Haruko is here commenting upon the story she had just told, but she is not yet at any distance from the events themselves. Following this exchange, a separation begins to develop between Haruko, still reliving the events of thirteen years before, and Akiye, who has begun to move toward the context of the present.

> Saying this, Haruko's eyes flashed as if she were reexperiencing old feelings. It was Haruko's nature to be energetic, and the way she had lured her husband to the hot spring seemed characteristically assertive.
>
> Akiye smiled at this. "Well, you certainly handled it well. And so, this became the place of reconciliation for the two of you?" (p. 221)

In the break into dialogue Akiye sums up the event, performing the readerlike function of identifying the central significance of the tale. She has returned to a sense that this is retrospective time, while Haruko has yet to be jolted into the present.

At moments like this, the shifting relationship among memory, thought, and speech and the strands of three separate consciousnesses are skillfully interwoven in the text. Sata's deft manipulation of dialogue, description, and narration here represents an obvious advance over the perceptible separation between the snatches of conversation and descriptive passages in "Kyarameru kōjō kara." The only clear transitions come at those points where the narrative moves from one tale to the next. For the tales are dealt out, as it were, with measured care. Thus, although Shigeko seeks to alleviate Haruko's embarrassment at having exposed this event from the past by mentioning that she herself has had a similar episode in her own life, Akiye suggests that they postpone its discussion for another time.

This is another of those points at which the sensitivity of the women to one another's feelings indicates how suited they are for their overt role of sympathetic listeners (and by extension, paradigms of the "ideal" reader). The complexity of mutual responsibility provides the background against which the tales are set. Shigeko had offered her remark as a consolation for Haruko, but she now becomes aware that such discussions of married life may be painful for Akiye, the only one of the three whose husband has died. Nevertheless, for reasons not yet apparent, it is Akiye who insists that Shigeko tell her tale on the following day. A shift in the roles of the women takes place here. Haruko, after telling her own story, had remarked that the snowfall, should it continue on the next day, would make her happy: "At least one of my responsibilities would be discharged." Now, in fact, as one of the organizers of the trip, two of her responsibilities have been discharged: the first as a guide, leading them to this inn, where snow was now falling as promised; and the second as a model, telling the first of the story's tales.

At this point in the narrative, Akiye's perspective begins to gain strength. The eye that views and interprets the falling snow is almost uniformly Akiye's, and now hers are the internal reflections the narrator chooses to share. Akiye seems to step forward as stage manager, urging Shigeko not once but twice to tell her tale. At the story's conclusion the reader can only assume that it is the weight of Akiye's own unshared confidence that impels her to insist, but at the time, Shigeko is puzzled by the insistence. Nevertheless, after hesitating, she is finally persuaded to tell the second of the story's tales. It follows the general format of the first recital, detailing an episode of her husband's unfaithfulness, with the main events given through indirect discourse.

Just as in the first case, the telling of the story introduces a reflective pause. But this time we follow only Akiye's reaction. She seems completely able to share in the narrated experiences, but since, as a widow, her own circumstances differ from those of her companions, her projections about the situation her friends have had in common are sympathetic but theoretical.

> She felt she had to agree with Shigeko's remark about the way people are; yet, perhaps because she knew Yoshizawa, she could not bring herself to censure him. If her own husband, Tamiya, had still been alive, she, too, might have had a similar experience by now. Akiye did not reject the notion; she had no conviction that her family would have been any exception, for during this time Akiye had been searching her own heart and asking such questions of herself. (p. 225)

Although she readily and easily extends this theoretical understanding and even empathy to her friends, Akiye is apparently less confident that they will be able to project themselves into her own as yet mysterious circumstances. She cannot decide whether to speak up in turn or to remain silent and privileged outside the circle of her friends' experience.

> But it had happened only in her imagination, she now decided, not without a certain melancholy. Looking at the experience more objectively, she could see that it had been a sentimental wavering of the heart. It might in fact be good to talk about it, but what would Shigeko or Haruko say if she were to mention it? (p. 226)

This is the most fully developed hesitation that any of the women exhibit, and it makes the third and last tale more significant. At this point, we, as readers, knowing that "something had happened" but not what that something is, want to know; structurally, too, there is a demand that the cycle of tales be completed. In the face of the recalcitrance of its would-be narrator, strong narrative pressure is exerted.

> The three of them talked about the fact that they had come so far for such a short stay, but that it had been worth it just to see the snow. For Haruko, moreover, it had been a place of deep associations, and Shigeko maintained that coming so far had freed her feelings and made it possible for her to reveal her personal secret. The experience had

brought them all closer together. Therefore, Akiye felt that it was now her turn to speak. (p. 226)

When Akiye finally does decide to tell her tale, the established formula holds for the most part. Her story, contained within an outer frame of conversational exchanges, is once more cast in reported discourse. The, by now, almost obligatory interruptions occur at the story's conclusion, but in this case the first narrative shift from represented speech to direct speech comes within the defined space of Akiye's telling. Because her husband had died at work, she had retained a young lawyer to help her in negotiating for a settlement with the firm. Akiye finds herself attracted to the lawyer, although her husband's death was very recent.

> One might say that Akiye, while bitterly longing for her late husband, was reaching out for the physical presence of a man.
> "He, too, was aware of me in that way. You see, there was one day during the summer rains...We had gone for the umpteenth time to the company to negotiate, and on our way back we walked all the way along the palace moat from Hibiya clear to Kudan." Akiye said this, but at this moment it seemed as if she were speaking of someone else. (p. 227)

This shift from direct to indirect discourse within the limits of the tale proper seems a bit problematic, but it does make this particular incident stand out more immediately and vividly from the muted background of the story. Here once again we find the weakening of the separated narrative which signals an invitation to dialogue in the work, and Haruko's intrusion at this point is predictable in the pattern of the previous tales.

> In her mind's eye Haruko could picture the figures of the two of them walking under the fresh green leaves of the willows on the embankment as the rains fell softly on them, and it made her own eyes shine. "My, how splendid. But what were you talking about?" (p. 227)

Again there is a sense of the strong dislocation in time that the tale creates upon its listeners, but more significantly upon its teller. Akiye, in fact, returns to the present in two steps, not in one, for she recounts an incident when she later encountered the lawyer.

> Smiling, Akiye spoke in a different tone. "Yes, well, very recently I ran into him in Shibuya. We merely greeted one another with the usual commonplaces and then parted, but at the time I happened to be rather

dressed up. And after we had gone our separate ways, I couldn't help thinking that it was a good thing that I had been looking my best that day. That's a woman's reaction for you. I still have these feelings." Akiye laughed, amused at herself. (p. 228)

The psychological assurance of this passage makes the reader smile in recognition, too. In a way very symbolic of their stay at the inn, after Akiye recovers her sense of the present moment she turns once more to look at the snow, which by this time has become the controlling image of the work.

The fourth of the story's presences tells no tale, and yet it is most responsible for the telling of them all. Through their relationships to this other presence at the inn, the snow, we are able to measure the true proportion of the three other protagonists' share in the central consciousness of the story.

When the story opens, Haruko clearly is the proprietor of the snow. It is a presence in her past, one that she seeks to recapture for the benefit of both her companions, but most especially for Akiye, whose "reward" the trip is intended to be and who had expressed a desire to see the snow country in the first place. Ultimately, however, it is upon Akiye's consciousness that the snow produces the most profound effect. The snow, the stories, and the relationship of the three women are all associated in her mind, to the point that she struggles to find some analogy for its significance to her that will touch upon the deep sense of connection she sees between the falling snow and their own lives: "The snow, while whirling round and round, was drifting down. Might not her own life up to this time have been exactly like that?" she asks herself earlier (p. 323). But the fittest ending for this short story must be what it is—Akiye's parting injunction to that fourth presence at their talks, "Dance, snow!"

The strongest residual impression of the story lies in the connection between the swirling snow and the levels of relationship among the women. And through the artfulness of the story, the falling snow makes a perfect counterpoint to the tales told around the warmth of the *kotatsu*. In covering over the outside world, the snow, like the trip itself, removes the women from their everyday Tokyo lives, providing them with a reflective space: "The whole area was enclosed by a sheet of whiteness, as though a thin silk curtain had been drawn around it" (p. 223). Within this space, the women tell their separate stories and together arrive at a shared understanding of incidents that had until then been private sources of pain or uneasiness. Thus, experience, recollection, and judgment; narration, thought, and dialogue; speaker and listener (narrator and reader); past and present are interwoven in a dense text. The text itself, unusual among Sata's works in its separation from the everyday world, from the intercalation of social and personal concerns, provides an opportunity for the examination of her art, not in terms of the dichotomies of content and form (or base and superstructure) or history and ideology, but in the continuum of praxis.

And yet, the very artistry of the story and its reflective setting mask the fact that it is not without significant social content. Perhaps that content is too plain to see. Written for the public of a woman's magazine, it retraces in the tales the social patterning inherent in the Japanese concept of marriage. These, in a sense, are another generation of the well-dressed matrons on Hiroko's morning train. On vacation they, or at least two of them, apparently have nothing better to do than complain about their husbands' unfaithfulness. But then, very obviously, they have nothing better to be, in their social context, than the wives of their husbands. That is why their husbands' affairs threaten their sense of themselves and potentially endanger their secure relationship to a society that still defines women primarily in terms of their familial role. That Akiye, the only one of the three who can be called independent (achieving self-determination only upon her husband's death), is unfaithful only to her husband's memory and only in thought, not deed, indicates the flourishing condition of the Japanese double standard.

In this story Sata, always aware of the particular constraints on women in her culture, clearly acknowledges the psychological force of such role patterning. While presenting the contradiction between the appearances one maintains in the social world and the private pain that can arise when personal relationships are threatened, she nevertheless affirms the importance to most women of these traditional social roles. The characters of "Yuki no mau yado," then, have no less social significance than Hiroko, although readers, caught by the personal dimensions of the narrative, may fail to recognize the social patterns and the cultural morés that give rise to the tales so naturally and so effortlessly as anything other than "the way things are."

Although the women are not directly financially exploited by the operation of an inhumane economic system, they are relatively dependent upon fixed social definitions of the appropriate role of women in society and unable to conceive of operating outside those definitions. Because so many readers share the broad cultural assumptions underlying the story, the social content goes almost unnoticed; but "Yuki no mau yado" is, in its way, no less a model of social process than "Kyarameru kōjō kara."

As different as "Yuki no mau yado" appears to be from "Kyarameru kōjō kara," it is nevertheless visibly the product of the same hand, though a hand grown at once more delicate and more sure. The same sharp eye for the visual creates both the material detail of a workroom at the close of day and the symbolic imagery of the snow falling through the night. The same ear for nuances of dialogue captures the conversation of workers and the confidences of old friends. Language and syntax remain relatively uncomplicated, but the narrative range permitted within this simplicity has grown from the dual perspective of "Kyarameru kōjō kara" to the communal perspective of the later story, where the narrator of the whole is more sensed than seen. In both cases time shifts rapidly within the sequences of sentences; but whereas the emotive time of "Kyarameru kōjō kara" is darkened by a downward turn projected into the future, temporal interaction in "Yuki no mau yado" is between the past and the present.

Almost all of Sata's stories, whether autobiographical or not, represent a series of soundings in time and are influenced in their overall tone by the chronological and psychological distance between the surface moment (the present) and the depth (the past) and by the prevailing mood of the times in which the "sounding" is taken. Taken together, the two stories we have considered indicate the considerable range afforded by such developed artistry.

The sense of the interconnectedness of human lives, glimpsed briefly in "Kyarameru kōjō kara" in the context of the shared burden of the workers is made explicit in "Yuki no mau yado." In this story meaning and the synthesis of past and present are achieved through verbal exchange. Incidents long isolated within the individual consciousnesses of the protagonists remain emotionally undigested, until, once recounted, they become the subject of discourse and interpretation. So the past becomes open to the present and to revision, and the shared present expands backward into a past made communal.

In "Kyarameru kōjō kara," although only the narrator refracts Hiroko's experience for the reader, Hiroko remains isolated in her own present. But in "Yuki no mau yado" the repeated cycle of narration and discussion suggests an inclusive model that allows Sata's own process of literary production to be rehearsed. Thus, a work that is not autobiographical reveals the intent and significance of the works that are. Like *Toki ni tatsu,* like *Kurenai,* like "Kyarameru kōjō kara," "Yuki no mau yado" assesses the closed material of history as the subject of a new discourse. But whereas each of the more autobiographical narratives is confined ultimately within the boundaries of authentically lived events, limited by the personal and social dimensions of the reported past and controlled by the perspective of the interpretive moment (although gaining strength from just this conjunction), "Yuki no mau yado" makes the process of narration a focal part of the narrative itself.

Indeed, Sata is aware of the self-replicating nature of the process. Her critical relationship to her own past work becomes a further extension of this. In the series of afterwords by the author that accompanies her *Zenshū* as a continuing thread (appropriately entitled "Time, People, and Myself"), she is aware of the subtle and contingent relationship she has toward her own past production. In the last of the volumes that present her fiction, she says,

> At this point I feel myself directly confronting a segment of my own past. The task of writing this afterword, since by its nature it involves casting a retrospective glance upon the past, probably produces this effect all the more. My past, in its own way, must ultimately reside within me, but even though that sphere has been determined upon, one might say that as far as going back and forth to it are concerned, the process is endless.[12]

It would seem that the past is never final, but continues to be accessible to present consciousness, a consciousness itself continually subject to revision in the course of time.

It has been Sata's project throughout fifty years of writing to examine experience in the contexts (social, political, and personal) of

---

[12] *Sata Ineko zenshū,* vol. 15, p. 401.

changing times. Her art evolves from the early stories, which, although faithful to the personal dimension of human existence, nevertheless evidence an urgency in articulating the social crises of the era. From the mid-1930s onward through the early 1950s, she faced pressures on many levels. The proletarian movement, in which she had found a community of like-minded individuals and a sense of mission, had been dispersed. The forces of oppression within her own country had triumphed, and she allowed herself to be drawn into the support of a war effort that was diametrically opposed to her own most cherished beliefs. The complexities involved in the reexamination of the past had multiplied, but Sata remained committed to such discipline. Works from the middle of her career thus concern themselves both with personal defeat and compromise and with the necessity of building the possibility for personal growth upon such unpromising ground. Inevitably, the stages of human life—childhood, youth, maturity, and old-age—are ever more clearly articulated in the works of her later years, and a sense of both the disintegrative and reintegrative force of duration becomes an ever-present motif within them.

Her artistic life is almost coterminous with the Shōwa era, and her corpus, by combining the broad social concerns of proletarian literature with the personal dimension of autobiographical fiction, has the unique quality of representing the tension and interplay between history and the individual consciousness. Sata's writing in the later decades of her career evinces a genuine recognition of and ability to reproduce the complex experience of the life lived in a layered and shifting context. Her *zenshū* evokes some fifty years of change in a nation and in an individual from a perspective that the reader comes to trust, in part because of its own admitted waverings and uncertainties. Narrated in a voice that, in spite of a variation in tone and an extension of range over the course of years, remains recognizable and relatively unchanged, her works are ultimately deserving of an assessment not unlike that which she accorded Ichiyō. More than her predecessor, she has made her own life the foundation of her work, and as much as Ichiyō, she "clearly yet subtly reflects the constrictions of the society of her time along with the aspirations of human beings." From the force of duration itself her works gather strength and depth, and it is not the least significant aspect of her particular gift as a writer that she is able to render the effect of time upon the individual with astonishing clarity.

CHAPTER FIVE

The Sibyl of Negation: Kurahashi Yumiko and "Natsu no owari"

KURAHASHI YUMIKO'S prize-winning initial effort, "Parutai," was published in 1960. While some ground might be found for a comparison of "Parutai" with Sata's purely proletarian works, it would have to be comparison based upon ideological opposition, for, despite their active writing careers having been concurrent for eleven years (until Kurahashi lapsed into nearly a decade of silence),[1] there are seeming light-years between the style and intent of their writing.

Certainly they are women of different generations, and a contrast between their writings is only to be expected. In addition, Kurahashi's background has less in common with Sata's than Sata's has with Ichiyō's. They may be termed, in fact, women of different classes. Born on October 10, 1935, in Shikoku, the eldest daughter of a dentist, Kurahashi graduated from Meiji University in 1960. She cannot be said to have experienced the poverty and hopelessness of the urban lower class firsthand as did Ichiyō and Sata. Nevertheless, in her case, as in the cases of both Sata and Ichiyō, we can find evidence of parental interference with her education and plans for her life. Kurahashi's father insisted that she gain qualification as a dental assistant. Although she consented to the completion of such training, she managed at the same time to gain entrance to the French Department at Meiji University without her father's knowledge, and had launched herself successfully as a writer before graduation.

Even in the postwar generation and when we are speaking of a writer termed "one of the most daring and prolific of avant-garde writers,"[2] then, there is a strong indication that the pressure of fami-

---

[1] Which ended with *Shiro no naka no shiro* (Tokyo: Shinchō, 1979–1980) and subsequent works.

[2] In the introduction to her story "To Die at the Estuary," which is included in Howard Hibbett, ed., *Contemporary Japanese Literature: An Anthology of Fiction, Film, and Other Writing Since 1945* (New York: Knopf, 1977), p. 247.

ly authority was exerted to get her to conform to an acceptable pattern. Beyond that, however, the nature of the pattern involved is instructive. Education, its form and its availability, has a great deal to do with the situation of women in society and, therefore, of the woman writer's interaction with that society. It is one of the major areas in which societal intentions for the patterning of women on a social level are most clearly manifested.

In 1945, after the war, women finally received the vote. They were admitted to the more prestigious national universities for the first time, and were elected to the Diet. Political and educational power had apparently been won. We would expect such a victory to be evidence of a profound shift in the opportunities open to women and a new freedom from traditional constraints. Women, it might seem, had been enabled to take an active role in the democratic, progressive, postindustrial nation that Japan had become in the postwar period.

The educational policies of the new Japan, however, fail to mirror such sweeping change. Since Kurahashi's writing career began, there has indeed been a revision in the Ministry of Education's aim for women in society. In 1971 a new curriculum was announced by the ministry and scheduled to be put into operation in 1973. Among other changes were the following stipulations: "General housekeeping becomes compulsory for every girl. The theory and practice of 'everyday manners' will be taught to make girls more genteel and to break the 'trend of argumentativeness.'"[3] To break the trend of argumentativeness? *Plus ça change...* Apparently in Japan as elsewhere, the new freedom for women seemed to threaten traditional "feminine" accomplishments. And if women had gained the vote by fiat, perhaps revisionary regulation might restore more time-honored qualities—such as gentility and docility (read submissiveness). All three of the writers under study can be considered in the context of the kind of restraints being articulated in this ministry declaration, and, although Sata has actively opposed the government on many social issues, it is surely Kurahashi whose fiction most clearly embodies that "trend of argumentativeness" that gave the Ministry of Education pause. Her stance vis-à-vis the society of present-day Japan is,

---

[3] *Far Eastern Economic Review*, March 13, 1971, p. 32.

however, for all its "daring," a primarily rhetorical rather than politically activist one.

Sata's fiction explores the relationship between the individual and the social world; Kurahashi rejects such a relationship. Both writers are depicting the same society at the same historical moment. Nevertheless, the juxtaposition of two stories they wrote in roughly the same era—"Yuki no mau yado" and "Natsu no owari" (The End of Summer)—produces a jarring impact on the reader. The two works hardly seem to be products of the same culture, and, in a real sense, they are not. Although the social situation addressed may seem to be temporally and historically the same, the stances of their fiction toward that situation could not be more opposed. Sata's humanistic outlook and her concern with the exploration of individual consciousness within the framework of traditional narrative verisimilitude represents the extension of aesthetic concerns formed in the social and literary contexts of the early Shōwa era, and "Yuki no mau yado" is a performative model of what may be called the dominant fictionalizing process during much of the twentieth century—that restructuring of personal experience that has its most extreme statement in the *shishōsetsu* form. Kurahashi's work is, in a deliberately provocative way, far more impersonal, Westernized, and modernistic, and her theory of fiction is aggressively avant-garde. She shares with Abe Kōbō and other writers less well known in the West a certain project of negating current societal values and focusing her fiction on sex, violence, alienation, and antirealism.

Curiously enough, although writers like Kurahashi directly challenge certain established aesthetic and sociological views of Japan in the West, Japan's avant-garde has met with a relatively enthusiastic reception here. Abe Kōbō and Ōe Kenzaburō, two of the other experimental writers of the present age, have a respectable readership in this country, and Kurahashi herself has had three of her short stories published in *New Directions*;[4] a fourth, "To Die at the Estuary" ("Kakō ni shisu"), appears in *Contemporary Japanese Literature*.[5]

---

[4] "The Ugly Devils," *New Directions* 24 (New York: New Directions Publishing Corporation, 1972). "Parutai," *New Directions* 26 (1973). "The Boy Who Became an Eagle," *New Directions* 29 (1974). All three were translated by Samuel Grolmes and Yumiko Tsumura.

[5] See n. 2; trans. Dennis Keene, pp. 248–281.

In addition, a full-length work, *The Adventures of Sumiyakist Q*, has also been translated.[6] Like Abe's and Ōe's, Kurahashi's works cannot be said to appeal to those admirers of Japanese literature who prize such traditional values as delicate sensitivity and allusive language. Moreover, the social background provided in works by these three and other modernists directly contradicts many of the current views held by leading American Japanologists. Thus, two images of Japan, sociological and "new" aesthetic, have assumed sharply contrasting configurations.

To a certain extent both views are fictions, or at least partial metaphors for a reality that in its complexity has something of each. Consequently, any examination of the intersection of text and context in the Japan of recent decades needs to recognize that at least two separate image-making processes are in operation in the West. One, the sociological, has its origins in a Western desire to understand and interpret the economic emergence of Japan as a superpower. The other, the aesthetic, represents the generally enthusiastic international reception of a current modern Japanese literature containing negative views of Japanese society and incorporating a kind of brittle cosmopolitanism. Obviously, influence can no longer be seen as a one-way street. For example, in Ezra Vogel's *Japan As Number 1: Lessons for America*, we are presented with an image of Japan as a socioeconomic exemplar, highly successful in adapting to the economic realities of the present age and yet able to resist pressures of social disintegration that have threatened other industrial nations. And the Japanese model is suggested as a viable one for America, with certain modifications.

> [T]here is no reason why, with greater central direction and sensitivity to the needs of various groups, to the mechanisms of maintaining solidarity, and to the practice of broad consultation, America could not adopt policies more suited to the postindustrial age and recreate a sense of community in a form adapted to postindustrial society.[7]

From such a point of view, the Japanese experience becomes an icon

---

[6] Japanese title: *Sumiyakisuto Q no bōken*. Trans. Dennis Keene (St. Lucia, Queensland: University of Queensland Press, 1979).

[7] Ezra Vogel, *Japan As Number 1: Lessons for America* (New York: Harper and Row, 1980), p. 255.

of successful modernization.

And yet, as coherent as such a presentation may be in its own terms, it suggests a perspective that necessarily has distanced elements in contemporary Japan that may be deemed irrelevant to its central argument. Consequently, when Vogel discusses the organized opposition to the opening of Narita Airport, it is for the most part in his chapter "Crime Control: Enforcement and Public Support," and his emphasis is upon the police role in maintaining order. Commenting upon "the overwhelming force" amassed by the police in meeting opposition, he observes,

> In 1978 for example, when gasoline was first taken to the Narita Airport over the protest of resisters, over six thousand riot police took charge of protecting the oil from the danger of intruders. They failed to prevent damage to the control tower, but thousands of well-trained, courteous riot police prevented any incidents in the first months of the airport's operation despite a group of highly skilled opponents determined to cause trouble.[8]

Certainly, the police effort in those times was impressive. Anyone who has seen a Japanese policeman in full riot gear, or who passed through Narita Airport in those early days of operation, might, however, be forgiven an additional, more visceral, response. With the visor of the full helmet and the chest protector in place, the policeman's appearance strikes the imaginative as having more to do with the fantasy world of science fiction than with the well-ordered universe of the diligent salary-man and assembly-line worker.

Since artists are by definition imaginative, that they should register the impact of such powerful social images in their work is no surprise. Even the Western observer of the contemporary Japanese scene can occasionally glimpse aesthetic representations of the confrontation between the forces of social order and of defiance. Thus, one of the most striking illustrations in Roland Barthes' *L'Empire des Signes* occurs in the section entitled "L'Écriture de la violence."[9] It is a double-page closeup view of helmeted students, their faces swathed in cloth to protect themselves against tear gas. Armed with battering rams and sticks, they are waiting with folded arms for what

---

[8] Ibid., p. 220.
[9] Roland Barthes, *L'Empire des Signes* (Geneva: Skira, 1970).

Barthes sees as a ritual of violent protest.

Even without a stylized interpretation like his, however, the picture conveys a meaning other than that which is extracted from Japan's astonishing economic leap forward. In the picture, as in Japanese society of the 1960s and 1970s, the student is clearly a figure defying an ordered, well-regulated, and virtually unstoppable social machine. And, since modernistic fiction in Japan has predictably tended to emphasize images of opposition, the figure of the student tends to loom large, especially in the early works of its proponents. Kurahashi is no exception. In her case, however, the idealism of youth is suspect, too; from "Parutai" onward parody and satire enter into her handling of organized student protest. Her aesthetic vision of her society entails not merely opposition, but total denial. In this, as in her handling of sexuality, where her use of metaphor is distinctive, Kurahashi must be differentiated from the other modernists.

Before we consider Kurahashi's idiosyncratic vision of her society, however, it might be well to locate her works within a more generalized view of the avant-garde writers. Although, as previously stated, the reception of Japan's modernists has been generally favorable, indeed occasionally flattering, many Western critics with a sense of the Japanese literary tradition are less tolerant of avant-garde mannerisms and the "degeneracy" of the movement as a whole. D.J. Enright, for example, in his review of Abe Kōbō's *Secret Rendezvous*, launches a frontal attack against contemporary Japanese writers (and their admirers): "Japanese fiction resembles British drama in that it started off at the peak and thereafter slid downhill."[10] His assessment of the view at the foot of the hill is accordingly bleak. Characterizing the trend of postwar letters in Japan as downward from the "sexuality of the nerves" of Tanizaki and Kawabata, "*raffiné* and perverse (and increasingly geriatric)," to a present stage of pornography and near pornography, he composes a sweeping indictment of Abe in particular and the modernist in general.

In the course of his argument, Enright raises some issues that might, I think, be related to Kurahashi's work at least as readily as to

[10] D.J. Enright, "Hooray for Monsters," *New York Review of Books*, 27 September 1979, p. 27.

Abe's. As he observes of the attitude of more sycophantic critics:

> Then, if a suggestion of allegory or fable can be detected in the book, we have all the more reason to choke back any old-fashioned, shame-faced complaint. Related is the phenomenon of "disgust," a highly metaphysical state of affairs which can be seen as lifting the writer into a higher category. Thus Kōbō Abe's new novel is, or may be held to be, a blend of Beckett, Nabokov, Masters and Johnson (vigorously extrapolated), science fiction—and Kafka too. All tokens of respectability.[11]

At this point, Enright is discussing two features of the modern Japanese text that he obviously considers highly objectionable: one, its degraded sexuality, and the other, its derivative nature, its dependence upon foreign sources for intellectual validation. No reader of Kurahashi can miss the application of such strictures to her work, and we will be discussing them in connection with "Natsu no owari." But there is yet another observation Enright makes, attacking not only the works themselves but also the admirers of the current mode in Japanese fiction and their dogged attempt to read deeper meanings into the works of its proponents than those that appear on the surface of the texts themselves.

Enright subsequently discusses the action (or inaction) of Abe's *The Ruined Map*, (*Moetsukita chizu*), which he terms quasi-*policier*. He compares it unfavorably with Kafka's *The Trial*, and goes on to declare it empty of meaning.

> Every clue misleads, every witness lies, every discovery mystifies further—and all on principle it seems. The book ends in utter inconsequence, for what is really missing is the story and its characters. But of course, the less there is to meet the eye, the more chance of someone supposing there is more than meets the eye.
>
> That is to say, allegory.... But like science fiction, allegory requires a measure of reality, of openness to participation by the reader, if it is to work.[12]

With the acuity of detestation, Enright has isolated the salient features of modernist production with which the reader must in some way come to terms. In his opinion, in addition to their perverse sex-

---

[11] Ibid.
[12] Ibid., p. 28.

uality and derivative pretentiousness, such texts are devoid of signification and make no attempt to incorporate the reader. They are, in Enright's terms, physically, intellectually, epistemologically, and psychologically repellent. The question is why. Any consideration of modernist production that does not, on the one hand, involve the kind of reverence that Enright scorns as a modern-day reading of the entrails, or, on the other hand, join in his own (implicit) demand for a purging of the temple must find some other basis for interaction with the text.

The first recognition that must be made in dealing with the work of Kurahashi (as with that of other modernists) is that we are in many ways facing a hostile text. The question for the critic then becomes that which Frederic Jameson calls "the most urgent and visceral issue...why he or she should be expected to find aesthetic pleasure and satisfaction in a work whose impulses are often so ugly and ideologically offensive."[13] In other words, why does the reader read the text?

But a further question arises. Why did the writer write the text? Why does the writer create a work so deliberately hostile to the society from which it arises and hostile even to the reader whose reactions it sets out to provoke? These are the questions underlying those other elements from which Enright recoils, the perverse sexuality, the occasionally quite ostentatious imitation and/or parody of Western works, the intentional obscuring of meaning, and the repudiation of the reader. What can be said about the intersection of the word (literature) and the world (society), when it is the intent of the text to repudiate not only its social but also its aesthetic context?

There can be little doubt that such, in large part, is the intention of Kurahashi's early fiction, a fiction that creates a bizarre anti-world with patterns of its own. Kurahashi's description is explicit in the dimensions of its denial.

> I abhor the intrusion of the disorder of "facts" into the world of words I have constructed. The iron-clad rule in reporting facts or events is the clarification of the five W's—when, where, who, what, why—but my stories reject these restrictions entirely and instead build castles in the

---

[13] Frederic Jameson, *Fables of Aggression: Wyndham Lewis, the Modernist as Fascist* (Berkeley/Los Angeles/London: University of California Press, 1979), p. 20.

air. At an uncertain time, in a place that is nowhere, somebody who is no one, for no reason is about to do something—and in the end does nothing: this is my ideal of the novel.[14]

Aside from the connotation of wistful fantasy suggested by the words "castles in the air," the description is an accurate one when applied to the fiction that Kurahashi had written up to that time (1966), and her project is clear—the substitution of a verbal world "that is not" for the physical and social world "that is." Even that verbal world, however, is based upon denial of the conventions of signification, and the writer insists here upon total control, the exercise of an almost Caligulan verbal power. Moreover, Kurahashi's sense of control goes beyond the text to the critical reception of her work. Although she is not beyond making disclaimers of a sort about her past fiction, in the statement above she exerts every effort to control the contexts of the texts themselves. In other words, her antistructural structure is quite firm. And it is defined in negatives. Her ideal of the novel (for which we may read the short story as well) is that it should refuse any relationship whatsoever with the world of facts.

At least, so runs Kurahashi's early theory of fiction. And how does this work out in practice? One of the things that strikes readers about her early fiction is that her verbal castles, as different as they are in form from one another, and lacking the "disorder of 'facts,'" do utilize a number of repeated motifs. "Natsu no owari," the story we will be considering at some length, was published at the end of her first, very prolific year of writing. It is more conventional in some ways than the preceding stories of that year (1960), making it somewhat easier to handle in an exposition of the influence of context upon text; but it does contain the hallmarks of the early Kurahashi style, and it handles the same themes as her more grotesque creations do. Nevertheless, it might be well to examine some of those earlier moments in the "world of words" that Kurahashi has constructed.

---

[14] Quoted in the introduction to "To Die at the Estuary," *Contemporary Japanese Literature*, from "Shōsetsu no meiro to hiteisei" [Negativity and the Labyrinth of Fiction], 1966.

In "Zōnin bokumetsu shukan," written before "Parutai" but published later in the year, the action concerns the extermination of inferior members of society by government decree. K-sensei is the first of Kurahashi's initials-only protagonists to put in an appearance. In the entire period, stories are told only from the standpoint of *watashi* (I) or *boku* (I/male) or else from the standpoint of K. The initial does not stand for a constant. In "Parutai," a story we will discuss briefly in terms of its similarities to "Natsu no owari," the protagonist is *watashi*, a student who addresses what may be seen as an explanation to her lover on the occasion of her leaving both him and the Communist Party. The atmosphere of "Hinin" is as bleak as those of earlier stories, but made more grotesque by the fact that its characters have tails and exude unpleasant secretions.

"Hebi" exhibits some of the elements that are most bizarre in Kurahashi's work at the same time as it presents a typical relational pattern. In this story, the student K wakes up one morning to discover that he has swallowed part of a snake and is unable to dislodge the creature. In the course of a rather complicated plot, the snake and, consequently, apparently also K, who after all had first swallowed the snake, swallows K's girl friend L (K is always male, L female). K's fellow students had decided to use the incident to make a political martyr of K, but the swallowing of L presents an additional complication. Ultimately, the government conducts an investigation, but while K is being interrogated, the snake emerges from him and swallows K, too. This simplifies the government's task, because the officials are able to decide that the snake is now the basic entity in the relationship. With K reduced to the classification of foodstuff, the awkward K-incident is regarded as having been tidily resolved.

In her explanation of this story at the end of the first volume of her *Zensakuhin* (Collected Works),[15] Kurahashi offers the information that the work was inspired by Abe Kōbō and Kafka. Enright's queasiness begins to seem justified. Why the insistence upon foreign sources? Why write a story like the subsequent "Kon'yaku," in which K for once is tied down to a historical personage (and that none other than Franz Kafka), or like such later stories as "Taishōjuku," in which Abraham and Sarah (and God) appear, or

---

[15] *Kurahashi Yumiko zensakuhin*, vol. 1 (Tokyo: Shinchōsha, 1975), p. 266.

"Miira," in which the protagonist (Rimbaud) is addressed as *anata* (you) by an unidentified narrator? And what is the significance of the repeated K and L pattern in all its variations, whether the incestuous twins of "Uchūjin," who ended up sleeping with a hermaphroditic and imbecilic character from outer space, or the matricidal twins of "Sasori," ("The Scorpions"), who cap a vacation trip during which they cause the deaths of their three companions by murdering their mother, or of any of the other K and L combinations of lovers who are not twins?

To continue cataloging Kurahashi's fiction would merely be to continue raising such questions, and the examination of a single short story will allow many of the same issues to be dealt with within a controlled context. Nevertheless, any survey of Kurahashi's writings does raise one final question for us, and that is why in a "world of words," where everything is apparently in question, does the recurrence of certain techniques and motifs suggest a kind of sense of its own? Although Enright might warn us of the danger of reading meaning into works without meaning, works in which "at an uncertain time, in a place that is nowhere, somebody who is no one, for no reason is about to do something," the relationship in Kurahashi's work between the single text and the many is worth some consideration.

The insistence upon a replication of consciousness, the commodification of the event (since motivation, or at least its emotional basis, is dissolved or denied), and the hostility of the text itself are aspects of Kurahashi's writing that will confront, and may affront, the reader of any of her stories. Thus, if the work selected for discussion here contains neither some of the more bizarre features of other, more "experimental" Kurahashi texts nor the more realistic situations depicted in her later fiction, it at least allows a critical assessment to be made of these persistent aspects of her fictional world.

In "Natsu no owari" most of those aspects already exist in the opening paragraph. The apparently flat prose in which the narrator details the summer plans for murder is studded with very characteristic Kurahashi touches. The second and third sentences of the paragraph serve as a veritable demonstration model:

> Our resolve had not changed. K must be transformed by our own hands into a heavy, dead lump. Just as we had jointly possessed him

as a lover, my sister and I were completely united in this *idée* also. (p. 229)[16]

Most obvious, perhaps, is the commodification of the flesh which appears in K's projected transformation into "a heavy, dead lump" and the reference to him as "jointly possessed." But even before that, the familiar initial "K" appears as the subject of the second sentence, albeit a subject whose function is to be acted upon. "Natsu no owari" is somewhat unusual among Kurahashi's stories employing this device, however, in that an origin is given for the practice as the story progresses. Instead of being taken as a given, if mystifying, element in the work, this use of the initial has a history.

> My sister asked what he had said his name was.
> I answered with the initial K. This abbreviated symbolic way of naming him amused my sister. I was rather pleased with it myself. We decided to go on referring to him in this way. (p. 230)

As a history it is brief; but it does suggest some of the possible functions of the process. Before they had arrived at the stage of planning to reduce him to "a heavy, dead lump," the sisters had already deprived him of the greater part of his name and identity. The narrator has decided to call this renaming process symbolic, and, pleased with her cleverness, fits it into what amounts, as we shall see, to a secret code that operates between the sisters when they deal with a third party. That is why, when her sister later uses the initial K before their lover, the narrator is shocked at this breaching of the code, although she laughs. At least, this is the explanation she offers for her reaction, but given the context at that point in the text, we have reason to suspect that both her account of her relationship to her sister and her description of her own emotions have been distorted.

There is no hint of unreliable narration in the opening paragraph, however, although the reader already has ample reason to regard the text as a hostile one. Even if one accepts the essentially amoral attitude involved in the content, and does not experience qualms in accepting the objective description of the sisters' delight at the prospect of murdering their lover or balk at the concept of their

---

[16] The page citations refer to the appended translation, "The End of Summer."

joint ownership of him, other elements in the style have an alienating effect.

First, perhaps, is the introduction of the French word *"idée,"'* used in the *katakana* phonetic system, when there are perfectly acceptable Japanese words that would convey the same meaning. We must assume that it is not only the meaning that is important here, but the effect. Why does Kurahashi use the word *"idée"*? Very possibly for the same reason that, when she describes the sources for the story, she lists Camus' *L'Etranger* as well as Mishima Yukio's "Manatsu no shi" ("Death in Midsummer") and a foreign film. Even in English a French *idée* has a more prestigious sound than a mere idea, and the *idée* is the central mechanism upon which the plot hangs. Here it is more muted than a similar usage of the word *"honte"* (shame) as the central concept, the "authentic" emotion, in "Parutai." In that case its double alien/alienating nature is more obvious, for in a running Japanese text, the word *"honte"* written in the Western alphabet leaps out of the text repeatedly, even when one simply glances at the page. The reader experiences a visual shock.

Although many of the foreign terms (*gairaigo*) used in the text are simply part of the Japanese language and some refer to such cultural imports as Charlie Parker L.P.'s and polo shirts, several usages seem set apart from ordinary language. *Idée* is one of these. Along with it, *imaaju* (image) and *sekushuaru* (sexual) appear to be appealing to Western systems of signification, a sign that the meaning of these terms in the stories is influenced by Western concepts and is not to be taken in an ordinary, domestic, Japanese sense. Other foreign terms in the text do have a way of exoticizing aspects of the use of images and sexuality; *totemu poru* (totem pole) and *masuku* (mask), for example, could be seen as linguistic signals of the alien nature of some of the images, and both occur in conjunction with the central relationship within the text. The formation of the initial liaison between the narrator and K is described as being deliberately created "as if we were carving a totem pole." Since the effort to fashion a visual image from this metaphor strikes even the Western reader as a bit forced, one can only wonder at the effect of such exoticism on the Japanese reader. The possible hierarchical implication of the image, at least in its Western usage, is virtually lost in the elaborate manner by which it is inscribed on the text. Paired with it is the image of "the dialogue of a classical play," a device that seems to work a little more smoothly. The mask image follows immediately upon the other two, obviously picking up on the reference to the play and its performers, but because of the use of the Western word, it has an intensified alienating effect that contributes to a sense of the younger sister as audience and yet performer—a masked audience as it were, about to insist on taking a role in the performance.

Other foreign terms cluster around the *sekushuaru* and are by and large the relatively innocuous *kissu, amuburassu* (embrace), and *karessu* (caress), all combined with the Japanese *suru*, which makes nouns into verbs. Apparently, then, just as the ideational content of the story, the central *idée*, is to be identified with matters Western, and perhaps even alien, so the mechanics of sexuality are tagged with the terminology of the alien and exotic. Finally, at the close of the story Kurahashi uses the French word *"objet"* to refer to the sisters' plan to transform K into an eternal possession: "Whereupon we would be able to have joint ownership of the then bleached bones of our love made into a fixed *objet* outside of ourselves." Here the sense of the alien is double, in the appearance of the word itself and in its meaning in context. Since this usage occurs after a repetition of *idée*, the impact of the French suggests an almost causal relation between the *"idée* of death" and the *"objet"* that is to be its concrete actualization.

If this were not enough to deny the reader a strong sense of connection with the protagonists, a further feature in the opening paragraph would certainly have that effect. That is the insistent use of first-person pronouns. Playing off the "abbreviated symbolism" of the reduction of K's personal identity and his status as jointly owned (*kyōyū shite ita*) property, is a dominant use of *watashi* and *watashi-tachi* (we). Normally, Japanese tend to forego personal pronouns except where absolutely necessary for clarity, but since Western grammar is very pronoun-centered, the full effect of the Japanese pronouns cannot be captured in translation. First-person pronouns occur in every sentence but one in this first paragraph, and they are assertive and controlling as well as frequent. The passive object K, then, is to be completely at the disposal of the controlling consciousness of the story, a consciousness that appears to be shared rather nonchalantly by "I," "we," and "I and my (younger) sister." The relationship between the narrator and her sister is to become increasingly significant as the story develops, but even in these opening sentences, its basis in complicity and control is hinted, and a powerful sense of a dominating ego is conveyed to the reader.

The first paragraph, then, outlines the potential plot of the story, introduces the central relationships of the work, and exhibits many of Kurahashi's linguistic mannerisms. In addition, the imagery that controls some aspects of the work is introduced, and the readers are presented with the problem of their relationship to a text that already seems hostile to their inclusion in its discourse, especially if they give in to the suspicion that the content is intended to shock and the language both to alienate and to express a kind of intellectual dominance. The imagery and the deliberate attempt to repel the reader are developed concurrently in the ensuing paragraph, which is strangely split in focus. Imagery has already been used to suggest both physical discomfort and emotional resentment as elements in the affair with K, which is likened to "the wound from a noxious cactus spine festering under the skin," and the obvious voraciousness of the protagonists' imaginations is built upon the assertion that "we would cram K into the maw of death," the details of which plan in several technical variations are evidently a source of greedy anticipation: "We took great pleasure in savoring the nuances of each one on our tongues." But in the second paragraph that image of voracious sexuality becomes strengthened as a curious split between the ideational level of the text and its figural and emotional level appears.

There is nothing particularly hidden in the sexual imagery, which develops in the paragraph from the point of "the completely closed buds" of summers past "that had never opened," being "buried intact" to "the glare of the sky above the ocean" yawning "open like the crimson flesh inside of fruit"; but more ambiguous is the emotional tenor of a passage in which these images awaken "shudders of horror and joy," whereas the fact that "last summer mother had died at this villa" provokes a carefree mood because "the dead could spread no protective wings above us." Kurahashi is here going Camus one better. Whereas Meursalt in *The Stranger* is merely indifferent to his mother's death, the sisters are pleasantly relieved. Without the supervision of their mother, they are free to make of the summer what they will: "This summer would belong to us alone."

And the imagery of the opening paragraphs indicates that whatever other plans they may have had in mind for summer vacation, sexual experimentation is a definite possibility.

By this point the reader of Kurahashi has enough information to classify "Natsu no owari" as belonging among those texts that deal with the complicity of siblings who launch a destructive campaign against the world, although more typically they would be the incestuous twins, K and L. In these stories the siblings are totally detached from relationship to the world, consider themselves an elite of two, and develop a private code of complicity that substitutes for morality in the amoral world of the conscious manipulation of sexuality. There is, however, no room in this world for emotion. The physical and mechanical aspects of sex and violence are fully indulged for the edification of the conscious mind, but the emotional basis of human motivation is repressed.

In "Natsu no owari" the result is a clash between the text's ideology and its psychology, and that clash takes place in the heart of the relationship that is the story's central core and principal conceit. We face a textual discontinuity between the conscious ideological level of the narrative and the figural representation of the repressed and unconscious emotional level of the text. Again Jameson seems to be describing the dilemmas of this work when he suggests "ideology, psychoanalysis and narrative"[17] as necessary coordinates for his own study of Wyndham Lewis. Furthermore, he suggests a pattern that may be present in an altered form in Kurahashi's replicated pairs. In his context the pseudo-couple is always masculine, and that is not the case in Kurahashi, where it is never an entirely masculine duo. Nevertheless, Jameson's definition of its functioning gives us a sense that behind the pattern is a meaning of some sort.

> The male pseudo-couple might be understood as a kind of compensation form, a curious structural halfway house in the history of the subject, between its construction in bourgeois individualism and its disintegration in late capitalism. The partners of the pseudo-couple are neither active, independent subjects in their own right, nor have they succumbed to the schizophrenic fetishization which characterizes contem-

---

[17] Jameson, *Fables*, p. 1.

porary consciousness. They remain legal subjects who nonetheless lack genuine autonomy and find themselves thereby obliged to lean on one another in a simulation of psychic unity which is little better than neurotic dependency.[18]

Unlike the dynamic that Jameson discovers in Lewis's work, where the pseudo-couple is frankly antagonistic to one another, in Kurahashi's fiction the repeated pair is never presented in the ideological narrative as being in conscious opposition. Quite the contrary, a great deal of the narrative energy of the text is expended in the assertion of their unity in body and mind. Clearly, her fictional configuration embodies some specific need through the unity of the pair, some construction representing another kind of "halfway house in the history of the subject," between the individualism of the nineteenth century and the schizophrenia of the modern subject. Although she does utilize a schizophrenic personality in "Aiko-tachi" (1965), Kurahashi does not repeatedly return to the theme as she does to that of replication. Replication, then, does not seem to serve the same ends as fragmentation, and its manifestation on the level of the characters must be intended to suggest some other function.

An examination of the qualities that the relationship of the sisters shares with similar relationships in other texts may help clarify the dynamic of the pattern in Kurahashi's fiction. In an essay "Concerning Incest," Kurahashi commented upon the significance of the incestuous couples in her fiction, and these, as we have said, function generally in the same manner as do the sisters in "Natsu no owari." "In this fictional crime I can detect the complete union of matter and temperament in the parties to it, and *nevertheless* I like to write about those accomplices in this elite crime, who by their will to evil possess a joint love which becomes even more highly charged, and bestows upon them the standing of the union of a high-born prince and princess." This is to attribute significance of mythic proportions to the crimes of the united consciousness, and to set it apart from the dictates of society. Given the fact that the sisters of "Natsu no owari" are not homosexual, the closest they can come to this kind of union is through their joint possession of a mutual sexual object: "Since our close resemblance made us completely in union in terms of phys-

---

[18] Ibid., p. 59.

ical appearance, we felt that the act of possessing K in turn could be mutually explored" (p. 235).

Although in terms of the incestuous ideal, where the sex act need not take place outside the shared consciousness, the sisters' relationship is only a makeshift accommodation; the complicity between them is like that between the incestuous twins of other stories. It implies the exclusion from the relationship of the unlike and allows the parties to it to deny all other human relationships while permitting them to make physical use of other people. Thus the objectification of K is necessary if he is not to become a divisive factor in the experience of the replicated pair. And the conscious narrator sees no ideological difficulty in the change in her relationship with K, which takes place after her sister sleeps with him for the first time, merely stating that there was "the necessity for a slight alteration in the concept of possession. Not a monopoly, but a graceful joint ownership" (p. 234).

In much of Kurahashi's fiction, sex does not imply a necessary closeness to the object one makes physical use of. Thus, in "Parutai" the protagonist, who apparently had been in love with the *anata* of the story, has a casual affair with a worker.

> When I looked at the Laborer's skin, it was tinged red like pig iron. I began to feel the same kind of interest in the Laborer that I might feel for some unknown animal.
>
> As for the incident that followed there is hardly anything to tell. I somehow touched the Laborer's body and found it was made of hard muscle. He was surprised. His interest in me aroused, he immediately forced me open and went about being loved by me, pouring his hot breath over me. It was more unpleasant than painful. I was pushed completely open. Even though the Laborer was inside me he was as alien as ever, and I was annoyed by his distance, as if two animals of different species happened to meet and just have intercourse on the spot.[19]

She finds the Laborer difficult to deal with because he is "without language, and his reality was nothing but that simple concrete life," and when she later encounters him, she no longer has any idea who he is. For the sharers of a single consciousness, this separation from

---

[19] "Partei," *New Directions* 26, p. 14.

the reality of others is even more pronounced. Lovers are all alien unless they are united in body and mind by the close ties of blood and shared consciousness. Sexual acts beyond such relationships are with mere objects, and the K and L of "The Alien" are only carrying the process to an extreme in their relationship to the hermaphrodite pet from outer space.

In such a context the sexual act becomes an affirmation of estrangement. It has little more than a mechanical significance. And, in the conscious narrative of "Natsu no owari," the narrator keeps sexuality under the control of intellectualization, objectifying it as performance. Generally, in Kurahashi's fiction, if a sexual relationship is not in some way shared by the accomplice/pair, it becomes a trivial exercise. In those works where one of the pair (usually L) becomes engaged in an entirely conventional manner to an outsider (usually S), the engaged party pays virtually no attention to the fiance/e and embarks on a crime spree with his or her opposite party in the pair. So much for the conventional relationships upon which society puts so much emphasis. They have virtually no bearing upon the relationship of the replicas.

In "Natsu no owari" outsiders leave hardly a ripple on the surface of the existence of the duo. Thus, when the sisters' father shows up at the villa, he makes a scene, but, vanquished by his daughters' wide-eyed stares and silence (agreed upon in advance), he disappears the next day. Father's scenes and mother's death make no apparent alteration in the quality of the relationship. But what is that quality, and why is it so constant a configuration in Kurahashi's fiction? Obviously the configuration is not simply sexual, obviously it has only a negative relationship to the social conventions of the outside world, and obviously it involves the denial of relationship with those outside its confines.

Thus, its essential nature must be in replication. Since the possibility of such a shared consciousness as the sisters exhibit, at least according to the narrator's construction, might occur in the case of two like-minded but biologically unrelated individuals, why is it always presented in the form of incestuous twins or in such close sibling relationships as we see in "Natsu no owari"? Because both parties in the couple must be doubly the same. The incestuous twins are generally far more physically similar than would be likely in a pair who by nature of their sexual differentiation must be fraternal rather than identical. The physical sameness appears to be necessary for the perfect functioning of an ideal configuration in the Kurahashi context.

This is an antisocial, antirelational construction as it appears in Kurahashi's works. It has no ties with the world of social reality ("I abhor the intrusion of 'fact' into the world of words I have constructed.") Thus, it does not mirror the social pressures that produce the shattered ego. Replication differs profoundly from the fragmentation of the subject; here is no splitting of the self into separated drives, but a doubling of the power of a single consciousness, usually interpreted as malign in conventional social terms. For the consciousness whose fundamental dynamic is denial of the world of facts, the social world, the only objective validation possible lies in another, like, consciousness. For this reason, "my sister and I" must be as one, but not one. Negation receives its affirmation in an answering negation.

And in that necessity for an ideal identical receptor/image lies the conflict inherent in this dynamic. For "my sister" is, in part, not the same as the narrator; she plays the role of audience for the narrator's *idées*. And by becoming the perfect reader (for that reason there is no real need for the reader who has been put off by the text), she has already been differentiated from the original. She is the replica who receives impressions and affirms them in their negative power, but insofar as she is actually like her sister, she retains capacity to initiate action.

Moreover, we are no longer in the potentially completely enclosed world of the incestuous twins. The fact that the sisters must move outside their relationship is a second, more disastrous wedge in the flawless unity of the identical front with which they face the world. So in order to maintain the ideological purity of the concept of their unity and separation from the world of other beings, the narrator must expend enormous effort in bringing the sexual under the control of the objective intellect. To do so, while she can admit the sexual act as a performance suitable for objective analysis and open to discussion with her duplicate self, she must exclude from her conscious narrative its possible emotional consequences. Thus, sex as object becomes the subject of an intellectualized discourse, and emotions become the object of repression. The more frank and objective the narrator becomes in her description of the controlled physical side of the three-way relationship, the more suspect her narration becomes. She is bent on an ideological defense of the single consciousness perfectly reproduced; the images and the evasions construct another picture. Nothing may be allowed to threaten the rhetoric with which her world of words is built; everything must be contained, restrained in words.

She first has sex with K after seeing him in her sister's arms, although the idea had occurred to her earlier: "I felt strangely jealous of his beautiful profile. Soon this feeling was transformed into the desire to possess him in his present sharply defined form" (p. 231), but this is not an act of appropriation in the conscious text. When she and K perform "as a pair of lovers in joint possession of the image of love," there is no statement that her sister might resent this extension of the privilege of joint possession of anything to an outsider, nor that she might wish to replicate the narrator in her present role. Instead, a physical explanation is given for her rather peculiar appearance at that time. She does not seem delighted with the performance: "She was still forbidden to swim because of her physical condition, and presumably for the same reason she would watch us languidly with only her eyes standing out in a weakly smiling mask" (p. 233). When the position is reversed, so is the reaction, but the fixity of the narrator's attention gives the reader pause: "When my sister offered her lips to be sucked, she slightly exposed the moist, gleaming darkness inside her mouth. I looked at her thrown back head, with its closed eyes, and the teeth shining like knives inside her mouth. My attitude was tolerant even to serenity. It was my desire to achieve a balance between the external and internal aspects of the performance" (p. 233).

The narrator assures us that the whole situation is under intellectual control at all times, but when she does discover her younger sister sleeping with K, there is a doubling of this verbal assurance.

When I finally entered the room, I saw K and my sister stretched out together on the bed. My sister burst out laughing and said, I borrowed K. I also laughed at my sister's use of the initial K in front of him. Asking, how was he—K, I made it a threesome. I felt no jealousy. You might say that I couldn't discover any of its poisonous fangs or dangerous slivers lodged in my emotions. (p. 234)

No jealousy, simply a rearrangement in the terms of possession, runs the text of the narrator's ideology. But the poisoned fangs or dangerous slivers were already implanted in her sister's mouth where her teeth were "shining like knives." To cover this description of the original projection of the narrator, the language of the text rises to new rhetorical heights of intellectualization. She and her sister must remain united in mastering the situation and in translating the three-way relationship into objective terms.

> This was something that resembled sport. We talked together about performing all kinds of acts with K, made comparisons, and examined them. And either one of us, but sometimes both of us, tried out our theories on K. He became the subject of investigation, the chemistry of passion translated into the dynamics of the flesh. (p. 235)

The tension between the emotional unsaid and the theoretical explanations of the narrator is increased, and the reader is struck by the widening circles of the duplicity of the text. On the evening of the scene with her father, there is another more disturbing scene between the narrator and K. He has already begun to pale in their eyes, if she is to be believed: "More than anything else, the lack of light" in his room at the inn "showed K as a lazy, lethargic youth" (p. 235). When, after returning with her to the villa, he refuses to leave when she wants him to, she experiences a shock at his failure to accept direction.

> Then for the first time I realized that something resembling uneasiness had tumbled into my secure existence. I looked at him quivering. His skin had begun to peel all over. Under the peeled patches I saw the dark, pitted underskin. Dropping all pretenses, I almost felt hatred toward him as he stood there like an ugly clod of earth. (p. 236)

At this point, K remarks that her sister has been pressuring him to express a preference for one of them. The narrator replies that the whole thing has merely been a game, a position she has maintained from the beginning. Yet when K denies this and says that something will have to be done to resolve the situation, the narrator also raises the issue of choice.

> Still which of us do you really love? I asked. Of course, this question had no special significance. In a wary tone, K answered that it was me he loved. I realized that an unbridgeable gap had opened in our concept of joint ownership. (p. 236)

Fissures, then, are opening up throughout the relationship. But even this disintegration is not allowed to effect the narrator's strong concept of her bond with her sister. That must be maintained against the erosion of the joint-ownership policy no matter what. So, although she has essentially forced K to verbalize a preference for her, the dynamics of the interaction of the three are not allowed to exhibit any change.

> My sister and I felt no strain on our relationship. Although a foreign body had intervened in the person of our joint property, K, that did not change our relationship. You might say, to borrow K's words, that we had not lost the flawless symmetry of two casts from the same mold. And if it was I whom K loved—and I didn't entirely believe that—it was nothing more than sheer chance. It was true that at first K had loved only me. However, K had begun to break down. Therefore, in our love, which placed a premium on shared ownership, he had bit by bit begun to lose substance. (p. 237)

The narrator is not quite sure she believes K and the readers are no longer sure they can believe the narrator, but in the passage above, the insistence on the maintenance of the "flawless symmetry" between the sisters is strongly evident. Has K in making a choice of a kind between the two really lost his value to the relationship? Or has his intrusion into the relationship and her own wavering forced her to choose either allegiance to the negative world of the shared consciousness or an admission of the repressed emotional substrata of the story? It is just at this point that the *idée* occurs. All will be resolved by the murder of K. And we are returned to the point where the narration of the story began. Once the resolution of the dilemma created by the counterarguments of the ideological and emotional texts has been achieved by raising the proposition of joint ownership to an eternal dimension, and incidentally ridding the sisters of a major irritant in their own relationship, the story's initial projection will have been realized. However, that projection remains open to challenge.

> Sometimes people try to assert total ownership by destroying their own property. However, K's death, the death of our love, rather than meaning destruction or loss, was the one transformation necessary to make our possession of him eternal.... whereupon, we would be able to have joint ownership of the then bleached bones of our love made into a fixed *objet outside of ourselves.* (p. 237)

The last phrase of the quotation is especially significant, for just at that moment, when everything seems to be hastening to the conclusion envisioned by the sisters and anticipated in the narration from the beginning, the most threatening invasion of the private world of the narrator occurs. The narrator suspects that she may be pregnant, and a series of scenes ensues. The pregnancy marks a totally unacceptable intrusion of the physical world into her life and one she bitterly resents: "Conception and pregnancy, these were inadmissible foreign substances to me; the image that they called to mind was nothing more than a carcinoma or a cancerous cell" (p. 238). For once emotion seems to surface in the text without the control of an intellectual screen. She refuses to consider giving birth to the child, although K sounds very much like a representative of the real world of society in urging her to do so. And she registers the most violent emotions that have been permitted in the text—in fact, the only emotions that have been directly presented to this extent.

> Even then the thought that inside my body a being that was not mine was eating up time and swelling ever larger filled me with nausea. The only idea that could counteract that nausea was that of K's death. The conviction I had had when I first repudiated the world, that at least I was alive and healthy, had changed before I knew it into a dark, corrupt fruit within my vitals. I desired the caretaker's death, my father's death, and even my sister's death. Only a great number of deaths were worthy of the sea, lapping at the sand like a mollusk. (pp. 238–239)

Now the context of death has widened. The (potential) baby, which began by suggesting a cancerous cell, is projected as swelling malignly within her, and the profound affront to her physical well-being and integrity in the protected isolation of this villa at "a certain cape" arouses her resentment and anger, which spill out over all those around her. K, the caretaker, her father, and even her sister—she wishes them all dead. For the invasion of this carefully constructed world of words, not by the mechanical, performative, initiatory elements of the sexual act, but by its biological, relational maturation in conception—with all that that implies in terms of future ties to a social framework in which others exist—is death to her antiworld. What would suggest life and fulfillment in the outside social world to which the sisters are indifferent means death and engorgement in the world of "Natsu no owari."

In this world are the devouring sea, the mother's death, and isolation from relationship. Now, all these things, positive in her world, negative in ours, begin to assume their final connective form. The narrator had seen the end of summer as the consummation of death, and through the rhetoric of the ideological narrative had justified it as the ultimate, perfect, and inevitable end of the summer of the sisters' initiation.

And now, under the midsummer sunshine, love truly resembled death.

August moved toward its end; while squandering its store of sunlight, it relentlessly approached the death of our love like a brain draining of its blood. (pp. 237–238)

That is why, when the "love" that was supposed to have found its ultimate meaning in death seems to produce life, and that, dependent life, she becomes so angry and even momentarily rejects the uncontaminated half of her own consciousness—her sister—upon whose existence, in fact, the validation of the narrator's ideology depends.

K's death was to have both purged and completed the world of the end of summer and to have restored the sisters to the sole united possession of their realm. As the story nears its conclusion, everything seems to aim at the final moment of K's destruction. But in the purging of the world at the end of summer, her sister, too, is swallowed up by the sea. The murder of K had been their last act in unison, and the negation of the world ends in the death of the shared consciousness. The narrator has lost her only affirmation and her image of herself. Summer has indeed been swallowed up in death.

For a text that begins with a voracious image of female sexuality, devouring, powerful, and dominant, for a text that contains a tension between the ideology of the elite shared consciousness and an emotional configuration repressed and considerably distorted by that ideology into a series of sexual games and performances with no significance, the movement of the final action is profoundly repressive. Although appearing to be enjoying the "good life" to the fullest and to be greedy for the physical and sexual possession of another, the sisters had maintained their allegiance to their private realm. The advent of K presented increasing difficulty and the disruption of their careful, consciously controlled unity; they were forced to choose between the world of negation and, if not the world of affirmation, at least the "real" world of human relationship. By electing for the death of K, they choose the antiworld. But life in the antiworld is lived in the embrace of death, and there its ultimate consummation is in the rejection of life itself. Thus, when the sisters seek to destroy the alien, invading life and to protect the purity of their own world, which depends upon the reversal of the real world, they are forced into a negative pattern. The narrator and K, two living beings, had in sexual union apparently produced life: "A love on the verge of death gave birth to life." That pattern had to be negated in its reversal. Thus, when the moment comes for the destruction of K, the younger sister (not contaminated by the threat of pregnancy) joins him in giving birth to death.

Of course, with the sister's death, half of the antiworld is destroyed, and all the ideological basis of the story is undermined. The perfect union of the shared consciousness is gone, and the narrator can only hope to recreate that union in a world of words which can no longer be addressed to the other part of herself, the almost perfect replica (but probable rival), her partner in crime (but possible victim), her audience, her ideal reader. The narrator instead must seek the less perfect reader who necessarily lives in the world of relationships and who has been held off from the text by the presence within it of a closed and complete circle of communication in whose unity of body and mind the extratextual being cannot hope to fully share.

"Natsu no owari," then, represents a working out of Kurahashi's antiworld, but it already contains within its language the dynamic of destruction inherent in its rhetorical negation of the real. In destroying the "real" world, the story brings about its own destruction. It is perhaps unfair to Kurahashi's fully developed craft to have selected so early a work for extended study. The five "anti-tragedies" of 1968–1971, for example, handle the collision between myth and reality in a far more subtle way. In those works, Greek myths are retold in a contemporary Japanese setting, thus robbing them of their tragic dimension but maintaining the evocative power of the myths themselves. Nevertheless, "Natsu no owari" does provide in its language a clear working out of the metaphoric dilemma of modernist fiction in Japan: How does one create meaning in a fiction whose central vision is that the world is without meaning except through the creation of an antiworld? "Natsu no owari" does, I think, illustrate both the metaphor and its self-destructive dynamic.

Beyond that, the early stories are a direct challenge to many of the hallowed concepts of critics about fiction by Japanese women. In Kurahashi's work, the delicate emotional sensitivity and subjective tone frequently considered hallmarks of "women's literature" have been banished from the "world of words." Intellectuality, a quality normally reserved for male writers in Japan as elsewhere, is very consciously emphasized. On the level of content, also, underlying cultural assumptions about the nature of women and their role in society are denied; and the family, the central unit of social organization (projected on a grand scale in the "paternalism" of commercial and industrial corporations and in the *kokka* 'national family') becomes the object of attack in both rhetoric and content.

If, in her later fiction, Kurahashi does grow in technical skill and subtlety, it is, nevertheless, in her early works that her as yet unregenerate modernism, her denial of social taboos and conventions, and her assertive intellectuality are more clearly evident. The insistent philosophic questioning of meaning and a parody of the earnestness of human inquiry into "meaning" and "reality" find extended thematic treatment in the novel *The Adventures of Sumiyakist Q,* the only full-length work by Kurahashi to appear in English translation.[20] That work, like the earlier short fiction, creates an antiworld of abstraction which ultimately ends in destruction. The very radical nature of her denial of the world of facts and the self-consuming quality of the worlds of words she had created as its opposition may well account for her long years of silence. The novels that have appeared since her emergence from that silence, including *Shiro no naka no shiro* (The Castle within the Castle, 1979–1980), are less daring in their experimentalism and more realistic in subject matter and tone.

What does not change as the author changes and as the later works assume configurations of their own is the intent of the original project of the early fiction—its attitude of opposition to its social context, its aggressive defiance of Japanese mores and the radical (but entirely verbal) effort to create another world—one which does not depend upon the obedient adherence to one's proper role in society

---

[20] See n. 5.

and the acceptance of an intricate hierarchical relational network, but upon a total rejection of connection with that world and the assertion of the conscious will of the individual. If the modernists' project was doomed to fail, to pass away into more conventional forms, or to be repeated endlessly in the creation of more and more self-destructing antiworlds, it nonetheless is testimony to the feeling of many of today's leading writers that art must challenge a culture's image of itself, must represent a defiance of the ideology propagated in the interest of creating a harmonious overview of a well-ordered and peaceful industrial society where everyone works together, each in his or her own proper place. It is not so much a matter for the modernist of which image is right as it is of their sense of the necessity that these images confront one another. For that reason, when these writers construct their metaphors for the relationship between the individual consciousness and the social context, they use that of the antiworld, expressing its negation in as shocking as possible a language, imagery, and content. To that extent this world of words, doomed to end in self-destruction, is meant to explode on impact.

Since the images you demand
cling to me
I cannot form my own image.
I am forced to live
by your images,
I am always living like that,
so
I understand
revolution is really body aching.

Nishi Junko, "Revolution"

COMPARISONS

Between Osan and Koharu: The Representation of Women in the Works of Hayashi Fumiko and Enchi Fumiko

ALTHOUGH LITERATURE BY WOMEN in the past century, when looked at in its manifestation in specific works, shows, as we have seen, a wide range of linguistic modes and of attitudes toward the social and literary contexts from which it arises, some Japanese critics are influenced by the standards of the past as they attempt to characterize feminine writing (*joryū bungaku*). Thus, emotional sensitivity, delicacy of language, and a subjective point of view are still held to be particularly "feminine" qualities in a writer. This despite the fact that until the modernist movement such qualities might be termed characteristic of almost all twentieth-century writers in Japan, male or female. Characterizations of "feminine style" in this vein tend to ignore the operation of the specific social context in favor of an unchanging standard based simply upon what is seen as a biological/psychological constant. Such a basis of classification in fact works to reinforce the very social constraints that the literature was created to question and resist.

The whole area of feminine stylistics is, moreover, peculiarly loaded with culture-based stereotyping both in Japan and the West, but because of the influence of Heian women writers upon all of their successors, it may be a less viable concept in the Japanese context. Even in the West, however, as Rosalind Miles has amply illustrated in *The Fiction of Sex: Themes and Functions of Sex Difference in the Modern Novel*, it is risky to attempt to differentiate maculine and feminine writing on the basis of the language of specific texts. "Do men and women write differently from one another? Of course they do; but from one another as individuals rather than as sexes. All writers who can claim the title write differently, that is all."[1] Each of the three writers we have considered in Part Two may, in fact, be said to have more in common with other Japanese writers whose social, literary, and aesthetic values are in sympathy with her own than with members of a constant subgenre of "women writers." The texts themselves not only make but illustrate this point.

A natural challenge to this position would then be, "If women writers are not to be looked upon as a subgroup within the Japanese literary tradition, why consider them together at all?" Aside from the obvious fact that this grouping highlights the variety of their work, the situation of Japanese women writers has two fascinating aspects that make it of interest to Westerners; one is the past as a literary tradition, the other is the present reality of a changing social context. The first involves consideration of a literary history very different from our own, and we must ask ourselves, I think, what the effect of past success has been upon the modern Japanese woman writer and how it has served to differentiate her literary realm from that of Western women. The second seeks to distinguish the efforts of modern writers from the specific modes of expression and the social and moral dictates of an earlier age and to trace those aesthetic qualities that are outgrowths of historical shifts in the controlling ideology of Japanese society as a whole.

As important as the understanding of the particular social and historical context in which she writes may be, however, no consideration of the Japanese woman writer can be complete without an examination of the aspects of her work that distinguish it from that of her male contemporaries. The purpose of this chapter, is, therefore, to isolate the factors separating two women writers, Hayashi Fumiko and Enchi Fumiko, from the two men Kawabata Yasunari and Tanizaki Jun'ichirō, whose works will be examined in the following chapter. All four writers place a woman at the heart of their works. The differences between them lie in their representation of her rather than in any readily identifiable stylistic features. As in the West, male and female writers in Japan visualize the being of women very differently. In works by men, as we shall see, women tend to be depicted through images of Otherness, which are represented

---

[1] Rosalind Miles, *The Fiction of Sex: Themes and Functions of Sex Difference in the Modern Novel* (London: Vision Press, 1974), p. 33.

symbolically and signal a rupture of human time. Women created by women writers, however, are generally represented thematically as living with the normalized (both progressive and regressive) time of personal relationships and are shown as having only a human capacity either to suggest or to undergo the transcendence of experience.

To indicate the dimensions of the difference between the male and female perspectives, we have to approach the works of the writers from the standpoint of the way in which female being (and being female) is thematized. Inevitably, this involves examining a number of works by each writer, so that her or his characteristic pattern of representation can be identified. Because fewer full-length novels by Hayashi and Enchi than by Kawabata and Tanizaki have been translated into English,[2] a certain amount of plot detail from significant untranslated works must be included in the comparison. This is doubly important because, from a critical perspective there are marked differences in the ways women are portrayed; works by women thematize the experience of female protagonists within the context of plot-related events, actions, and relationships, whereas the aspect of aestheticization becomes a central focus in fiction by male writers, whose representation of women heavily emphasizes her signifying function as an object of "beauty." Concomitant with this in the works of the two men is a privileging of the position of women who embody the "feminine ideal," while other women, who fulfill less transcendent social functions, are ordinarily relegated to the sidelines in their work.

Before considering the work of each writer in detail, however, it would be well to develop an outline of the literary model in which the social roles of women in Japanese society have tended to be cast since the heyday of Edo letters. Both male and female writers recognize the cultural vitality of this model, for which we can find an archetype in the works of the great dramatist Chikamatsu Monzaemon (1653–1724), but they utilize the model in far different ways.

Obviously, no single pattern of representation and no single literary model can suit the complexities of any one of the writers in-

---

[2] Many of the major works by Tanizaki and Kawabata have been translated, but although a number of short stories by Hayashi and Enchi have been translated, only two full-length novels, Enchi's *The Waiting Years* (*Onnazaka*) and *Masks* (*Onna-men*) are currently available in English translation.

dividually. Nor is the aim of the comparison to reduce the writers collectively to one theme. Rather it is intended to examine ways in which the act of thematization itself represents a significant difference in perspective and in the process of symbolization. Equally obvious is that in seeking to define "feminine consciousness" in women and to compare it to the "consciousness of the feminine"[3] in men, we will be drawing near to the shoals of feminist, antifeminist, and afeminist criticism.

Even within the relatively familiar confines of our own tradition, the areas of feminine stylistics, feminine consciousness, and feminist poetics are difficult to delineate and define, and all these areas are heavily culture-determined.[4] We may, however, find in works like Patricia Meyer Spacks' *The Female Imagination* an isolation of a specifically "feminine" content that sets works by male and female writers in definite contrast and one that has considerable applications to the Japanese context. Spacks makes it her aim "to look for evidence of sharing, seek persistent ways of feeling, discover patterns of self-depiction that survive the vagaries of change."[5] In the discussion that follows, we, too, will restrict ourselves to such areas as we examine works by Enchi and Hayashi whose female protagonists seek to define themselves as women within the Japanese framework. Both Enchi and Hayashi repeatedly create "patterns of self-depiction" in their protagonists by placing them again and again in

---

[3] The term "feminine consciousness" is defined and utilized in Sidney Janet Kaplan's *Feminine Consciousness in the Modern British Novel* (Urbana: University of Illinois Press, 1975) with reference particularly to the stream-of-consciousness mode in modernist fiction. Japanese women writers cannot of course be readily confined to one mode, but I mean here what Kaplan does on the broader level, the way in which women writers represent a female protagonist's view of her experience as a woman.

[4] Miles, in fact, in *The Fiction of Sex*, states that "sexual definition is the obligation and pastime of all cultures...sex definition is both a cultural and a personal activity. These are not necessarily distinct—what is called a well-integrated personality is perhaps one in which exterior and interior definitions correspond" (pp. 11, 12). The writer, however, is found at work in the space that opens up between the cultural and the personal and perhaps by definition is not well integrated. Miles also points out the heavily stylized nature of sex distinctions in art and literature, wherein male and female are frequently used "as symbols of opposed or complementary qualities" (p. 24).

[5] Patricia Meyer Spacks, *The Female Imagination* (New York: Arthur Knopf, 1975), p. 3.

similar situations in which they must explore the physical, economic, social, and, yes, emotional conditions of a woman's life in detail. Neither writer can be termed either representative of or acquiescent to prevailing cultural stereotypes of the woman, and each in her own way creates images of consciousness that are at the same time recognizably feminine in most cultures and specifically Japanese in their implementation.

It might be well, therefore, to remember that, just as the Heian classics were the work of women who were aristocratic as well as "feminine," so the writing of women in the present day arises from its own context, and that context, from the Meiji period onward, has been in a continued state of flux. No longer are all women writers members of a small, privileged, homogeneous class. Instead, among the most prominent women writers of the past century a significant number are partially, even largely, self-educated and allied by birth and by sympathy with what might be termed the lower classes of society. Of the two writers we will be considering in this chapter, Hayashi, like Ichiyō and Sata, can certainly be so described. The intent of the preceding studies has been to examine closely the ties between various chronologically progressing social and literary contexts and specific short works produced within them; and, in the works considered, the interests and conditions of various classes have been portrayed. An intimate correspondence between text and context was, after all, a precondition of the reemergence of the woman writer as a literary force; the recognition of that correspondence is likewise a precondition for understanding the real role(s) she has played in modern Japanese literature. Now, freed from aesthetic and linguistic conformance to a standard inherited from the classical age, the woman writer can once again find her own style and literary perspective and convey her own conception of the social world to which she has returned as an observing, verbally responsive member. She is free, in other words, to write, and to write as writers will, about the limits to the freedom of being. Very naturally the writers already examined (Ichiyō, Sata, Kurahashi) have chosen differently on the levels of language, ideology, and narrative strategy. But they are all women, and although women have once more gained a degree of aesthetic autonomy, they remain aware in common of particular and powerful social, economic, and cultural restraints.

Principal among those restraints is, of course, a single institu-
tion that has, since Tokugawa times, played a dominant part in
determining the cultural limits of the woman's role in Japanese society.[6] A nation that has historically come to describe itself in terms
of the *kokka* (national family) obviously is investing the concept of
"family" with the strongest possible significance, making of it a single image encompassing all social groupings. Each family unit then
becomes a would-be microcosm of an idealized national harmony,
and, in accordance with Neo-Confucian orthodoxy, is thereupon subject to a model of authority with mythopoeic dimensions.[7] Between
the individual and society itself (the classic battleground of much of
Western fiction in recent centuries), between the "me" and the mass,
a powerful mediating configuration comes into being, and is visible
as such, in much of Japanese literature—but most especially in literature by women.

For all of the differences already indicated, the three writers
whose works have been examined in preceding chapters recognize in
the family that central structure of authority that has essentially
encoded their lives and the lives of others "as women." A concern
with the nature of familial relationships may consequently be pointed
to as a near constant element in their works, even as the differing
tone of the individual stories—resignation, reflection, or
defiance—indicates that the family can be viewed as the determinant
of an individual character's way of life, as an economic unit, as the
only sphere of a woman's proper activity and the source of her iden-

[6] The importance of the point is central to discussion in Takamure Itsue's two-
volume *Josei no rekishi* [A History of Women], (Tokyo: Kōdansha, 1963); see especially
vol. 1, chap. 3, pp. 373–421. See also Inoue Kiyoshi, *Nihon joseishi* [Japanese
Women's History], (Tokyo: San'ichi Shiseidō, 1967), pp. 50–143; and Murakami
Nobuhiko, *Meiji joseishi* [A History of Women in the Meiji Era], (Tokyo: Kōdansha,
1978), vol. 1.

[7] Maruyama Masao refers to the basis for this dynamic in Confucian thought in
Studies in the Intellectual History of Tokugawa Japan (Tokyo: University of Tokyo and
Princeton University Press, 1974), pp. 193–194 and in the ensuing discussion in his
chapters on Chu Hsi philosophy and the Sorai School revolution, pp. 195–222.
Although the emperor became the focus of authority replacing the shogun in National
Learning (*kokugaku*), extensions of the model in the Meiji, Taishō, and early Shōwa
periods retain much of the connection between the national ideal and the individual
family unit, a connection that remained explicit as long as the *ie* itself retained the legal and social force of the old Tokugawa model.

tity, or very simply as the enemy of the individual. In Ichiyō's "Takekurabe," for example, it is the family that determines what Shōta, Nobu, and Midori will become; they have no option to make choices other than those that might be considered inherited. In "Kyarameru kōjō kara," Hiroko's life is controlled both by her family's poverty and by her father's authority over her. While the women of "Yuki no mau yado" are by no means in the same position as the naïve child exploited by both her father and her employer, they are nevertheless so constrained by social mores concerning the woman's proper place in society that their identities are clearly tied to their success as wives. Kurahashi's depiction of the family does form a definite contrast to that of the others, for her fiction frequently portrays the family as violent (there is matricide in "Sasori" and the killing of children by their mother in "Shiroi kami no dojo") or it encourages the breaking of societal taboos against incest. "Natsu no owari" is less aggressive in its attack against the family than many of her other works, but the indifference of the sisters to their mother's death and their dismissal of their father's wrath indicate that family feeling is one of the societal ideals they have rejected. Whether the authority over the individual that the family wields, then, is yielded to or opposed on the level of wish, will, or outright action within the texts themselves, it is obvious that for the authors some common sense of cultural closure is completed within its configuration.

This is a consciousness more clearly focused upon in works by Hayashi and Enchi. Whereas Ichiyō might accurately be labeled a "neoclassical" writer, Sata a "proletarian" writer, and Kurahashi a "modernist," writers such as Enchi and Hayashi would most probably be identified initially as "women writers," an identification arising largely from their chosen themes and patterns of representation. Predictably, in their works, the family, with its significance in the Japanese tradition, serves as a central symbol, but the two writers illuminate the limitations of socially institutionalized women's roles from contrasting perspectives. Convention both excludes and confines, and its inflexibility is generally presented by Hayashi from the standpoint of protagonists who are outside its boundaries. Enchi's protagonists are generally confined within them.

This is not to say that Enchi is conventional and Hayashi unconventional. No such distinction can be made between them on the basis of their writings. Rather, in their direct representation of women either excluded from (Hayashi) or entrapped within (Enchi) traditional conventions of feminine behavior, they have tended to project recognizable patterns of both the respectable (good) and the fallen (bad) woman. As in the Heian period, but to a much different effect, social class plays a role in determining the content of their works. The strictures of respectability limit the behavior of the middle-class women who appear in Enchi's fiction, whereas many of Hayashi's female protagonists, struggling with poverty and uncertainty on the fringes of society, regard the protection provided by accepted and codified roles as beyond their attainment.

I place the terms "good" and "bad" in parentheses advisedly because, in spite of the Western literary convention of the prostitute with the heart of gold, the moral judgments implied in such terms, even when employed parenthetically, are rooted in a Judeo-Christian and not a Japanese ethic. The roots of an only roughly equivalent convention in Japan can be traced to a model first articulated in the Edo period. This new model designed for women in drama and fiction had a strong origin in class distinctions that were also being reformulated at this time and portrayed women whose classes of origin had not been represented in earlier fiction. While the role of the respectable woman within the *ie* was becoming increasingly codified and theoretically applied to women of almost all socioeconomic backgrounds, the existence of another feminine role, that of the geisha, began to grow in cultural significance. Flourishing pleasure quarters like the Yoshiwara provided the arts with a new and alluring subject matter. But, as we have seen, the licensed quarters absorbed many of the daughters of the poor, women from the same class that would later supply them as labor for the mills and factories of a rapidly industrializing nation.[8] In Edo literature, however, these daughters of the poor were to play one role in a new polarization of the male ideal of the feminine, which posed them, romanticized as lovers and glamorous courtesans, against an increasingly merchant-class stan-

---

[8] See Mikiso Hane's description of both contexts in *Peasants, Rebels and Outcasts: The Underside of Modern Japan* (New York: Pantheon Books, 1982), pp. 173–225.

dard of female respectability.

In line with the separation of feminine roles into those relating to the all-important *ie* (wife, mother, daughter) and those that the pleasure quarters served to exemplify and glorify (geisha, famous beauty, lover), literary formulas developed that juxtaposed the two for maximum effect. Both roles were apparently deemed necessary, for legal codes developed to control the spheres of each,[9] but in no simple sense were they seen as the good and the bad. Saikaku's fast-paced tales might warn of the dangers inherent in the licensed quarters, but the puppet plays of Chikamatsu articulated an ethic in which the demands of each sphere had their place. Especially in his domestic tragedies, we find the archetypal representation of a new conflict in the ideals of the feminine. *Shinjū ten no Amijima* (The Love Suicides at Amijima), for example, embodies the conflict in the characterization of Osan and Koharu.

Neither woman is "good" or "bad" at the expense of the other, since both are acting out the dictates of society within the format of the conflict between *giri* (social responsibility) and *ninjō* (human passion). Clearly Osan, the respectable and dutiful wife, who comes from a solid merchant family, is committed to submission to *giri* by virtue of her class and her role in life, just as Koharu, the geisha (who uses what money she can manage to save to support an impoverished mother), is assigned the area of *ninjō*. In light of what would seem an unbridgeable gulf in their backgrounds, however, the relationship that develops between the two women is especially intriguing to the Western reader. Its nature is clearly revealed in the pivotal scene of Osan's confession. After her husband, Jihei, had become entangled in a love affair with Koharu, Osan had secretly written to the geisha, begging her to sever the relationship. Koharu agrees to do so for the sake of both Osan and Jihei, but she conceals her decision from Jihei behind a mask of indifference. Jihei, believ-

---

[9] The married woman's role is defined by her position in the *ie*, and the geisha's by government regulations of another kind. The "pleasure" quarters were licensed quarters and their regulation a matter of national policy. Discussed in Murakami's *Meiji joseishi*, vol. 4, pp. 8–166, and Takamure's *Josei no rekishi*, vol. 2, pp. 30–43. Joseph De Becker's *The Nightless City or the History of the Yoshiwara Yūwaku* (Yokohama: M. Nössler, 1905) gives an account of the pleasure quarters that is nearly contemporaneous with Ichiyō's portrayal of it in "Takekurabe."

ing in Koharu's apparent duplicity, sarcastically comments to his wife that he has heard a rumor that Koharu is to be redeemed from service by his former arch rival. Since Koharu had once vowed that she would kill herself rather than be redeemed by that man, Jihei sees the rumor as another example of Koharu's two-facedness. Osan, realizing that Koharu indeed meant the vow she had made, blurts out the whole truth.

> "I was determined never to tell you so long as I lived, but I'm afraid of the crime I'd be committing if I concealed the facts and let her die with my knowledge. I will reveal my great secret. There is not a grain of deceit in Koharu. It was I who schemed to end the relations between you. I could see signs that you were drifting toward suicide. I felt so unhappy that I wrote a letter, begging her as one woman to another to break with you, though I knew how painful it would be. I asked her to save your life. The letter must have moved her. She answered that she would give you up, though you were more precious than life itself, because she could not shirk her duty to me. I've kept her letter with me ever since—it's been like a protective charm.... Alas! I'd be failing the obligations I owe her as another woman if I allowed her to die. Please go to her at once. Don't let her kill herself."[10]

Both women appear to recognize and respect the necessities of the other's situation, and each is aware of a responsibility to the other. There is a kind of mutual recognition, of feminine complicity—a feminine consciousness—hinted at here.

Remembering that when Chikamatsu wrote, masculine depictions of the role of women in society were virtually unchallenged by works by women, we are struck by two aspects of his representation. They even seem to be contradictory. The first is a surprising (to us) recognition of what might today be termed a "sisterhood" among women, transcending the limits of role models and asserting a commonality and a mutuality in women's experience. The second is the necessity of both roles from the male perspective; there is a split between the duties of the respectable wife and the passion of the beloved. As we shall see, Chikamatsu's remarkably even-handed treatment of both roles is exceptional. But in the following chapter we will be discussing the ramifications of the division of roles itself

---

[10] Donald Keene, *Four Plays by Chikamatsu* (New York: Columbia University Press, 1981), pp. 191–192.

as it still survives in the writing of men about women, using works by Kawabata and Tanizaki as a basis for discussion.

We should not be too surprised, however, that women writing about women in the modern age tend to develop experience only on one side or the other of what might be termed this "great divide" of convention. In a society that provides women only the alternatives of being inside or outside the fixed boundaries of the culturally endorsed family unit, women writers, although rejecting the separation that objectification makes possible, must approximate one established role in their representations in order to preserve fidelity to social experience and to imitate a real-life imperative. While such representations may well be similar to that of one figure in the Koharu-Osan model, they will never be identical to either, essentially because the marked contrast between the two seems to be a necessity of the masculine perspective and because practical experience (living) takes place between the poles established by ideality or abstraction. This will become clearer as we discuss aestheticization and its relationship to the split categorization of the female in Tanizaki and Kawabata. What we are concerned with at present, because we are exploring the differences between male and female representations of the feminine, is a division of another kind—not the frequent split and paired objectification of the feminine by male writers, but the separation between that process and the process through which a feminine consciousness is developed in writing by women—a consciousness that must recognize the division of roles the culture demands but can experience only one of those roles, and that only partially, as lived. Except in its most specific dimensions, such a separation is, of course, not unique to Japanese literature. In the West, too, as Louise Bernikow observes in *Among Women*, a woman writing about a woman, "a woman looking at another woman sees differently from a man. Sometimes. Often we wear their lenses. On the whole, we do not see mythologically. We do not see Eve, the mother of evil and seduction. We see less Sacred and Profane Love, Madonna and Whore, Good Girl and Bad. Fewer red, red roses. Less 'loveliness.'"[11]

---

[11] Louise Bernikow, *Among Women* (New York: Harper Colophon, 1981), p. 184.

The Japanese reader, the Japanese writer, male or female, would be uncomfortable with the moral judgments conveyed in the above language but would instinctively understand the function of the role separation they enforce. Bernikow makes it plain that the Western reader and writer, when a woman, is sometimes equally uncomfortable with such judgments. At any rate, the male-oriented societal structure of Japan, and its male-originated literature, function along the lines of a similar division, albeit without its moral overtones. The descendants of Osan and Koharu have found their way into works by male writers ever since Chikamatsu. Works like Kawabata's *Yama no oto* (Sound of the Mountain) and *Yukiguni* (Snow Country) and Tanizaki's *Tade kūu mushi* (Some Prefer Nettles) and *Kagi* (The Key) can be seen partially in this light. But a significant difference exists between what happens in these works and the frequency and importance of such split and paired renderings in fiction by women. There, we see it less, it means less, and even when it does occur, as in Enchi's *Onnazaka* (The Waiting Years) and Hayashi's *Ukigumo,* its lines are blurred by the recognition of a common—feminine—consciousness.

Born as was Sata in the first decade of the twentieth century, Hayashi (1903–1951) and Enchi (b. 1905) passed through much of the same national and historical experience. Although both published before the war, and Hayashi in particular achieved spectacular success with her autobiographical *Hōrōki,* they wrote their most important fiction in the postwar period. In fact, Japan's experience of defeat was to broaden the application of Hayashi's conception of the outsider's position in society, and Enchi's physical and psychological burdens in the postwar years enabled her to increase the depth and scope of her exploration of the female experience. To this day, however, the common distinction made between them on the basis of the appeal of their works to the reading public—Hayashi as a popular writer, Enchi as *belle-lettriste*—reflects significant differences in their personal backgrounds and literary concerns. Neither represents the Heian "aristocratic" ideal, but they do represent significantly different societal strata in many of their works.

The initial success of *Hōrōki,* which detailed Hayashi's life as a child and young woman, was hard-earned. After years of wandering with her mother and stepfather, who were itinerant peddlers,

Hayashi struck out on her own. For a long time she lived in poverty as she attempted to make a living for herself in Tokyo, working in a hospital, in a celluloid factory, and as a maid, a waitress, and a street vendor. Throughout this period, Hayashi had a series of relationships with various men interspersed with unsuccessful marriages. All this is detailed in *Hōrōki*, and some of the themes in that long autobiographical account were to become recurrent patterns in her later fiction. Financial insecurity and a persistent rootlessness are, understandably, among them. So, too, is the vulnerability to men, which Hirabayashi Taiko sees as part of Hayashi's inheritance from her mother.[12]

In "Inazuma," for example, Hayashi portrays the inheritance of a socially unacceptable sexuality, as she considers the circumstances and characters of the four illegitimate children of one woman by a series of men, focusing particularly upon the three daughters. In spite of the fact that each of them plays a respectable female role in the opening pages—one is married, one newly widowed, and the third, a suitably virginal schoolgirl—the sisters' sexual nature flares into conflict as all three form a relationship with the same man in a curious reversal of their mother's odyssey from one man to the next.

The two works indicate much of the appeal of Hayashi's relatively popular prewar stories; they outline situations that the bulk of her readership would consider extreme (and therefore interesting) and deal sympathetically with protagonists whose poverty or unsettled way of life or both puts them outside the limits of ordinary family structures. True, *Hōrōki* and "Inazuma" contain a strong element of the sensational, the "true confessional" mode, and Hayashi might well have continued to be seen as a merely popular writer were it not for the events that took place in the last decade of her life. Because the war put a period to the publication of almost all fiction, and because Hayashi was to live only until 1951, her postwar production is truly remarkable both in quantity and quality. In fact, Hayashi (somewhat like Ichiyō) could almost be said to have written herself to death, for she collapsed and died under the pressures of overwork

---

[12] Hirabayashi Taiko, *Hayashi Fumiko* (Tokyo: Shinchōsha, 1969). Hirabayshi uses the term "outsider" to identify both Hayashi and her protagonists. Her discussion of Hayashi's relationship with her mother is extended.

and a weak heart while writing the novel *Meshi* The stories she completed in the brief period from 1946 to 1951 include some of her
finest fiction, among which we might include "Fubiki" (1946),
Uzushio (1949), and *Cha-iro no me* (1951), as well as the better known
"Shitamachi" (Tokyo, 1948), "Bangiku" (Late Chrysanthemum,
1948), and *Ukigumo* (1952).

The perspective that Hayashi had already developed in her earlier works seemed to gain scope in a postwar world where all of
Japanese society found itself wrenched out of the traditional security
and order of prewar experience, a situation that made the poverty
and uncertainty that had been largely the heritage of the peasant,
working, and urban fringe classes a more nearly universal experience.
In describing the women writers of the postwar period, Okubo Norio
singles out both Hayashi and Miyamoto Yuriko,[13] making the distinction between them, however, that a period that represented personal joy and triumph for Miyamoto was one in which Hayashi
could speak to the deepest feelings of the reading public. Whereas
Miyamoto was able to look forward to a reunion with a husband
who had been imprisoned for his leftist politics before and during the
war years, and her literature in the postwar period has some sense of
personal liberation (*kaiho*), much of Hayashi's postwar fiction centers
directly upon the experience of defeat (*haisen*) as it registered both
nationally and personally.

In fact, a single dynamic runs throughout much of Hayashi's
postwar fiction, setting it apart from that of the prewar period and
bringing the experiences of her protagonists into greater conformity
with those of the general public. In a recurring pattern, a lone woman during the war years or the immediate postwar period is separated
from her husband because he is missing ("Tokyo"), believed to be
dead ("Fubiki"), or indeed dead (*Uzushio*). A principal reason for
her tenacity throughout her struggles lies in the fact that she has a
child or children whom she must support, and she finds some emotional solace in another man whom she encounters in the course of
her struggles. Among the important works of Hayashi's later years,
"Late Chrysanthemum" and *Ukigumo* stand outside the pattern, but

[13] Okubo Norio, "Sengo bungakushi no naka no joryū bungaku," *Kaishaku to kanshō* 37 (March 1972): 47–52.

Cha-iro no me contains it as a single element in its plot dynamic.

The pattern itself is a significant one, for it enables Hayashi to transform the marginal protagonists of her earlier works through alterations that bring home those fears and uncertainties of the postwar period shared by almost all Japanese—but especially Japanese women. The homeless wanderers of the earlier stories are mirrored in the uprooting that the war had made general, the poverty of the marginal few is extended to near universality as a result of the war's devastation and duration, and the security of marital relationships is disrupted by wartime separation and destroyed by death.

Kane of "Fubiki" fits the pattern well. Her household includes four children and their grandmother, and because she has received notification of her husband's death, she is in desperate circumstances. Food is becoming scarce in her mountain village and the winter is harsh. Only with the help of Katsu, a kindly neighbor, does she manage to get by. Although she loved her husband, she is attracted to the sympathetic Katsu. Given the family's desperate condition, Kane's turn to another man does not arouse much comment or condemnation in her village until word reaches them that her husband is alive and in a hospital in Utsunomiya. The would-be lovers go to visit him, and the three agree that for the sake of appearances Katsu must leave the village for Tokyo before her husband's return. Kane's grief and suffering and the reawakening of love and hope ends in confusion, not tragedy, and a semblance of the prewar forms will be resumed.

For a while, however, all the bases upon which Kane's life had been established are shaken. Distinctions that had clarified a woman's position break down. Wives and mothers are suddenly marginal, becoming the abandoned and the needy. Even officialdom, now staggering under the responsibility for the military debacle and domestic collapse, only creates confusion: the original death notice brought about the crisis in the first place, but Kane never receives official notice that her husband is alive. The existence of children makes her survival of more than personal significance, adds to the poignancy of her plight, and amounts to an unbearable pressure for her to reestablish some kind of security in her life, but Kane shares with earlier protagonists an emotional and physical need for a man. That need remains unchanged, but the supporting environment has become so altered as to make the woman on the margins of existence the very emblem of the national experience.

The best known in the West of Hayashi's stories is "Tokyo." Riyo, its protagonist, has not heard from her husband, who is a prisoner in Siberia, for six years, and is barely making a living for herself and her son in Tokyo, to which she has just come. While selling tea from house to house, she meets a man, Tsuruishi, with whom she strikes up a friendship. He is kind to her son and cares about her and the difficult life she is leading; a day's excursion ends with their lovemaking at an inn. Two days later he is killed in an accident, but although Riyo grieves at his death, even this brief interval has given her the courage to go on. *Uzushio*, a novel exploring the same theme, follows its widowed protagonist, Chiyoko, through many trials. More educated than most of the women in these stories, she finds that her husband's death and the national defeat have brought about a radical change in her social and economic status. Forced to place her young son in a boarding school in Ninomiya while she takes work as a waitress to support them both, she is sexually harassed by her employer. She is attracted to another man, Sugimoto, who has long admired her, but his family objects to the fact that she is a widow with a child. Having finally determined to marry Chiyoko, regardless of his parents' wishes, Sugimoto tells her,

> "It's a fatalistic way of putting it, but you and I were destined for this. I don't want to go on living among people on the basis of hard common sense. Was I born only to make the family happy? I went to war thinking it was for my family and my country. Now that it's over, all that's left is reality. It's my own damned fault. So much for schemes and common sense. Love is the one place where you ought to trust your instincts.... So then, what do you say? Shouldn't we be together?"[14]

Here the male rather than the female character voices the credo to which almost all of Hayashi's female characters would also subscribe.

Yukiko of *Ukigumo*, the best known in Japan of the postwar protagonists, is clearly of Sugimoto's persuasion that "Love is the one place where you ought to trust your instincts." She is outside the

---

[14] *Hayashi Fumiko zenshū* [Complete Works of Hayashi Fumiko], vol. 6 (Tokyo: Bunsendō, 1976), p. 377.

pattern we have outlined; she has neither a dead or missing husband nor a dependent child. Yukiko does get pregnant by her lover, Tomioka, but she has an abortion. She has more resemblance to a Koharu than to a lost and abandoned Osan. Her lover is married, and although Yukiko and he dreamed, when they had been working for the Forestry Service in French Indochina, of returning there after the war, Tomioka's wife is ailing, and he decides to stay with her. Yukiko must get along by herself, and she does. She enters into a brief relationship with an American soldier but still sees Tomioka from time to time. On a trip that they take together they even discuss the possibility of a "love suicide" (though it seems more like defeat malaise). The trip does not lead to suicide, but it does involve Tomioka in an affair that will end in a murder. At the hot springs he is attracted to the wife of a bar owner who follows him to Tokyo, but the bar owner eventually catches up with her and kills her. Only after his own wife dies, too, does Yukiko have any chance of capturing Tomioka's attention. Stealing a large sum of money from her employer, Iba, she tries to persuade Tomioka to marry her. Eventually, she manages to wear him down to the point where she is allowed to accompany him on a new job he has managed to obtain from the Forest Service, but she dies soon, apparently of tuberculosis, after their arrival at Yakushima.

The reader is struck by the unexpectedness of Yukiko's death and cannot help wondering why a character notable for resilience so suddenly gives way to an interior weakness. Given her apparent amorality and transient existence, Yukiko is the outsider par excellence in the postwar books, and it is her will to survive and to possess love that supplies much of the vitality of the undoubtedly melodramatic *Ukigumo*. For all of its soap-operatic story line, however, the work does succeed on several levels other than the merely popular and sensational. The flashbacks to Indochina supply what seem to be authentic glimpses of an exotic setting (a travelogue from the victors' point of view), and these, in turn, make the environment of Tokyo stand out all the more starkly. The dream world is gone and "all that's left is reality." The black-market schemes, the wheeling and dealing, the frustration of defeat, the sounds and smells of poverty and occasional luxury are almost tangible.

Yukiko, too, with all her inconsistencies, is vividly realized, and, in spite of the various nefarious activities in which she engages, there is an almost charming incongruity between her financial calculation and her emotional extravagance. The American is summed up for what he is worth, but she recognizes that his loneliness matches her own. On Iba she wastes no compassion at all. He is a relative as well as her employer and had sexually exploited her when she was a young girl living in his home. The emotional investment in Tomioka, however, is staggering. He is not worth it, and she knows it, but that is entirely beside the point. As the object of her desire, he becomes the focus of her indomitable will to live and to love. Perhaps, once he can no longer get away, she has nothing to live for. Yukiko was apparently made to triumph over defeat; she cannot survive victory.

She embodies many of the other Hayashi outsiders in her desire for love and her courage. These outsiders are negatively empowered by inheritance or by history to respond to the situations, the opportunities and defeats, and the emotions that fall outside the norm. Born outside of comfortable normality, or abandoned there when normality itself disintegrated, Hayashi's outsiders must make new choices, must recognize needs usually masked by convention. Kane ("Fubiki") realizes that the desperate circumstances in which she and her family find themselves must take precedence over the reticent luxury of prolonged mourning. Chiyoko (*Uzushio*), physically without a man, acknowledges that, although she can envision surviving as a celibate woman like her former teacher, Tanimura, she would find such a life empty.

Kin, of "Late Chrysanthemum," just as emphatically opts for the single (if not celibate) life. A former geisha, she has used her past relationships with men to accumulate property and security for a fast approaching old age and views the preservation of her beauty in calculated, almost technological, terms. She enjoys the admiration of the lovers who have become increasingly rare as she reaches her mid-fifties, but, although she considers "a life bereft of men too dreadful to bear thinking of," she dismisses the thought (and the duties) of marriage.

> Kin had never been in the habit of giving her men a meal. She had not the slightest wish to be the kind of woman who prepared meals carefully and laid them proudly before a man in hope of winning his heart

with her cooking. Domesticity had no appeal for her. What need had she, who had not the faintest intention of getting married, to put on a show of domesticity for men?[15]

Clearly, Kin does not accept the conventions of womanly behavior. Having secured financial independence, she has no wish to accept dependence as long as she will not be "bereft of men." But Hayashi is characteristically using the protagonist's circumstances, once again not those that could be considered average or normal, to focus on discussion of the actual physical and emotional needs of women as she sees them.

Hayashi is most concerned with depicting her characters when and as long as they remain outside the boundaries of convention. Clearly, then, when she thematizes the woman's experience, Hayashi is not generally inclined to pose one woman against another in alternative roles. Rather, she explores the context of a given woman's life in terms of needs that she sees as present in all women. From Chiyoko to Kin, her protagonists are seeking to combine their desires for security and love. As we shall see in the special case of *Cha-iro no me*, she is perfectly capable of portrayals of the "respectable lady," but her compassion lies elsewhere—with the rootless, the unprotected, the physically, financially, or emotionally needy, who must act outside the limits of what is "proper" in order to hold on to life.

In a literature that has a marked abundance of passive and reflective main characters, Hayashi's women have passion and energy. They go on living as best they can, taking life as it comes, but wanting more. They have fully articulated (but not consistent) personalities. Consistency, after all, is the outward sign of the already formulated symbol—the stereotype.

Hayashi's protagonists are perceived more directly, if not more distinctly, than those of most Japanese male writers. Since the highly formalized dimensions of gender definition help to make accessible to all writers certain conceptual sets that are generally endorsed as "masculine" and "feminine," such sets can become the stock in trade for any writer who wants to utilize them. Thus, Kawabata and Tan-

---

[15] Hayashi Fumiko, "Late Chrysanthemum," trans. John Bester, in Ivan Morris et al., eds., *Modern Japanese Short Stories* (Tokyo: Japan Publications Inc., 1960), pp. 190, 191.

izaki can make use of convincing feminine personae in such stories as "Hokuro no tegami" (The Mole) and *Sasameyuki* (The Makiokoa Sisters). These fictions work, just as does fiction by the women considered in this volume when they project the consciousness of a male protagonist; nevertheless, when the representation of the female is central to a work it is thematized differently by men and women.

When the consciousness of the feminine is filtered through a woman's perspective, the sharpness and certainty of objectification are yielded up to the more intricate balancing of identification. The reader, reading a text that depicts a woman's perspective as a woman projects it—and perhaps most especially if the reader, too, is a woman—is beyond the reification of Otherness and behind the eyes of the Same. Experienced as it were from within, Hayashi's women are not aesthetically pleasing. They are not aesthetically imaged; they are not images (except through the eyes of men or in the totally cold blood of "Late Chrysanthemum"). They fall between "wife" and "mistress," Osan and Koharu, sometimes closer to one pole than the other, but always in some way outside the safety of tradition and the dichotomizing eye which sees Otherness as objectified.

And yet, in one of her last works, Hayashi does employ something very like the Koharu-Osan model. That work is the almost completely atypical *Cha-iro no me* (1950). Although the author points out its tripartite point of view, the work's central consciousness seems to be that of its male protagonist, an aging office worker named Nakagawa Juichi, driven by the nagging management of his wife, Mineko, to dream of divorce and a relationship with an attractive fellow worker, Mrs. Sagara (a widow with a dependent child). What is especially intriguing about *Cha-iro no me* is that in adopting a male persona as the central consciousness of the work, Hayashi automatically seizes upon the split and paired dynamic of masculine representation of the female. We have the situation of a woman looking at women the way a man does. It may be true that "often we wear their lenses," but in this work, at least, Hayashi sometimes wears those lenses as a man. The result is fascinating. Hayashi herself declares in her author's afterword to a reissue of the work that the novel represents a complete departure for her, a new "detached" style. Although she tells us that she has been accused of cynicism in its creation, the term irony would be more apt. The tone seems present in the afterword itself.

> My eyes are brown. The title at a glance takes its hint from my brown eyes. The protagonists of *Cha-iro no me* [Brown eyes] are all people whose existence is my own. I, the author, am like Mineko, the wife, like Mrs. Sagara, and even like Juichi himself. It wouldn't be exaggerating to say that I wanted to depict a certain "air pocket" for people going through middle age by fragmenting it into three aspects.[16]

And, if she confesses having depicted Mrs. Sagara with a certain compassion because she "couldn't dissect Sagara with the condemnatory eye of a Mineko,"[17] we would not be apt to accuse her of such compassion in her handling of that respectable wife (*okusan*), whose obsessive righteousness becomes the target of deft satire.

Sex and money, duty and love, impulse and responsibility, all themes present in the treatment of the female since *The Love Suicides at Amijima*, are in this novel parceled out in more discrete packages than is usual in Hayashi. She normally homogenizes all these themes in her depictions of a woman's experience from the point of view of a purely "feminine consciousness." Certainly Juichi's male perspective tends to curdle when his wife, Mineko, is its focus. He remonstrates with her when she condemns a young woman boarding with them, who, although she is from a "good" family, finds herself reduced to the status of a bar hostess. Mineko sees a "fallen" woman, where he sees someone struggling to survive in a postwar world where traditional supports for women have collapsed. He can also understand that his wife's acrimony and righteousness are part of what she cannot admit to be her own tenuous status. As he first considers the possibility of divorce, he realizes that his wife, a middle-aged *okusan*, has no real way of making her way in the outside world. She has lost any market value she may once have had as a beautiful woman, and by tradition and training has no aptitude that would allow her an independent life. When Kaname in Tanizaki's *Some Prefer Nettles* examines the similar situation of his own wife, he can at least salve his conscience by consigning her to a

---

[16] *Hayashi Fumiko zenshū*, vol. 16, p. 279.

[17] Ibid., p. 280. Mineko is the character who actually has the brown eyes of the title.

new lover. Mineko has no such option. In her terms, she is a "good wife" and would scorn the thought. Desperate for control, she ultimately is able to break up the budding relationship between her husband and Mrs. Sagara by confronting her "rival." This Osan does not plead, she virtually commands, and this Koharu, who, after all, has the credentials of respectability herself, retreats, leaving a farewell note for Juichi.

In winning her battle, Mineko may very well have lost the man. This is not Edo Japan, so there is no love suicide, but something of the Osan-Koharu formulation persists in Juichi's perspective. His O(ku)san, however, has become a bit of a harridan. In Hayashi's fiction, those who have the protection of tradition and convention and use it against the marginal open themselves to satiric treatment; but behind Mineko's strategems and deviousness, denunciations and control, lies a force of personality, a determination, not unlike Yukiko's. Here, at last, is Hayashi's full-length portrait of the other side of convention—the place of the Insider, threatened and defending her ground (the *ie*, both house and family, though Mineko, significantly, has no children) with tooth and claw.

The comfort and normality and the "protection" of traditional roles look different from the inside. And that is the perspective that Enchi Fumiko tends to adopt in a great deal of her postwar fiction. She is as natural a channel for this viewpoint as Hayashi is for that of the outsider. The daughter of an important scholar of the Japanese language, Ueda Kazutoshi,[18] she was well versed in the Japanese classics and in Edo literature from her childhood, and her continued adherence to these literary traditions (which finds expression in *Onna-men*, translated as *Masks* by Juliet Winters Carpenter) went hand in hand with an interest in more modern trends in Japanese literature and society. Her earliest successes were in Japan's prewar modern drama, and her political sympathies were markedly left-wing. Following her marriage in 1930, she gradually began to shift her efforts to the writing of fiction, principally short stories, but it was not until well after the war that she was to gain acclaim as a novelist.

---

[18] Also read as Ueda Mannen.

After years of struggling to achieve success with her fiction and in the wake of two serious operations, she began to receive recognition for her short stories and novels. In 1952 she won the Women Writers Prize for "Himojii tsukihi"), in 1957 the Noma prize for *Onnazaka* (The Waiting Years), and in 1970 the Tanizaki Jun'ichirō prize for her three-part autobiographical novel *Ake o ubau mono.* In addition, Enchi translated the *Genji monogatari*[19] into modern Japanese and in 1957 received a second Women Writers Prize for her *Namamiko monogatari*, a work set in the classical period describing the life and death of the Empress Teishi. As successful as Enchi was with this last work, however, and as skillfully as she evokes the atmosphere of the classical age, she is even more successful in relating the traditions and conventions of the Tokugawa and Meiji eras to the conditions of the modern Japanese woman in a domestic setting. We will be tracing the convolutions in her work of a pattern that finds its historical development in *The Waiting Years.*

The narrative dynamic resembles two of the tales of Sata's "Yuki no mau yado," a wife unhappy with an unfaithful husband. The dimensions of domestic suffering in Enchi's work, however, run from an extreme statement of patriarchal oppression in that part of *The Waiting Years* set in the Meiji period, where Tomo, the protagonist, dutifully appears in Tokyo in the opening pages to select a live-in concubine for her husband, Shirakawa, to that of later works like "Yo" (The Enchantress), wherein a mutually agreed upon distance is maintained between husband and wife. In *The Waiting Years* and in "Otoko no hone," both set partially in the Meiji, the husband is initially loved; but in many of the works set in later periods, such as "The Enchantress," "Himojii tsukishi," and especially the *Ake o ubau mono* series, the protagonist never did particularly care for her husband but was unaware of the major flaws in his nature when she married him. Unhappy in her marriage and tormented by the physical signs of aging (false teeth, graying and/or thinning hair, hysterectomies, mastectomies, deafness, loss of memory and the sense of smell, nearsightedness, etc.), the protagonist seeks an escape from the bleakness and boredom of everyday life in some combination of erot-

---

[19] As did Tanizaki.

ic fantasy ("The Enchantress"), literature and art ("The Enchantress," *Kizu aru tsubasa*), or a lover (*Kizu aru tsubasa, Niji to shura*).

The *Waiting Years*, until the publication of *Masks* the only full-length novel by either Enchi or Hayashi readily available in translation, serves as an excellent basis for considering the historic tradition from which much of the definition of the married woman's role even in the present day is derived. In Tomo, Enchi depicts both the strength and the vulnerability of a woman raised in the Tokugawa mold, but there is a separation between what the narrator can know from her vantage in the present and the somewhat mystified obedience that is Tomo's "choice." Although the narrator provides us with the political background of the times, Tomo knows little of the world outside her home.

> Toward the Emperor and the authorities she showed the same vaguely submissive attitude as to the feminine ethic that had taught her to yield to her husband's wishes in every respect, however unreasonable they might seem. Born in a country district of Kyushu near the end of the feudal period and barely able to read or write, she had no shield to defend herself other than the existing moral code.[20]

The extreme limitation of that code becomes clear to Tomo when she selects Suga as the first of two concubines who are to become a part of the Shirakawa family. Threatened by the physical relationship that Suga has with the sensual Shirakawa and that marks the end of her own, Tomo realizes that she herself has no way out of the present situation and no possible means of survival except within a code that denies her any expression of her own emotion.

There is no opportunity for a direct challenging of the injustice involved in her new role, and the narrator implies that a more articulated consciousness would only compound Tomo's difficulties.

> Innocent of learning, she had never been taught how to understand a person intellectually and was constitutionally incapable of letting her actions follow the natural dictates of her instincts. Only this made it possible for her to live in unswerving allegiance to the feudal code of feminine morality and to take as her ideal the chaste wife who grudged no sacrifice for her husband and family. But now an unmistakable mis-

---

[20] Enchi Fumiko, *The Waiting Years*, trans. John Bester (Tokyo: Kōdansha International, 1980), p. 43.

trust in the code that had been her unquestioned creed was making it-self felt within.[21]

Denied the luxury of expressed opposition and recognizing the precarious nature of her own social and economic position, Tomo can only resort to the circumvention of her former rule of complete obe-dience. She secretly keeps back the remainder of the money that Shirikawa had given her for the purchase of a concubine and hoards it against the quite possible day when she might be ousted from her own position.

Silent about her husband's relationship with Suga; with Yumi, the second of the concubines arriving some years later; and even with Miya, their son's wife, Tomo's only moment to speak comes when she is approaching death. She had for long years hoped for the triumph of survival, but only death promises her freedom from "that unfeeling, hard and unassailable fortress summed up by the one word 'family'."[22] Only now can Tomo reveal her own will in both the legal and intentional senses of the word. *The Waiting Years* ends with a double reaction, when her husband at her request reads the document in which Tomo leaves the money that she had accu-mulated from the original secret sum to her grandchildren and to Suga and Yumi, a wish he will grant, and when he refuses a second request conveyed to him as Tomo's death approaches that she not be given any funeral, but that her body be dumped in the sea. This is the only manner in which she can now formulate freedom from the strangling bonds that have confined her all her life, but this too will elude her.

"Otoko no hone" (1956) returns to this theme, with its origins in the feudal family structure, but generalizes it somewhat more. Again there is a separation between contemporary consciousness and a feudal past, but that separation is more clearly defined. In this sto-ry, the narrator, whose friend Shizuko is showing her an obi that had been handed down from her grandmother to her mother and then to her, reports their discovery of a letter hidden within it. The origins of the letter itself are obscure, for although it is inscribed as "a mes-sage in Chise's blood" by a hand that appears to be that of Ritsu,

---

[21] Ibid., p. 52.
[22] Ibid., pp. 189–190.

Shizuko's grandmother, it is unclear just which of her grandfather's discarded lovers the writer of this farewell message might be. Its discovery, however, prompts Shizuko to tell the narrator about her grandmother's life with her perennially unfaithful husband and the concubine who lived with them. Essentially the same story as Tomo's, it ends as the narrator and Shizuko visit the cemetery plot where all three are buried together. Again the wife is the first to die after a lifetime of silence behind which lie feelings glimpsed only in the hidden letter and in an equally obscure story that her grandmother had told Shizuko about a man with a wife and a concubine living in apparent harmony. In this story a man walking in the garden hears a strange noise coming from the annex and accompanied by the scent of aloes. He peers into the room to find his wife and concubine playing go. While he watches, their hair begins writhing in the air, its ends turning into large snakes, hissing and striking. This unpleasant vision makes him aware of the force of the rivalry and jealousy concealed beneath a calm surface. The story conveys to an older Shizuko much of what her grandmother, too, must have felt beneath a submissive exterior, and the narrator follows her as she constructs connections between what she had known of her grandmother and the fuller story she now perceives.

Although there are obvious similarities between the works, the element of narrative complication serves to make "Otoko no hone" particularly suggestive of Enchi's mature writing. Whereas *The Waiting Years* is quite straightforward in its narration of the events of Tomo's life from the time she appears in Tokyo until her death, with the narrator's impersonal function being that of adding material from history and politics to amplify Tomo's own consciousness, the shorter form of "Otoko no hone" contains an intricate balance between the hidden past—the suppressed but transmitted messages of the letter and the story—and a present in which the women discover, decipher, and intuitively piece together the fragments. A relatively clear image appears of women emerging from a feudal past in which protest is not only futile but forbidden, nevertheless secretly relaying their stories to coming generations, and, again, of a kind of complicity, a shared burden. "We do not know when, where and to what end the woman called Chise, who wrote the message in blood, was fleeing, but only because her lament was carefully sewn inside the obi by Ritsu was an attachment so difficult to renounce kept alive through sixty or seventy years and conveyed to Shizuko."[23] Osan preserves Koharu's letter and Ritsu keeps Chise's. Why? The narrator and Shizuko speculate too. "Although the message in blood was doubtless written by this Chise, Shizuko wondered if it wasn't because her grandmother somehow or other had the same feelings within her that she had then sewn these words within the lining of the obi, where, against all expectation, they remained hidden from the light of the sun and preserved for all this time."[24]

The historical setting of the two stories places this problem of an unequal and unhappy marriage at a comforting distance. However quietly unhappy the lives of Ritsu and Tomo may have been, the specifically Meiji trappings of the texts would seem to suggest that that kind of domestic oppression is a thing of the past. On the contrary, Enchi's fiction set in subsequent periods demonstrates that this is not so on any fundamental level. Like Shizuko's grandmother and like Tomo, Saku of "Himojii tsukihi," for example, does not outlive her husband. She dreams of release from the paralyzed and querulous Naokichi either through divorce or survival, but her only real gain in the power to rebel lies in being able to directly voice her own complaints. Although his habitual womanizing had early given her a disgust for him, and although her resentment is deep, she is horrified when her young son, Koichi, suggests that they should kill him. Rejecting action upon his verbalization of the darkest impulses of a rebellion they all feel, Saku continues to struggle to make a meager living for the family until she collapses and dies. She, too, is destined to be buried beside her husband's first wife, and her life translates the experience of Tomo and Ritsu into more modern terms. As she struggles in a difficult postwar world to provide adequately for her family, her final days are enveloped by the poisonous atmosphere of a home pervaded by the smells of the invalid, the malice of the daughters, and the bland criminality of the son. In all these works, then, the home becomes a place of oppression and protest (silent or spoken, but never acted upon) and ultimately manages to stifle the life of the protagonist whose role it is to serve that home and family.

---

[23] *Enchi Fumiko zenshū* (Tokyo: Shinchōsha, 1977), vol. 2, p. 285.

[24] Ibid., p. 285.

Some of the themes and situations that find expression in "Himojii tsukihi" are more fully implemented in the series of novels subsumed under the title of the initial volume, *Ake o ubau mono*. Although the first volume recounts the childhood and young womanhood of the central character, Munakata Shigeko, and ends shortly after her marriage, it opens with a scene in which the middle-aged Shigeko is having all of her teeth pulled. She has already undergone a mastectomy and a hysterectomy, and the loss of her teeth seems a third massive indignity inflicted upon her flesh. As the opening of what might otherwise be termed a female *bildungsroman,*[25] this passage is striking, for already carried in it is the threat of a painful decay that is both actual and a metaphor for the decaying of the protagonist's hopes as the novels follow their course. Shigeko's mature experience is to reverse a promising beginning. In spite of a cultured background, in spite of early success as a modern "leftist" playwright, and even in spite of a love affair with the married Ichiyanagi, for reasons explored in the closing chapter Shigeko consents, after an initial refusal, to marry an archeologist and teacher, Munakata Kanji.

It is especially in the central volume of the trilogy, *Kizu aru tsubasa*, that the common themes of Enchi's fiction are most fully developed. This work deals most extensively with the disillusions incumbent upon a loveless marriage. In "Himojii tsukihi," Saku, then pregnant with Kyoichi, is forced to beg her husband's superiors to keep him on after a scandal erupts over his sexual harassment of a female colleague. Similarly, in *Kizu aru tsubasa*, while Shigeko's daughter, Yoshiko, is still quite young, Munakata is the object of numerous complaints from young women and even a young office boy where he works, and Shigeko, too, must plead his case, an unforgivable humiliation for the daughter of a highly respected scholar. The marriage is doomed, but, although it is her dearest wish to obtain a divorce, worsening conditions on the national scene argue

---

[25] According to Annis Pratt in *Archetypal Patterns in Women's Fiction* (Bloomington: Indiana University Press, 1981), the female *bildungsroman* very often ends unhappily. Although specific myths that she isolates as frequent in fiction by English and American writers do not occur in fiction by Japanese women, the four categories into which she divides fiction by women—the *bildungsroman*, the novel of domestic enclosure, novels of Eros, and novels of rebirth and transformation—do seem to apply.

against such an action. What she had seen as a "springboard" to freedom, taking her out of her own family environment once her beloved father had died, threatens to become the equivalent of a tomb for her hopes.

In turning away from emotional involvement in this marriage, Shigeko has three things to sustain her: her daughter, her relationships with other men, and her work. The first two represent difficult areas in prewar Japanese society, and, in an impersonal tone that reminds us of the narrator of *The Waiting Years*, Enchi informs us about Japanese law at that time. A mother with young children could not expect to be granted their custody, and although a husband's adultery was not a prosecutable offense, a wife's was.[26] Her anxiety about her daughter's future, a hesitancy to endure the disdain society accords the divorced woman, and the certainty of an unequal distribution of property keep Shigeko within the external boundaries of marriage; but unlike Tomo, Ritsu, and Saku, she is unwilling to forgo physical and emotional satisfactions, which are unavailable to her in that relationship. She resumes the affair with Ichiyanagi, and it continues until she expresses a desire to have a child by him. Given the framework of Japanese law, he not too surprisingly withdraws.

This leaves Shigeko with her work as a principal solace, and here we pick up a thread already visible in "Otoko no hone." Throughout *Kizu aru tsubasa* and *Niji to shura*, Shigeko will struggle to find a mature voice in which to express her vision of the world, for as the opening chapter of the former work reveals, she envisions writing as the only possible way she can achieve financial independence from her husband. Financial security and aesthetic expression are fused. Not the impersonal dictates of law and convention but the failure of her own will and talent seems to block her path. If she does not write, she feels, she will not only remain financially entrapped, but she will effectively be silenced. Writing becomes of desperate importance to her; "hungrily, avidly, living like a bird with a crippled wing, she longed to fly."[27] When she looks back at her

---

[26] *Enchi Fumiko zenshū*, vol. 12, p. 138 for discussion of children and pp. 223–224 of adultery.

[27] Ibid., p. 145.

early plays, however, she sees a falseness in them and is shaken by the fear that she cannot write: "But if I don't write...if I don't write, I can't live. If I don't write, I am nothing at all."[28] The very universal nature of her situation makes it all the more somber: "The miserable state she had lapsed into as a wife and a mother was doubtless that into which thousands and tens of thousands of wives, carrying children in their arms, had fallen. These women, however, had no way of fleeing into the construction of words."[29] She recognizes already that her own writing represents a retreat from everyday reality, but not until much later will she comprehend the paradox that only by turning to the very experience of "thousands and tens of thousands of wives" can she succeed in writing. For it is their story she has to tell.

Niji to shura continues the story in even darker tones. Shigeko has trouble recovering from her second operation, a hysterectomy, and sees her life as a woman as being over. Still saddened by the death of Ichiyanagi, having lost her home but not her husband, Shigeko faces the problems of dealing with a difficult teenaged daughter, while struggling with poor health and the despair of unsuccessfully attempting a literary comeback. Only slowly is she able to resume a normal, if subdued, life; and even though she ultimately has an affair with Kakinuma, a man who has loved her for years and who believes in her gifts as a writer, his death at the end of the work seems to signal the end of Shigeko's physical ties to any man. He has, however, suggested to her that she seize upon the material of the lives about her and reveal the beauty and the horror hidden within them. Thus, Shigeko comes to a realization resembling that of the narrator of "Otoko no hone," that the lives of wife and lover alike are written in blood and have as the same subject the failure of wholeness, the need to fly on wings crippled or clipped by constricting views of a woman's needs and a woman's proper role in relationships and in society.

Even Chigako of "The Enchantress" uses art as an alternative to mere acceptance. In the room where she sleeps, lives, and works separately from Keisaku, the husband of many years with whom ag-

---

[28] Ibid., p. 146.
[29] Ibid.

ing is her only tie, Chigako muses and dreams. Almost grotesque in her pursuit of an ever retreating attractiveness, and hovering between life and death in her own imagination, Chigako represents the fusion in failure of both illusion and reality. But in her ability to capture this fusion on paper, she achieves a kind of power. She makes from her own life on the hill a "kind of romance," transforming herself from an old wife into a young wife with a lover to whom she gives her husband's treasured antiques. It is the real Keisaku's most precious possession, a Ming vase, that the fictional lovers are pictured as breaking.

> By portraying a woman's feelings in introducing another man into the house unbeknown to her husband, she who had never herself done any such thing could enjoy in the story a kind of revenge on Keisaku. The breaking of the vase, of course, was itself a formalization of this revenge. After committing to paper this mixture of wanton fantasy interwoven with reality, she would stay quite still listening for sounds from the hill, the smile of the enchantress still playing around her eyes.[30]

If Chigako can realize her fantasies only on paper, remaining conscious of the weaknesses of old age rapidly overtaking her, Mieko Togano of *Masks*[31] comes closer to embodying the powers of an enchantress. A widow who had been unhappy in her marriage as so many of the other Enchi protagonists, she has a love affair in her past. But her present and Japan's past figure more boldly in the plot of this fascinating novel, which fuses Enchi's knowledge of Japanese literary history with a modern setting. Mieko's powerful personality controls those of her son's widow, Yasuko, and of her retarded daughter, Harume; and her interest in the Japanese classics, particularly the *Genji monogatari* and Noh drama, enables her to construct an image of women that attributes the power of ancient shamans to them. In fact, an essay she had published twenty years before describes her view in nearly Jungian terms. Mieko observes that although Murasaki herself seemed skeptical of spirit possession, her creation of Lady Rokujo in the *Genji* suggested the demonic power of

---

[30] Enchi Fumiko, "Enchantress," trans. John Bester, in Morris et al., *Modern Japanese Short Stories*, p. 91.

[31] Enchi Fumiko, *Masks*, trans. Juliet Winters Carpenter (New York: Alfred A. Knopf, 1983).

unconscious jealousy.

One cannot help wondering why she chose to write so vividly in her novel about a phenomenon in which she herself seemed to have little faith: in doing so, however, she was able to combine women's extreme ego suppression and ancient female shamanism, showing both in opposition in men....

Just as there is an archetype of woman as the object of man's eternal love, so there must be an archetype of her as the object of his eternal fear, representing, perhaps, the shadow of his own evil actions. The Rokujo lady is an embodiment of this archetype.[32]

She herself manipulates both daughter and daughter-in-law to her own ends and succeeds through that manipulation in producing a grandson in a household without males. Fascinating, however, is the way, in the work within a work that the essay is, that Mieko attests to both the mythic powers once believed inherent in women and to the real artistry of the classical woman writer. And just as Mieko, the character, manages to exert some of the force of the Rokujo lady, so Enchi, the writer, conveys both a testimony to and a modern equivalent of Murasaki's skill and psychological depth.

To recapture the shaman's power; to break the vase; to find the message hidden in the obi; to connect the present with a silenced past, fantasy with reality, all are the aims of Enchi's mature fiction. To display the enchantress in the old woman, the Koharu in Osan and the Osan in Koharu have been the aims of both Enchi and Hayashi. Chigako, the wife, finds her mirror in Kin, the aging geisha of Hayashi's "Late Chrysanthemum." By living and by growing old, by becoming more and more the same, they have forfeited any claims they may have had to Osan or Koharu ideality. For both, fighting the signs of aging with cosmetics and beauty routines has become a ritual. The cosmetic covering over of the real, however, whether in Chigako's near frenzy or in Kin's practiced calculation, implies a consciousness of the gap between the self as experienced and the face and body as perceived by others, an awareness not only of the ideal of beauty but of its distance from reality. However skill-

---

[32] Ibid., p. 57.

fully male writers may assume a female persona, it is not often that they choose a Kin or a Chigako as object of their art.

To project: One detects the smile of the Mona Lisa—a woman not young, not beautiful. And yet she sits for a famous, a gifted artist, so that her portrait may hang on her husband's wall. She has other things to do with her time, and the process of being transformed into an object of art is more than faintly ridiculous. (Da Vinci knows it too; he paints the smile.) The beauty of women is for Enchi and Hayashi never an ideal, it is an effect—dangerous for women like Tomo (who cannot or can no longer embody it) because for men like her husband it is an ideal. The whole area of beauty and art as Woman lies, then, between men and women, between the writing of women and men.

CHAPTER SEVEN

Creating Koharu: The Image of Woman in the Works of Kawabata Yasunari and Tanizaki Jun'ichirō

THE WHOLE AREA OF BEAUTY and art as Woman lies, then, between women and men, between the writing of men and women. Hayashi and Enchi, while evincing an awareness in their work of the "feminine" ideals and images their culture validates, each in her own way develops a picture, a thematic representation of the limitations of those ideals and images. Their works do not merely represent such conceptualizations but are personalized challenges to them. For the most part they have views of distinctly different levels of social experience, which is only to be expected when one considers the influence that their backgrounds must have had upon their choice of contexts for their respective protagonists. For both outsider and insider, however, the narrative arises from the process by which the space between the idealization of social roles, the Osans and Koharus of the male imagination, is articulated. Beyond this, however, by virtue of a perspective that seeks to make verbal art of the perceptions of a "feminine consciousness," modern women writers of any economic, political, or aesthetic persuasion are bound to eschew the thematics and the symbolization of the female that occur more conspicuously in works by males. The ground may overlap in part, but it is not the same, for in most works by male writers, when the gap between the real and the ideal of the Woman becomes a focal point, it is usually the ideal that is privileged and that becomes the embodiment of art.

In the works of Kawabata Yasunari and Tanizaki Jun'ichirō, for example, the idealization and aesthetization of the Woman is handled differently, but the perspectives have certain similarities. This might at first glance seem to be a fundamental contradiction; yet when the works of women writers are kept in mind, we begin to be aware of a fundamental agreement between the two arising from a "masculine" "consciousness of the feminine," one that contrasts distinctly with the kinds of "feminine consciousness" we have sought to isolate in the writing of Enchi and Hayashi. And, even though it is possible to identify Kawabata as more "feminine" than Tanizaki in the consciousness that he develops in certain of his works (an identification, of course, open to question when certain other works are considered), the effect of their aestheticizations—the idealization of Woman and the estrangement of women (in the guise of specific female characters)—is virtually identical. Witness for example the differentiation Enchi makes between the two.

> It is generally established that Tanizaki Jun'ichirō's literature depicts the beauty of the female figure with exquisite subtlety, but his depictions, consistently being the deft rendering of the masculine view of the woman from the outside, do not peel back externality to touch upon her internal emotions. In that sense, Kawabata's eye, by invading the woman herself, has a more fearful quality of coldbloodedness.[1]

Enchi's observation seems to call back the figures of the Outsider and the Insider in terms different from those we have used to designate them in her works and in Hayashi's and to identify Kawabata with an internal perspective that might seem to be closer to the feminine than Tanizaki's "masculine" view of the woman from the outside.

Strangely enough, however, Enchi describes Kawabata's eye in terms of an even greater alienation, "invading" the woman with "a more fearful quality of coldbloodedness." Enchi is neither wrong nor careless in her use of terms. There is something paradoxical in Kawabata's art—an intimate alienation, as it were. The paradox will become clearer as we examine his works, but something essential to its creation lies in the terms that criticism is almost forced to adopt in describing his work. Ekizawa Yukio, for instance, begins his article on gender-consciousness in the woman writer not with any woman writer but with Kawabata: "For example, the women Kawabata depicts are described as having more womanliness (femininity—*onnarashisa*) than the various women depicted by women writers."[2] The compound word *onnarashisa* says it all, for it trans-

---

[1] Enchi Fumiko, "Maihime ni tsuite," *Enchi Fumiko zenshū*, vol. 16, p. 257.
[2] Ekizawa Yukio, "Joryū sakka ni okeru seishiki" [Gender-consciousness in the

poses the being of *onna* (woman) into the idealization of *raishisa* (seeming), making of it a cultural construct that depends upon sex differentiation in terms of symbols of "opposed or complementary qualities."[3] In order to approach the actual representation of women by women, then, Ekizawa realizes that he must first deal with the cultural conceptualization of the *"onnarashisa"* that finds its aesthetic implementation in Kawabata.

We have chosen to reverse Ekizawa's order, to delineate women depicted by women before considering the *"onnarashisa"* of the male writer and to concentrate on the presentation of the complexities, ambiguities, and interrelatedness of being before going on to the cultural construct of a femininity represented as objectified, idealized Otherness, sharply visual in its outlines and dependent upon the identification of a female essence, purified of the dross of mere existence. Let us turn now to Kawabata's fiction and to the concept of "womanliness" or "femininity" revealed through his works, realizing that in considering Kawabata in advance of Tanizaki, we are making another choice—that of dealing with the "aesthetic object" (Woman) as it is depicted in Kawabata's work before considering the process through which aestheticization takes place (as it is foregrounded in Tanizaki's self-conscious and preternatural pursuit of the Eternal Woman in his fiction).

A natural point of departure is "Izu no odoriko" (The Izu Dancer), which is a clear articulation of a feminine ideal that will develop further in Kawabata's later fiction. Interestingly enough, the evolution occurs in the perceiving eye rather more than in the object herself (the dancer). The inherent qualities of this object—youth, purity, beauty of form, and a degree of unconsciousness—will remain relatively unchanged in almost all of the works from "The Izu Dancer" through *Yukiguni* (Snow Country), *Sembazuru* (Thousand Cranes), and *Yama no oto* (Sound of the Mountain), to *Nemureru bijo* (House of the Sleeping Beauties) and *Mizuumi* (The Lake). The perceiving eye, on the contrary, grows increasingly older or more estranged or both, even if we do not go as far as agreement with D. J. Enright's description of both Kawabata and Tanizaki as being deeply embued with a "sexuality of the nerves," "raffiné and perverse (and

Woman Writer], *Kaishaku to kanshō* 37 (March 1972): 63.

3 Miles, *The Fiction of Sex*, p. 24. See p. 140, 4n.

increasingly geriatric)."[4]

Kawabata's aesthetic of the feminine may indeed have become increasingly "raffiné and perverse" as his career evolved, but the change occurs in the way in which a relatively unchanging aesthetic object is responded to. The early (1926) "Izu Dancer" is essentially a story describing the encounter of a young student with the youngest member of a troupe of traveling entertainers whom he meets on a walking tour of the Izu peninsula. In some ways, the story line is not unlike that of Ichiyō's "Takekurabe," the awakening of a wistful sexual attraction in two young people who are not going to become lovers. But already, Kawabata's lifelong obsession with a purity/defilement differentiation is in evidence. Since the young dancer is untouched sexually, she is a worthy object of the protagonist's desire; but her social marginality indicates that this is a very tenuous state, and the protagonist chooses merely to look and yearn.

She is, moreover, a forerunner of Komako, who in *Snow Country* is not yet a full-fledged geisha when Shimamura makes her acquaintance. In the short period of his relationship with her, we see the projection of the Izu dancer's future. Komako, for all her energy and passion, is already marked or marred in her lover's eyes by a shop-worn quality, which makes her more poignant and more imperfect as well as more vulnerable to the counterbalancing attraction that Shimamura feels toward Yoko, the pure and unsullied image in the train window.

The Shimamura whom we see in the work is less a social Shimamura, father of a family and husband of a real woman (Shimamura's wife and children are very much off-stage and liable to be invoked in rather peculiar contexts. For instance, on his final visit to the hot spring in late autumn when the insects are beginning to die, "as he picked up a dead insect to throw it out, he sometimes thought for an instant of the children he had left in Tokyo.")[5] than a Shimamura who lives a life of leisure on inherited money; he is

[4] D.J. Enright, "Hooray for Monsters," *New York Review of Books*, 27 September 1979, p. 27.

[5] Kawabata Yasunari, *Snow Country*, trans. Edward Seidensticker (New York: Knopf, 1956), p. 132.

without a real profession, using his excursions to the mountains to indulge in his taste for beauty. Like his predilection for the Western dance, which depends upon not seeing it performed, his relationship with both Komako and Yoko depends upon the ultimate unreality that he attaches to them both as forms. He sees Komako "as somehow unreal, like the woman's face in the evening mirror."[6] He must see her so, for to consider her otherwise would be to enter into genuine relationship, to make of the stylized and aestheticized mountain scenery a real world.

In the context of *Snow Country*, then, real wives and children are out of place, but a counterbalance for the physical passion of Komako and the warmth and fire that are her image-associations in the text is found in the "cooly piercing" beauty Shimamura sees in Yoko, in her disembodied eye (the powerful image with which the work begins), and in her high voice, pure and sad, which seems to penetrate his heart. It is Yoko, a faintly Madonna-like figure, who cares for the dying Yukio "for all the world like a mother," Yoko who sings to the innkeeper's child in the bath, Yoko who tends Yukio's grave; it is she who represents the sacred, the pure, the as yet unsullied. With her presence in the work, Komako's passion and energy can be more clearly isolated as futile and contaminated, and her love for Shimamura revealed as "wasted effort."

In this lies the paradoxical quality of much of Kawabata's fiction, for even though he skillfully creates an image of the two women as contrasting objects of Shimamura's fancy, these symbolic creations empty Shimamura of himself. Thus, Komako's love for her Tokyo patron seems not so much empty of content as devoid of an object. For in embuing Yoko and Komako with such force—warmth and vitality in Komako's case, intensity and earnestness in Yoko's—Shimamura successfully externalizes the necessity of such qualities and cancels all but the power to perceive their absence in himself.

In *Toward a New Psychology of Women*, Jean Baker Miller points out that this is an almost inherent separation, which gender distinctions in Western psychology also fall back upon. "It has done this," she tells us, "without recognizing that these areas of experience [vul-

---

6 Referring here to Yoko's face in the train window.

nerability, weakness, helplessness, dependency, and the basic emotional connection between an individual and other people] may have been kept out of people's conscious awareness by virtue of their being so heavily disassociated from men and so heavily associated with women."[7] To apply Miller's terms, Komako's passion, Yoko's earnestness, and the emotional intensity of them both become the alienated experience of parts of Shimamura's own human potential from which he seeks a protection in projection. "Women, then, become the 'carriers' for society of certain aspects of the total human experience—those aspects that remain unsolved. The result of such a process is to keep men from fully integrating these areas into their own lives."[8] Because Shimamura endows the woman Komako with certain qualities, he can postulate his own emptiness of them and renounce connection: "He stood gazing at his own coldness, so to speak. He could not understand how she had so lost herself. All of Komako came to him, but it seemed that nothing went out from him to her. He heard in his chest, like snow piling up, the sound of Komako, an echo beating against empty walls."[9]

In using the images of women as symbols of unassimilated experience, Kawabata's protagonists manage to make of the female both the epitome of isolation and an embodiment of an almost inhuman physical perfection. In being viewed as the approximation of a physical ideal, the female figures in his works exist on the edge of an extreme vulnerability surpassing even the financial, social, and emotional insecurities that beset the women in Enchi's and Hayashi's fiction. Insofar as they are realizations of purity, perfection of form, and beauty, they are particularly prey to the inescapable ravages of time. The Izu dancer, whose lot is inevitably to be exposed to the assaults on her virginity that her tenuous social standing implies, can only exist in the pure form that is the young student's vision of her in the brief period during which he knows her. Like Komako, her existence as an ideal is ephemeral; flesh will thicken, voice tones will harden, and attainability will destroy the abstract quality of her aestheticization.

---

[7] Jean Baker Miller, *Toward a New Psychology of Women* (Boston: Beacon Press, 1976), p. 22.

[8] Ibid., pp. 22, 23.

[9] Kawabata, *Snow Country*, pp. 126–127.

As a result, there is a particularly strong thematic emphasis in Kawabata's works upon female figures as objects, which involves a near obsession with those physical details, sometimes relatively minute, that hint at the imperfection and/or defilement of their beauty and purity. The ideal of the feminine becomes specular—accessible to the eye—and any hint of defilement becomes ominous. Thus, even small imperfections are symbolic of defilement. In *Thousand Cranes*, for example, Chikako's birthmark serves to emphasize the disgust with which the protagonist, Kikuji, views her, and the very sexual availability of Mrs. Oda leads to her self-destruction just as, at the work's conclusion, her daughter Fumiko's sensual yielding apparently must result in her effacement, too. Chikako becomes the symbolic figure within the work for a feminine defilement that all of the women—with the exception of Yukiko, the virginal product of a "good" family who is offered for Kikuji's consideration as a prospective bride—are depicted as sharing.

Perhaps the clearest development of the connection between a visible mark of imperfection and the failure of relationship is in "Hokuro no tegami" (The Mole), a short story that may in some ways be seen as the model of Kawabata's development of a female perspective from within. The narrator in this story is a rejected wife who places the onus of her own unacceptability upon her insistent habit of playing with a small mole on her shoulder. An initial reading of the work confirms Kawabata's reputation as a master at rendering the female psyche, but careful reconsideration of its theme reveals what it shares both with Kawabata's male-originating narratives and with a broader culturewide stereotyping of the wife, and the wifely. The mole in the story comes to mean many things: it is an imperfection but an individuation as well, and it seems at one point to represent the failure of the narrator, Sayoko, to be completely submissive to her husband's wishes. He even beats her repeatedly in his aggravation at her failure to break the habit, and their relationship for a while seems almost a model of the sadomasochistic. But it is in the almost fully realized masochism of the narrator's point of view that the story diverges most fundamentally from female-oriented narratives by women. Sayoko's willingness, however plaintive, to take the blame upon herself for the failure of her marriage accords more with cultural stereotypes of wifely submission than with the actions of the female protagonists of women writers. Sayoko's perfect self-abnegation accords both with Kawabata's transubstantiation of the female into the aesthetic and with a broader cultural directive that female being should allow itself to become subsumed by masculine autonomy and authority. For just as Sayoko has a "liberating" dream wherein she removes her mole and offers it to her husband—reflecting afterward on how fitting it might be if her mole were absorbed in a mole her husband has beside his nose ("What a fine fairy story it would make if your mole really were to swell up because you had put mine in it"),[10] so the qualities attributed to other feminine figures become reified like Sayoko's bean-like mole. Yoko becomes an eye on a train window and a crystalline voice, Komako a flaming face in a snowy mirror; and in *Thousand Cranes* Mrs. Oda's being is absorbed in the images of a wave and a Shino tea cup which must be smashed in order to destroy the defiling mark of her lips on its rim and the power of her sensuality. The being of the women becomes thus objectified, aestheticized in things, and as a thing, and the progress of this process of aestheticization can be traced from "The Izu Dancer" through *The Lake* and *The House of the Sleeping Beauties*. The Izu dancer's potential attainability by other men torments the young student, but it is her unattainability for him that gives the story its romanticized poignance. The attainable is ultimately equated with the defiled, and in *Thousand Cranes*, the defiled with the destroyed. But in *The Sound of the Mountain* the two aspects of attainability/unattainability are met in the same figure. Like Sayoko of "The Mole," Kikuko is of little interest to her husband Shuichi. He sees her as "a child," while considering his mistress, Kinu, to be the embodiment of adult passion. To Shingo, Shuichi's father, however, Kikuko represents the unattainability of suppressed desire. Thus, when he awakens from the dream of a woman who is not Kikuko, he wonders if he had not borrowed the figure of another woman as her substitute.

Had not the girl in the dream been an incarnation of Kikuko, a substitute for her? Had not moral considerations after all had their way even

---

[10] Kawabata Yasunari, "The Mole," trans. Edward Seidensticker, in Donald Keene, ed., *Modern Japanese Literature* (New York: Grove Press, 1956), p. 373.

in his dream, had he not borrowed the figure of the girl as a substitute for Kikuko? . . .
And might it not be that, if his desires were given free reign, if he could remake his life as he wished, he would want to love the virgin Kikuko, before she was married to Shuichi?[11]

In a like manner, Kikuko herself represents a kind of reincarnation of an earlier, equally unattainable lover, who was the beautiful older sister of his own unbeautiful wife, Yasuko. The sister, who had married another man and died young, continues to exercise a power over Shingo's imagination that Yasuko cannot. And as with the other beautiful women of Kawabata's fiction, the sister is contained in imagery; her spirit becomes incarnated in the dwarf maple that had accompanied her to her husband's home and was returned after her death.

The desirability of the beautiful and its necessary distancing and alienation from the perceiving masculine eye receive extended treatment in the "raffiné and perverse" *House of the Sleeping Beauties* and *The Lake.* Both works may be said to carry a Shimamura-like passivity to its voyeuristic extreme, for in the *House of the Sleeping Beauties* drugged virgins are put to bed with impotent old men, whose imaginations are given full rein in a situation that may be said to represent a certain kind of masculine ideal, and *The Lake* traces the career of an actual voyeur. Although the elderly patrons of the *House of the Sleeping Beauties* are assumed to be incapable of physically deflowering their sleeping partners, the very unconsciousness of the young girls relieves their customers of any sense of responsibility, of mutual responsiveness. They are free to enjoy the sleeping girls as unconscious objects completely vulnerable to the eye, and nothing of the actual lives of either the old men or the young girls is allowed to intrude upon the consciousness of their partners. But at the story's conclusion, the very desirable unconsciousness of the sleeping beauties is carried to its logically objectified extreme, as one of two young women with whom Eguchi, the protagonist, is sleeping lapses from unconsciousness into death.

---

11 Kawabata Yasunari, *The Sound of the Mountain,* trans. Edward Seidensticker (New York: Perigee Books, 1981), p. 207.

In *The Lake* Gimpei, the protagonist, is equally an objectifier. A voyeur in fact, he spends days following women about the streets. After having been fired from a teaching job for having an affair with one of his students, he seeks out beautiful women, drinking in their beauty through his eyes. What is he seeking? As an encounter with a masseuse in a bath house indicates, he is seeking an ideal: "Her voice had aroused in him a sense of pure happiness and warm relief. Was this the voice of the eternal woman or the compassionate mother?"[12] All of the women in his life from his mother to his cousin Yayoi are intertwined with the fantasies he constructs around the chance-met beauties, and the almost pathological nature of his yearning is clear in his obsession with his last encounter with the ideal in the work. In the figure of the schoolgirl, Machie, whom he watches from hiding in a park, the dynamics of aestheticization/ objectification are vivid.

First in significance is the unreality of his fascination. Searching for Machie after their first encounter he constructs scenarios that have little to do with his (lack of) relationship with the actual girl.

Words seemed inadequate to describe the intensity of her long, tapering eyes, and as he walked along he traced the shape of a tiny beautiful fish around his own eyes with his thumb and forefinger. Heavenly music filled his ears.

"In my next life I shall be born with beautiful feet. You will be just as you are now, and we'll dance together in a ballet of white." The girl's dress was the white tutu of classical ballet and the skirt swirled and fluttered.[13]

Concomitant with this unreality is a sense of the ephemerality of the beauty he so admires. Gimpei becomes its master by maintaining the connoisseur's appreciation of the "right moment" for the contemplation of the desired object: "Unfortunately, such perfection doesn't last after the age of sixteen or seventeen, and even she will only be at her best for a few brief years."[14] Increasingly important, too, is the desired object's unawareness of the dreams and visions of their agent. The young protagonist of "The Izu Dancer" does not

---

[12] Kawabata Yasunari, *The Lake*, trans. Reiko Tsukimura (New York: Kōdansha International), p. 8.
[13] Ibid., p. 132.
[14] Ibid., p. 133.

speak of his love for the little dancer, but a tenuous tacit understanding exists between them. More and more the later works begin to remove the experience of desire from its object. Komako after all was capable only of emptying Shimamura of his own desire by herself participating too fully in it. In the later works the female object is barred from knowing or experiencing the transcendence that the protagonist achieves through her.

A final aspect of this aestheticization lies in its concentration/fragmentation of the whole into the part. The masseuse becomes a voice; Machie, "long tapering eyes"; and Gimpei's whole energy, his life, becomes absorbed by the powerful aesthetic pull of the detail, the image, and the form of an alienated beauty, which, unaware and unparticipating, is spread out before his eyes. The student of "The Izu Dancer," the wealthy Tokyo patron of *Snow Country*, the young office worker of *Thousand Cranes*, the old office worker of *The Sound of the Mountain*, the old men at the *House of the Sleeping Beauties*, and Gimpei, each in his own way, surrenders his energies to a vision of the female—beautiful, but alien to the realities of their everyday lives and concentrated in physical details that capture the essence of dreams.

Ultimately, at the heart of such dreams is the paradoxical appeal of the eternally unattainable and the perennially vulnerable. To retain an aestheticized and objectified power to represent ideality, real life is sacrificed to the image. The form of Yoko falling through flames, the shattered Shino bowl, the removal of the body of a dead sleeping partner, all testify to the necessity of preserving the perfection of the aesthetic image by destroying its physical embodiment. From the Izu dancer to the schoolgirl Machie, the idealized quality of the image of beauty remains unchanged. Only the perceiving eye has evolved, becoming farsighted with age, so that the details of the human face before it become blurred; and in *Sound of the Mountain*, a Noh mask can assume a living reality, provoking the desire in the aging Shingo to press kisses upon its inanimate lips. The line between living flesh and ideal is effaced through a constant interchangeability more and more obvious in the later works, until the Eternal Woman becomes served by a series of human women who are all in the process of outliving ideal status.

Mishima Yukio's short story "Onnagata" indicates indeed that there is no need for a real woman to become the avenue of the expression of the true essence of the *onnarashisa*; a female impersonator can more adequately represent the masculine ideal of femininity because it is closer to the male's own consciousness than to the experience of real women living in time. And the vivid detail, the transcending image, can remain in consciousness, lingering like a dwarf maple whose owner has died. The value of the *onnarashisa* is that it transcends the power of the individual to embody it; and in the images of Kawabata's works, with their compelling poetic power to suggest the ideal, the ephemerality of beauty, and the power of art, we see its essential dynamic.

But if the Eternal Woman and the essence of womanliness find their most vivid expression in Kawabata's works in a series of fragmented aesthetic images—a voice, an eye, a touch—in the works of Tanizaki Jun'ichirō the process of creating the Eternal Woman is the clear and conscious construct. From "Shisei" (The Tattooer, 1910) on, we are presented with a series of protagonists bent upon imposing that idealized image upon the actual flesh of living women. Less passive than Kawabata's male protagonists, whose eyes are lit by the occasional glimpses of their eternal ideal of the beautiful in women, the Tanizaki protagonist is aware of and takes an active role in the process of making life conform to the ideal. As Enchi's comment indicates, however, Tanizaki, concentrating primarily upon the female's externality, seems less inclined to suggest that the internal consciousness of his female characters conforms with an ideal or with a stereotypical social role. An interesting divergence of consciousnesses actually adds a dynamic of narrative complexity, therefore, for although Tanizaki's male characters are devoted to the pursuit and creation of the Eternal Woman, very frequently the actual woman whom they nominate as vessels of her essence have other ideas.

In contrast to Kawabata's writings, where the ideal of the female remains virtually unchanged while shifts take place in the nature of the perceiving eye, in Tanizaki's works from "The Tattooer" to *Fūten rōjin nikki* (The Diary of a Mad Old Man, 1962) there is considerable fluctuation in the form that the ideal woman is made to assume. In Tanizaki's fiction it is the idealizer who remains more or less the same, a "woman-worshipper," while the image desired undergoes considerable modification. Moreover, whereas wives remain rather firmly offstage in Kawabata's fiction, in many of Tanizaki's works, most especially "Ashikari" and *Kagi* (The Key), wives play an important part in the working out of the ideal. Just as Woman as a partial fleeting image plays a central role in the works of Kawabata, so in Tanizaki's another aspect of the aestheticization of the female—the creative process itself—occupies a central position. Tanizaki frequently intensifies our recognition of this by using arts other than writing to create embedded metaphors for this process. Sweethearts, lovers, wives, sisters-in-law, daughters-in-law, and casually encountered women become the raw material for transformation into an image of the Eternal Woman that will wear radically different faces in various works, but Tanizaki's protagonists are consistently less inclined to take these women as "givens" than are Kawabata's. They wish to play an active role in the actualization of their dreams.

Tanizaki was not only among the most conscious of modern Japanese narrative craftsmen, he was also among the most explicit in his visualization of the female as the flesh of art. Seeing the connection between the Japanese culture and its representation of the power of the Eternal Woman as being deep and necessary, he was fascinated, at times obsessed, with the narrative manipulation of various nonliterary aesthetic images of the feminine through which he sought to efface the external distinction between woman as being and as image, performer, or symbol. Art as creation and performance, in the plastic terms of the Pygmalion dynamic, becomes his metaphor for the female's physical presence to the masculine imagination. To Yeats' famous query "How can we tell the dancer from the dance?" Tanizaki's fiction seems to reply "We cannot, should not; we can only retell the moment, the manner and the power of their meeting." Thus, as does Yeats in his poem, Tanizaki frequently seeks to use the medium of words to capture the fusion of flesh and dream in embodied art.

Words and the images they evoke, reality and idealization, vision and its object, male and female, artist and art are counterpoised against one another in many of his narratives that translate the experiences of one art (be it visual, musical, or theatrical) into the verbalized dimensions of another. Tanizaki uses these arts to suggest and reenact the embodiment of the female as aesthetic force and to capture the moment when a Japanese Galatea, for good or evil, steps down from her marble block, becoming through that gesture not spectacle but performer. His 1921 short story "Aoi Hana" (Aguri) suggests how this dynamic operates. The protagonist, Okada, thirty-four years old but in poor health, has taken Aguri, a seventeen-year-old girl with whom he has been obsessed for three years, on a shopping trip to buy her some Western clothes. In the course of the story he visualizes her as many things—a Western beauty, a Chinese sing-song girl, a leopard, but most of all as a living statue.

> At the thought of Aguri his mind became a pitch-dark room hung with black velvet curtains—a room like a conjurer's stage set—in the center of which stood the marble statue of a nude woman. Was that really Aguri? Surely the Aguri he loved was the living, breathing counterpart of that marble figure.
>
> ...he could see the lines of her body through the loose flannel clothing that enveloped it, could picture to himself the statue of the "woman" under her kimono. He recalled each elegant trace of the chisel. Today he would adorn the statue with jewels and silks.[15]

Unlike the Kawabata protagonist, who perceives the Woman in fragmentary images of incredible power to suggest the inner being, Okada visualizes Aguri as a physical entity, but one that has an (almost obligatory) streak of cruelty and a mind and consciousness of her own. His ideal is internalized; although the acquisitive Aguri is willing to allow him to deck her out in whatever finery he desires, she is not expected to share in the fantasies taking place in Okada's mind. In an earlier work, "The Tattooer," however, Tanizaki had already demonstrated the extent to which he could verbally re-create the figure of a woman as the fusion of flesh and art. That is the story of the transfer of the power of the dream to the control of the envisioned woman, for in it the writer does not merely compare female flesh and art, but constitutes them literally as identical, inseparable. Translated by Howard Hibbett as "The Tattooer," the title of the original would, for our purposes, more appropriately be rendered as "The Tattoo," since much of what Tanizaki seeks to show in this story is that art, especially when cast in the female form, has an innate

---

[15] Tanizaki Jun'ichirō, *Seven Japanese Tales*, trans. Howard Hibbett (New York: Berkley Medallion Books, 1965), "Aguri," p. 130.

power to consume the life force of its creator and that, in the activation of his art, the creator becomes its creature.

Although Seikichi, the tattooer, is technically the protagonist of the story, the tattoo itself is the agent of its force. In the few short pages of "The Tattooer," Tanizaki makes what may be his strongest assertion of art's transcendent power. The tattooer of the opening pages is a master of his craft, capricious in his acceptance of commissions and indifferent to the sufferings of the customers whose flesh he transforms and, as it were, commands. But he is made vulnerable by the dream of an ultimate aesthetic act: "For a long time Seikichi had cherished the desire to create a masterpiece on the skin of a beautiful woman."[16] Thus, inevitably, when the ideal material for his art appears in the form of a young apprentice geisha, Seikichi immediately sets about creating the image of his own doom. Before she herself can share the artist's vision and become a worthy bearer of it, Seikichi instructs her in the true nature of her power, which he sees as innately cruel, by showing her two scrolls depicting beautiful women enjoying the torments of men who are subject to them. Even though the pictures speak to "something long hidden in her heart," the girl is frightened. She is still just so much raw material, for she remains only a woman and not yet a work of art.

But the artist in this case is peculiarly dependent upon his medium. Only through this girl can his dream receive living, breathing reality. Seikichi slowly inscribes the terrifying image of a huge black widow spider on the young girl's back, and, when it is finished, he tells her, "I have poured my soul in this tattoo. Today there is no woman in Japan to compare with you. Your old fears are gone. All men will be your victims."[17] Though he had once been in control of his vision, Seikichi has now surrendered to it, volunteering himself as her first victim. The power of the artist is transferred to the art object, and the story ends with a grotesque vision of the fusion of flesh and art as "her resplendently tattooed back caught a ray of sunlight and the spider was wreathed in flames."[18]

---

[16] Ibid., "The Tattooer," p. 108.
[17] Ibid., p. 113.
[18] Ibid.

Although the story's brevity demands a single-minded development of the image of art, perverse and forceful, in which "beauty
and strength are one," "The Tattooer" is almost too concentrated in
its objectification of art in a single image. Seikichi is all artist and the
girl all art. The spider is an image at once too vivid and too repellent
for generalization, and the world of the work has a nightmare quality
that separates it from the world of ordinary humanity. Nevertheless,
the very brevity of the story provides a concentrated pattern for the
image of the other arts in a number of Tanizaki's other works—a
specific figure in female form that suggests a powerful ideal—and the
story itself is a particularly clear and direct statement about the capacity art has for absorbing life.

Other stories involve a similar dynamic. In "Shunkinshō" (A
Portrait of Shunkin), for example, the beautiful and cruel Shunkin
exacts absolute service and adoration from her devoted disciple and
lover, Sasuke, but she in turn becomes a form for his own creation
after her death. So much is this the case that the detached narrator
of the story finds it difficult to separate the woman and the artist
from the myth: "I suppose that in the two decades in which he lived
alone, he created a Shunkin quite remote from the actual woman yet
more vivid in his mind."[19] His narrator's observation in this story
captures a distinction between Tanizaki's concept of embodied feminine beauty and Kawabata's. We might say that, whereas
Kawabata's art tends to describe beauty as if it were a "found" object, spontaneously occurring in the purity of a voice or the poignance of a maple tree, Tanizaki tends to emphasize a similarity
(indeed frequently an absolute identity) in the function of female
beauty and of art as "created" object. Here again the sharpness of
Enchi's observation that Kawabata's deeper invasion of the envisioned represents a "coldbloodedness" that implies that the object's
essence indeed lies in her image can be appreciated. By foreground-
ing the process of the creation of the "beautiful" as an act of the
masculine imagination, Tanizaki's narratives tend to keep us aware of
the separation that exists between the "actual woman" and her re-
creation as a desired object.

---

[19] Ibid., "A Portrait of Shunkin," p. 17.

Although "The Tattooer" presents us with an image of their union, "The Portrait of Shunkin" indicates the distance between the myth and the actuality. Likewise, in "Ashikari" a great deal of the atmosphere of a dream within a dream, conveyed by a narrative within a narrative, depends upon the careful building up of the vision of the Eternal Woman suggested by Oyu, a spoiled Meiji beauty who is able to live her life in the manner of a Heian court lady in "some old and mellowed picture." When the narrator of the frame tale, who had to that point been thoroughly engrossed in listening to a story told by one Serizawa (a mysterious curio dealer he met one night on a river bank), attempts to apply logic to romance, the whole is dissipated. Calculating that, if the middle-aged man he has met is the second generation of devoted worshippers of the fabulous Oyu, the woman herself "must be very old by now—almost eighty," the first narrator proves himself unworthy of the dream of the beauty of the Eternal Woman, and the curio dealer, the illusion (and the narrative) evaporate simultaneously in the final sentences: "But where he had been sitting, there was nothing to be seen save the tall grasses swaying and rustling in the wind. The reeds which grew down to the water's edge were fading from sight, and the man had vanished like a wraith in the light of the moon."[20]

Like Serizawa, however, most of Tanizaki's protagonists are faithful to a dream of eternal beauty, and although prone to attach artistic values to her, to find her image in art, or to make art of her image and her form, there is considerable variation in the specific dimensions that individual protagonists assign to their dream. Some stories, for example "Aguri" and *Chijin no ai* (Naomi)[21] present a feminine ideal in Western terms, but in others Tanizaki works with various images drawn from Japanese culture. Shifts in his own literary and personal values, which run from an interest in and emulation of such Western writers as Poe and Baudelaire early in his career to a deliberate turning to the Japanese culture in mid-career,[22]

---

[20] Tanizaki Jun'ichirō, *Ashikari and the Story of Shunken*, trans. Roy Humpherson and Hajime Okita (New York: Greenwood Press, 1970), p. 67.

[21] Tanizaki Jun'ichirō, *Naomi*, trans. Anthony H. Chambers (New York: Knopf, 1985).

[22] This is neither a smooth nor a consistent transition, but part of his movement toward Japanese aesthetic models is probably related to his labor of translating the *Genji monogatari* into modern Japanese. It is perhaps not coincidental that *Sasame yuki*

are mirrored in his fiction.

Especially interesting for us, therefore, is *Tade kuu mushi* (Some Prefer Nettles, 1928), which captures the shift toward the Japanese model as it takes place. Important in this work, too, is a certain "normalization" of the relationship to the presence of the female in art. Kaname, its protagonist, is neither an artist nor very active or original in seeking the concrete embodiment of his ideal woman. He is bored with his wife; they are considering divorce, and a continuing relationship with the Eurasian prostitute Louise has served merely to indulge him in "something of his longing for Europe." When Louise, in the course of the work, seems to have a dream of her own that would involve switching to the more regularized status of mistress, Kaname is horrified: "The picture of her coming into a narrow little room through an ill-fitting door and walking across the puffy insubstantiality of a badly made floor matting, her bobbed hair emerging from a wifely cotton kimono—somehow the picture had its disenchanting aspects."[23] Because she has been cast in the role of the exotic Western beauty, Louise's wish for a more mundane security offends Kaname's sensibilities. It is enough to tempt him to abandon toying with "European" sensuality and to accelerate that turn to the Japanese culture which is already in progress in his consciousness.

His present father-in-law had touched off this process by reintroducing him to the Japanese puppet theater, the *bunraku*, and had pointed out the distinctively superior Japanese character of the puppet dolls which, unlike Western puppets "were worked from the inside, so that the surge of life was actually present under the clothes."[24] In the opening pages of the work, Kaname is essentially uninterested in the art form itself, a true spectator, objective, aware not only of the puppets but of the puppeteers, whose manipulation of them is clearly visible to the Japanese audience. But here, as in "The Tattooer," "Aguri," and "The Portrait of Shunkin," human flesh begins to surrender its life to art, and the spectator senses a vi-

---

(translated as *The Makioka Sisters*), his most extended treatment of the feminine consciousness at least in part from within, was completed following the years devoted to the translation.

[23] Tanizaki Jun'ichirō, *Some Prefer Nettles*, trans. Edward Seidensticker (New York: Perigee Books, 1981), p. 168.

[24] Ibid., p. 23.

tality, a meaning that seems the puppets' own. Kaname, in characteristic fashion for a Tanizaki protagonist, is particularly drawn to
Koharu,[25] the female puppet, who evolves before his eyes from a
single dolllike form representing one character in a particular play to
a symbol of beauty, of art, of Woman. Koharu, the puppet herself, is
separated from the verbal text of the play, which is voiced by narra-
tors seated in plain view to the side, and even from the attentive gestures of the master puppeteer who manipulates her. As Kaname
watches her she seems to take on the full power of what Roland
Barthes terms one of *bunraku*'s strengths, "the silent writing" of
"emotive gesture." Kaname, no longer heeding narrator or puppeteer,
is absorbed by meditation upon the doll's power to suggest an ideal:
"Perhaps this doll was the 'Eternal Woman' as Japanese tradition had
her." A whole culture, this time his own, becomes concentrated for
him in the tiny figure. Suddenly the old forms of the *bunraku* are
transformed into something he has been looking for for some time, a
"vague dream" of "something in women or in art that might transfix
him," that "had to have about it a certain radiance, the power to in-
spire veneration."[26]

Koharu seems to him to possess that power, which, until now,
Kaname had seen no possibility of tapping. He soon realizes that his
father-in-law has already managed to create in his mistress, O-hisa, a
figure that comes close to being the actualization of such a dream.
Later, when he travels to Awaji with the two of them, he will become fascinated by the strong resemblance between O-hisa and the
puppets, although initially he had not considered this as particularly
attractive, dismissing O-hisa's place in the old man's life with the
comment, "She's one of the antiques in his collection, exactly like an
old doll."[27] The trip to Awaji, however, marks a stage in the evolution of his consciousness and in the concretization of his vague
dream of art and woman in terms of the puppet theater. In fact, the
very unreality of the life that his father-in-law has created for himself with O-hisa begins to exert a powerful influence upon Kaname:

---

[25] "Our" Koharu, in fact, since Chikamatsu's "Shinjū ten no Amijima" is the play
being performed.

[26] *Some Prefer Nettles*, p. 25.

[27] Ibid., p. 7.

"The old man's life—off to Awaji, appointed like a doll on the stage, accompanied by a doll, in search of an old doll to buy—seemed to suggest a profound spiritual peace, reached without training and without effort."[28]

Without training and without effort—this is not, of course, any longer the experience of the artist for whom training and effort are the costs of creation. Kaname is not a maker of dreams, merely a dreamer of dreams suggested by others. Yet he is not unaware of the process through which those dreams have come to have their being: "What of folk arts like this puppet theater—have they not become what they are with the help of fixed standards? The heavy-toned old country plays in a sense have in them the work of the race."[29] As dreamer rather than doer, Kaname hopes that he, too, might somehow acquire "the work of the race," without effort and without pain. At the close of the work, he is alone in his father-in-law's house with O-hisa while his wife and her father have gone out to discuss the impending divorce, and Kaname senses that his dream is coming closer. Just as he had come to view the puppet theater as an art with deep roots in the Japanese spirit, he now recognizes that what he terms the "type O-hisa," the doll woman has roots in his own spirit.

In O-hisa his father-in-law had re-created the vision of Woman presented in the puppet theater, and Kaname in turn appropriates the vision: "The O-hisa for whom his secret dream searched might not be O-hisa at all, but another, a more O-hisa–like O-hisa. And it might even be that this latter O-hisa was no more than a doll."[30] The interchangeability of Woman, doll, and dream become even clearer as he lies on his bed in the guest room: "For an instant he saw O-hisa's face, faint and white, in a shadowy corner beside the bed. He started up, but quickly caught himself. It was the puppet the old man had brought back from Awaji, a lady puppet in a modest kimono."[31] Now, whatever the dolls had come to mean for Kaname, their meaning clearly has its physical manifestation in the

---

[28] Ibid., p. 153.
[29] Ibid., p. 143.
[30] Ibid., p. 196.
[31] Ibid., p. 201.

figure of the actual woman who appears beside him in the dim light as *Some Prefer Nettles* ends: "The door slid open and this time, half a dozen old-style books in arm, it was not a puppet that sat faintly white in the shadows beyond the netting."[32]

It hardly seems to matter. *Some Prefer Nettles* closes with Kaname alone in the dim room with two white shapes beside his bed—one a doll and one a woman to whom it has a strong symbolic connection—as "The Tattooer" ends with a final glimpse of the tattoo blazing on a young girl's back. Dreamer and dream. In both works, as in "The Portrait of Shunkin" and "Aguri," a clearly marked image of art has added to the emotional reverberations connected with the female form. We can no longer tell the singer from the song, the dancer from the dance. In Tanizaki's work, the artist's nightmare and the dreamer's dream, the pain of creation or "a profound spiritual peace reached without training and without effort" alike find their realization in the Eternal Woman bodied forth in some real woman's flesh.

Although in works like these art serves as a metaphor for Tanizaki's own aestheticization of the female, the process of rendering a specific woman into the idealized Woman is equally central in many works like "Ashikari" and *The Key*, where no single, strong image of art is used to capture the fusion of ideal and flesh. Just as clearly many of Tanizaki's works play with a contrast between characters who represent the areas of *ninjō* and *giri* as he uses the traditional social roles of women to act as foils for his central image, the "Eternal Woman." Not only does the original Koharu figure prominently in Kaname's conception of this all-important figure, but she is counterpointed by the figures of Louise and O-hisa, who are the modern-day translation and semitranslation of her social function. Misako, Kaname's wife, although she has now taken a lover and become superficially Westernized, was for many years of their marriage the very pattern of a long-suffering, rejected wife.

The wife in "Ashikari" carries an Osan-like self-sacrifice to the extreme, for she helps to facilitate the love affair of her husband, the first Serizawa (unconsummated, we are assured by the second Serizawa), with her sister Oyu. In *The Diary of a Mad Old Man*, the eld-

---

[32] Ibid.

erly wife grumbles but is essentially in no position to do more when her husband, Utsugi, turns their highly Westernized daughter-in-law, Satsuko, a former dancer, into the object of his erotic fantasies. Utsugi even takes a kind of pleasure in speculating at the horror his Meiji-bred mother would feel at his present behavior: "Suppose Mother knew that her son Tokusuke, born in 1883, is alive today and is shamefully attracted to a woman like Satsuko—to her grand-daughter at that, the wife of her own grandson—and finds pleasure in being tantalized by her, even sacrificing his wife and children to win her love."[33] He finally comes to envision himself buried under those feet that have inspired him with erotic joy, for he fantasizes persuading Satsuko to allow him "to have her footprints carved on stone in the manner of the Buddha's and to have my ashes buried under that stone, my tombstone, the tombstone of Utsugi Tokusuke."[34]

But, except for *Some Prefer Nettles*, where the image of the Eternal Woman is inevitably colored by some of the devoted passion of the original Koharu, the women who act as the idols of Tanizaki's women-worshippers are all essentially cruel. Even in *The Key* (1956), a work in which the roles of both wife and mistress are combined in Ikuko, the wife, the cruelty is evident. She is apparently manipulated in the opening pages into yielding to her husband's feverish desire to indulge in fantasies about what he sees as her true "natural gift," an insatiable sexuality which makes him declare in his diary, "If she had been sold to one of those elegant brothels in the old Shimabara quarter, she would have been a sensation, a great celebrity; all of the rakes in town would have clustered around her."[35]

One more in that series of fatal women who go along with masculine erotic fantasies that center around their physical bodies, Ikuko, in the initial entries in her counterpointing diary, would have us believe that she herself wishes nothing more than to fulfill the conventional expectations of the Japanese wife: "My parents brought me up to believe that a woman ought to be quiet and demure, cer-

---

[33] Tanizaki Jun'ichirō, *Diary of a Mad Old Man*, trans. Howard Hibbett (New York: Berkley Medallion Books, 1965), p. 71.

[34] Ibid., p. 125.

[35] Tanizaki Jun'ichirō, *The Key*, trans. Howard Hibbett (New York: Berkley Medallion Books, 1971), p. 7.

tainly never aggressive to a man."[36] Nevertheless, she is drawn into a kind of game in which she allows herself to become overcome by drink and drugs, and lies passive and naked under her husband's scrutiny while he examines her body "with the most scrupulous care," awed by the "utter purity of her skin." The ailing middle-aged husband seems like Utsugi in *The Diary of a Mad Old Man* as he drives his blood pressure ever higher. The sessions conclude in lovemaking and eventually progress to his photographing the nude woman under heavy lighting. In a way the dynamics of these encounters are reminiscent of the episodes in *The House of the Sleeping Beauties*, with an apparently unconscious woman completely surrendered to the male imagination, but here we have a wife of some thirty years serving an erotic function from which the truly unconscious virgins of the Kawabata story are precluded. Both works conclude in death, but it is not surprising that a writer who created a story like "The Tattooer" early in his career, and consistently created images of the cruel beauty and the woman-worshipper in his subsequent works, would conclude this work with the death of the husband.

In *The Key* the duet of confessional "secret" diaries that comprise the structure of the work serves to intensify its tone of intrigue and duplicity. Only in her final entry does Ikuko admit that she allowed herself to be drawn into the game by other than the most wifely of motives—"I'd told myself I was behaving like a devoted wife, even from an old-fashioned point of view"[37]—but in fact she goes on to confess that she had entered into a physical relationship with Kimura, a young colleague of her husband's whom he had introduced into the game to fan his own jealousy, and had ultimately used her husband's obsession to bring about his collapse and death. Thus like Okada in "Aguri," Utsugi in *The Diary of a Mad Old Man*, and Seikichi in "The Tattooer," the woman-worshipper is consumed by his own desire while the object of his obsession survives.

Whereas death seems often to claim the ephemeral representations of beauty as Woman in Kawabata, the Eternal Woman whom Tanizaki's protagonists pursue shows a hardiness in keeping with her designation. Perhaps because his representation confines the mascu-

---

[36] Ibid., p. 10.
[37] Ibid., p. 123.

line realm to the surface, Tanizaki manages to convey the personality
of his female characters as something apart from the dream his protagonists seek so avidly to create. Thus even in two stories whose
surface structures have the similarities of *Sound of the Mountain* and
Diary of a Mad Old Man —an elderly man in love with a daughter-
in-law living in his home—the tone of the works is quite different.
Kikuko, the daughter-in-law of the Kawabata work, is a traditional
representation of wifely suffering from a husband's unfaithfulness, at
the very moment when she comes to represent the unattainable and
the pure to Shingo, her father-in-law, who tries to intervene in his
son's affair with Kinu. In Tanizaki's *Diary of a Mad Old Man*, in contrast, Satsuko, the image of the erotic in the work, is encouraged by
her victim to develop the cruel aspects of her nature, and Utsugi
himself is unrestrained in the expression of his passion except by the
impotence and senility of old age. Although Satsuko permits her
father-in-law limited physical liberties, she manages quite literally to
profit from his indulgence without losing her own identity. If the female figures in Kawabata, then, seem to be subsumed by the images
they present and to find their lives therein, in Tanizaki it is the male
protagonists who are living to find and to create such images. In
both cases the element of aestheticization is strong, but what is seen
as inherently residing within the Woman in Kawabata is recognized
by Tanizaki to be the product of the masculine imagination.

As we have noted previously, such aestheticizations are largely
absent in the representation of the female by women authors. That
is only to be expected if we realize that "a female consciousness"
does not look upon the female as other. Beyond this, though, in
works by women there is no evidence of a significant parallel
representation of the male in aestheticized terms. This is not to say
that they are incapable of aestheticization as such nor that they invariably avoid picturing a male consciousness, merely that they do
not depict male figures as aesthetic objects for the purposes and to
the degree that male writers tend to objectify, aestheticize, or idealize
the female. Nobu and Shōtarō of "Takekurabe" and Tomioka of
Ukigumo, for all their centrality in these works, are not rendered in
aesthetic terms, but in terms of the dynamics of their relationships to
others. Thus, even though Tomioka is the object of Yukiko's passion,
he retains a nearly total autonomy in the narrative, wholly apart

from Yukiko's desires, and she does not ascribe a significance to him that transcends the limits of his own actual existence. Moreover, even Enchi, among the women whose works we have examined perhaps the most continually conscious of the specific social dimensions of the Japanese woman's role in life, can nevertheless produce a sensitive depiction of a male protagonist. Her Yunosuke of "Yuki ore" is as convincing a rendering in its way as is Kawabata's narrator in "The Mole" and as are the title characters of Tanizaki's *Makioka Sisters*.

Yunosuke, an aging man, encounters Kimi, a woman he had known in her long-ago geisha days; and as they renew their essentially casual acquaintanceship, his loneliness and sense of alienation from his family and the world of the young and useful around him abate. But the tenuous sense of belonging that he experiences is shattered by Kimi's death as the story ends, and the point of view and narrative line convey a sensitive portrayal of the emotions, actions, and thoughts of its elderly protagonist. Similar portrayals of convincing male figures can be found in works by others of the writers whom we have discussed. By and large, however, nothing in such representations resembles either the patterns of representations we have observed in Kawabata and Tanizaki or the aestheticization of the male figure that occurs in the great classical model of feminine fiction, the *Genji monogatari*. Murasaki's "Shining Prince," Genji himself, does not find a modern counterpart in writing by women. This is another area in which the woman writer of the last century has diverged from the past, and the divergence itself is a manifestation of changes in the literary context since Murasaki wrote.

There has been a clear shift in the locus of aesthetic control. When the Heian classics were created, aestheticization appears from its verbal traces to have been meant as the recording of responses, the registering of sensitivity to the natural and sensual world. The aestheticized portrayal of Genji as a "thing of beauty" depends heavily upon the depiction of his unexampled degree of superiority in both demonstrating and evoking the most elegant sensibility. Thus, his choice of dress, high birth, grace in dancing, radiance of face, susceptibility of heart, fragrance of body, and exquisite taste in matters of art and literature conjure up a vision of the Heian ideal.

While the character of Genji is no doubt judged differently by the standards of later centuries, he nevertheless represents a construction of the desirable love object of his own times. That he was created at all suggests a kind of confidence on the part of his creator, not only in her own judgment and taste in imaging such a character, but in the fitness of such an activity for the feminine mind. No more than Michitsuna no haha need she question the importance of setting down her vision of the desirable, and no less than either does Sei Shōnagon exercise in *The Pillow Book* a similar right to discriminate between shades and levels of beauty, perfection, and acceptability. The right moment of the day for each season, the most delicate harmony of colors in dress, the most pleasing behavior for a lover are all subjects of discussion that offer the writer an opportunity to manifest her own sensitivity or responsiveness. In an age when the celebration of such subtleties was the purpose of literature, it is no wonder that the male ideal would also be delineated in aesthetic terms.

By the modern period both literature and society had changed drastically. Women were no longer virtually the sole arbiters of aesthetic taste in prose, writers were no longer aristocrats, and the activity of writing itself bore little resemblance to a refined occupation (the filling of idle hours by developing an exquisite sense of discrimination based upon a knowledge of the poignance and the ephemeral beauty of the world of things, *mono no aware*), becoming rather a way of making a living and of refracting new conditions that governed the experience of women. Consequently, there is not only a different motivation behind literary production, but from Ichiyō to Kurahashi we can trace shifting economic realities that controlled the writers' own lives and are mirrored in their writing.

More explicit, too, in modern fiction is the recognition of social and familial constraints as they influence the actual dimensions of well-defined social roles, roles that bear little resemblance to those of the Heian aristocrat but are not yet free of the history of more recent centuries. Since the Tokugawa period these roles, as first developed along the lines of Koharu and Osan—love object and (abandoned or ignored) wife—have been the staples of much masculine fiction, and the love object herself has come to be the fulcrum of an aestheticizing process that finds its fullest expression in fiction by men. Why, then, we must ask, is the interconnection of love or desire and objectified aestheticization largely absent in works by modern women writers? If they only rarely depict either male or female characters in aestheticized terms, why do they do this when they do, and what do they render in aesthetic terms in place of the human form?

Although we have dealt with only a limited number of texts by selected women in the present volume, even this sampling indicates how significant the whole area of comparative aesthetics must be in understanding the relative use of the concept of sexuality as theme, image, and symbol of power and authority in works by women and men. Here, a significant exception to the observation that women writers do not objectify the male as love object must already have occurred to the reader—Kurahashi's "Natsu no owari." There is no doubt that the sisters in this story are doing precisely what the Kawabata protagonists implicitly and the Tanizaki protagonists explicitly do. Even more obvious is the fact that Kurahashi is here making evident an intimate modern association between aestheticization as objectification and the assertion of power as an exercise in destruction and violence. Kurahashi's reference to K as *objet* in fact comes at a point of the text where the narrator describes the initial discussion of K's murder between the sisters. A less obvious instance of the connections between art, objectification, and power is can be found in "The Enchantress," where Enchi uses the destruction of the rare vase in the story within a story as "an act of revenge." The story nevertheless recognizes the use (and abuse) of the image of art as an assertion of control. But behind such relatively rare depictions and behind Kin's deliberate re-creation of herself as a beautiful, ageless object in Hayashi's "Late Chrysanthemum" lies an acknowledgment of objectified beauty as an instrument of power and of the fact that those who possess that power of visualization have the capacity to bring about either their own destruction or that of the imaged other.

Kurahashi's narrator, in her assumption of the authority to turn another human being into an *objet*, makes the rule clear by violating the convention. She defies a cultural assumption that such power is inappropriate in a young girl who "ought" to embody rather than project such a conceptualization, and it is part and parcel of the project of Kurahashi's early modernist stories that even the tacit assumptions of her society are thus openly confronted and reversed. The game in "Natsu no owari" is profoundly unsettling to generalized literary conventions concerning the woman's role in society. Even more unsettling, however, would be the concept of a modern woman writer who explicitly made it the aim of her literary career to depict the male object of love in that single unchanging instant of "pure beauty" that Kawabata searches for in his fiction and that Kurahashi's sisters kill to preserve. And almost unthinkable would be the notion of a second woman writer who depicted the protagonists of her works as being women in pursuit of the Eternal Man. A partial proof of the difficulty such a task would entail is captured in the story line of Enchi's "Fuyu momoji." In this story Enchi (the most frequently identified of our woman writers as "aesthetically oriented") created a middle-aged protagonist named Eiko, a widow in love with a young man she had originally thought of as a possible husband for her niece. Her vague yearnings and fantasies about the possibility of a relationship with the young man are shattered when Fujiki, a male friend of her own age, confesses to her that he is going to have to divorce his wife because his young mistress has become pregnant with his child. Eiko realizes suddenly how different her own circumstances and dreams are.

> Even though she was a year younger, the fact that she could never have children now changed the way in which she could love a man as young as that.
>
> Feeling acutely how separate were the experiences of men and women, the sadness of being only an old woman surged through her body, washing over Eiko like a chill fog.[38]

Enchi, then, makes explicit the recognition that time operates differently upon men and women and underlines the only marginal social acceptability of an aging woman having fantasies about the male in terms of youth and beauty. Clearly indicated in "Fuyu momoji" is the double standard, which suggests that only men may actively and appropriately pursue such a dream throughout their lives.

For women to depict women as having the power to turn the male into an object is only possible, it would seem, in the antiworld of modernism. Even Hayashi's Kin objectifies only herself, a woman, and then with a cynical but also resigned understanding of the way

---

[38] *Enchi Fumiko zenshū* (Tokyo: Shinchosha, 1977), vol. 3, p. 141.

in which her ability to have presented herself as an aesthetic object for so long has enabled her to wrest financial security from men while remaining free of the subservience of the domestic dependent. Women writers in the modern age, then, seem to perceive and present the aestheticization of the human as the prerogative of the male. Aside from Kurahashi's protagonists, the female characters in their works are time-bound, unwilling or unable to use the flesh of another as a symbol of breaking free from the life cycle. There seems in their works to be an understanding that a kind of violence or destruction is inherent in the artistic rupture of the flow of living in the name either of physically embodying a transcendent moment of pure and fragmented beauty or of attempting to concretize an eternal ideal in a mortal being. In their works, aestheticization occurs more frequently in the illuminating significance of the natural world (the snow in "Yuki no mau yado," the swirling waters of *Uzushio*), in underlining the significance of an event (the scrap of cloth in "Takekurabe"), in visions like that of Saku of "Himojii tsukihi" who has a liberating dream of a beautiful bird shortly before she dies, or in the creation of nonhuman metaphors for the aesthetic process (the title and developed metaphor of *Kizu aru tsubasa* [Crippled wing], where the need to write is envisioned as a crippled bird's dream of flight).

While similar instances of aestheticization may be cited in works by men, it is evident in their works that women, too, are partially envisioned as objects outside of normal social interchange, and they become a significant means by which the male writer seeks to project his desire to transcend the mundane conditions of normalized patterns. Thus, in those very centuries wherein the *ie*, the family, was formally instituted as a controlling structure in the life of the individual and fitted as the smallest social unit into the hierarchical structure of the nation as a whole, and when women's position in that family and that social structure was rigidly defined in terms of submission, obedience, and duty, an entire "floating world" grew up around those aspects of human experience that the Neo-Confucianism of the Tokugawa era cast as it were outside acceptable social structure.

Not normal social interchange, but economic exchange, however, was at the base of the visions of sensual pleasure that were the stock in trade of what J. E. DeBecker terms "the nightless city," and it is the "nightless city" of the pleasure quarters that became a principal literary focus not only for frankly erotic but for popular genres. Curiously, the "licentiousness" that the upper-class Heian female writers seemed to represent in the eyes of Neo-Confucian purists (in that they combined respectable social position with an apparent, though limited, sexual freedom) was replaced with a licensed "licentiousness," separating the experience of women into two categories. In fiction the male writer and his protagonist could slip from world to world, from *ninjō* to *giri*, and find or portray the woman who represented each; but it is not to be expected that women in either actual role would experience through it the sense of choice, of variation, that their simultaneous existence, appeals, and demands could suggest and would continue to suggest in masculine fiction. It was not, after all, in the Tokugawa period that the woman writer began to emerge and to recast the literary image of those times into the forms of her own experience; only in the Meiji era, as new trends of thought suggested a limited increase in social possibilities for the woman, did women writers finally begin to address their own age once more and to evaluate the heritage hidden within their centuries of silence.

Not too surprising, then, is the relative frequency of a return to the past in writers such as Enchi and the popular Ariyoshi Sawako, for the largely untold story of the women of the Tokugawa and early Meiji periods is seen as one of the sources of the modern woman's experience in Japan. *The Waiting Years* is just one of those works in which a writer looks back upon a past era and tells its history as a woman's experience. "Otoko no hone" is explicit in its endeavor to uncover the stories of buried women, and Ariyoshi in *Ki no kawa* (The River Ki) and *Hanaoka Seishu no tsuma* (The Doctor's Wife) is also seeking to reconstruct a past inhabited by women. In doing so, it seems only natural that they should avoid the aestheticization of both male and female characters and the disruption of human temporality. On the contrary, female characters in fiction by women are frequently constructed for the purpose of recovering the past, establishing a continuum of historical experience, emphasizing the influence of traditional ways of thinking on the roles that women presently play in Japanese society, and establishing the significance of women's lives in terms of duration and endurance. Given the historical and social context of the new literary age of the woman writer, it is natural, too, that depictions of the male figures in her works should not follow the path pursued by male writers since the Tokugawa, constructing a parallel mode of representing masculine characters as aesthetic objects.

Having been herself exposed to a literary tradition in which such objectification has been principally applied to her own sex, the woman writer is not inclined to be naïve about the cost of commodification to the human consciousness. Characterizations as early as Ichiyō's Midori and O-riki (of "Nigorie") indicate both the economic motivation that pervaded the "floating world" and the psychological cost of existence as a merchandisable, physical object. Nor do Ichiyō and the others ignore the tenuous nature of other roles available to women. In "Jūsan'ya" the unhappy young wife is made aware by her father that leaving her husband would have a disastrous impact upon her family's comfort and hopes. The future for the marginal workers in Sata's "Kyarameru kōjō kara" is even bleaker. Riyo in "Tokyo" faces no easier circumstances, and even the middle aged, middle-class women of Sata's "Yuki no mau yado" and those like them who abound in Enchi 's fiction are depicted as very much constrained by a definition of "feminine" social roles and codes of behavior that do not accord with the psychological realities they recognize. Living neither in instants of piercing ephemeral beauty nor in the eternal dimension of the symbol, these women have a different kind of "meaning." They "mean" to survive, to endure, to inscribe themselves on time in mortal terms.

However he may be depicted in the works of Japanese women, the Japanese male represents a factor of control, of authority, and sometimes, frankly, of oppression in creating the social dimensions that these writers see as limiting their protagonists' real options. As fathers, husbands, and lovers they achieve no status similar to that of Woman in the writing of Japanese men. Neither trivialized nor idealized in feminine fiction, they seem almost not to be "there" as aspects of formal art, for, since they serve as the delineators of the scope of the lives of wives, daughters, and lovers, they are so implicated in the social framework and economic necessities of which the female protagonists' lives are constructed as to be almost indistinguishable from the circumstances of life itself. Even where they are clearly the objects of a female protagonist's passion or desire they are seldom objectified. For objectification, to be successful, depends upon an assured relationship with the structures of real power within a society, just as objectification as aestheticization represents the refraction of real cultural authority. Obviously, the Heian woman possessed such authority in a very literal (literary) sense. Obviously, the modern writer can claim no such aesthetic power in a culture still clearly dominated by a formalized double standard. In literature, then, woman may exercise the power conveyed upon her by the masculine imagination. Tanizaki's fiction attests to this; Kin in Hayshi's "Late Chrysanthemum" is an interpretation of the role from within. But except for verbal acts like Kurahashi's defiance of the power of convention, the modern writer has no equivalent cultural empowerment in her own day to create an image of the male as the product of female imaginings.

If male critics, looking at the way in which men are depicted through the eyes of the woman writer, are inclined to agree with Yamada Yūsaku's statement that women writers do not represent a masculine consciousness in their works,[39] perhaps the reasons for this are more complex than obscure. Women's writing has less of the *onnarashisa* than does Kawabata's depiction of the "feminine" consciousness. The *onnarashisa*, after all, is largely a construction of male desiring, the imaging by a culturally dominant group of an Otherness termed Woman. However strong, however enduring, however deeply women may be shown to be embedded in the nation's culture and consciousness, they cannot be demonstrated to have the economic, social, and political status publicly accorded to the male. The opposite of Otherness escapes the notice of the dominant culture, for it lies in the most public aspect of that dominant culture itself. When women represent men in terms of their relationship to a female protagonist, in terms of mere events and mere actions, or in the terms of life's natural progression, as Enchi does in "Yuki ore," they are normalizing the male and making of "masculinity" a simple and direct part of human experience. Endowed only with the recog-

[39] Yamada Yūsaku, "Otoko o egaku joryū bungaku no me," *Kaishaku to kanshō* 41 (November 1976): 77–83.

nizable powers, privileges, and prerogatives that society has already accorded to masculinity, the male figure loses the mythical or magical dimension accorded to the human being whose own sources of strength are difficult to trace because difficult to document. And, having raised the *onnarashisa* to so high a degree of artfulness, the male writer may be less willing or less able to abandon his conceptualization of the feminine in favor of the merely female. There is no "Masculine Mystery" equivalent to what must seem the *hidden* powers of the "Feminine." The Eternal Woman of art is alive and flourishing; the Shining Prince is dead.

Is't love or fancy, maid or myth—
I cannot tell you—all that I know is
She with her innocent charm has entranced me.
Almost transparently fragile and slender
Dainty in stature, quaint little figure,
Seems to have stepped down
Straight from a screen.
But from her background of varnish and lacquer—
Suddenly light as a feather she flutters,
And like a butterfly, hovers and settles.
With so much charm and such seductive graces,
That to pursue her a wild wish seized me—
Though in the quest her frail wings should be broken.

Pinkerton to Sharpless, *Madame Butterfly*

CONCLUSIONS

CHAPTER EIGHT

Conclusion: Daughters of the Moon

"SINCE THE IMAGES YOU DEMAND cling to me," Nishi Junko begins her poem "Revolution," "I cannot form my own image." And yet the poem itself suggests a forming and dissolving of each image, a forming and dissolving implicit, sometimes explicit, in any comparison of the representation of women by male and female writers. Perhaps, after all, the Heian period was a time when actual men faded into obscurity before the Shining Prince. As the centuries since his creation elapsed, however, the voice of the Japanese woman writer grew still—until, that is, the past century, when something that cannot quite be called a dialogue began. Rather, like the contrapuntal diaries of Tanizaki's *The Key*, there are male voices and female voices. They are not actually talking to each other; they are not talking about the same thing in the same way; but what each one says has to do with what the others say, what the others see or want to see.

For the Japanese reader both kinds of voice are audible—and distinct. A partial refeminization of Japanese letters is underway. The number of women writers has grown steadily since World War II. By 1965 the *Mainichi Shimbun* had brought out an eight-volume anthology of short fiction entitled *Gendai no joryū bungaku*, which contains selections from the writing of more than sixty contemporary Japanese women writers. The Women's Writers Association, formed in the war years, has been annually awarding a coveted prize for women's fiction, and, with the exception of Ichiyō, each of the writers whose works we have considered has been a recipient of this award. That this does not represent a recognition of a subgenre within a broader literary perspective is indicated by the fact that the same writers have garnered the Noma, Tanizaki, and Kawabata literary prizes among them. But the Women's Writers Association and its prize makes the commonality of concerns of women writers visible, valorized, and public. Given the context of our discussion of the term *onnarashisa*, moreover, it is not particularly surprising to discover that the "refeminization" of Japanese fiction can be said to have been accompanied by a kind of "defeminization" of the Japanese woman's experience that removes it from the exclusive province of the male writer's conceptualization of it and her. Her self-images in literature have diverged from the way the roles of women have been depicted and from the images through which they have been represented in the centuries when male writers dominated the field of prose. Available to readers in Japan, then, throughout the century just past, has been an ever growing number of works that see the Japanese woman's position in her society as something different and something more.

From the Meiji period on this was inevitable. The "new woman" envisioned by progressive male thinkers was to be late in emerging as a figure in writing by women themselves and differed markedly from the masculine projections, probably because such writers as Ichiyō adopted a less idealistic but more experiential view concerning the weight of past tradition upon the potential of their present. Again, especially among socialist intellectuals, male writers of the early twentieth century evidenced a concern with the working class woman's plight considerably before a strong core of women emerged in the proletarian school of literature. But however praiseworthy it may have been for Nakano Shigeharu to urge that Sata tell the story of the proletarian woman and the children of the working class, it was the experience of Sata's own life and the dimensions of her own perspective that would validate the stories that she wrote. In them, she chooses to thematize the woman's actual experience of her own times in the context of a double view. The personal conflicts involved in maintaining a political and social commitment in the midst of domestic strife inform her novel *Kurenai*. Not the ideal, but the discrepancy between ideal and real becomes a locus of concern in her works and remains evident beneath even the idyllic surface of stories such as "Yuki no mau yado." Such thematicizations are evident in Enchi's work also; and when Hayashi chooses to deal with women as the marginal and the impoverished, she broadens the justification for actions in conflict with traditional mores. Her most significant fiction was produced during the period of upheaval following the war, when history reinforced her emphasis upon the vulnerability of women in their struggle for survival.

Having thus divested herself and her writings of the images that had been projected upon them by man's desiring, the Japanese woman found herself confronting her own history rather than the dreams of others, and the power of her writing rises from this act of self-creation. In the 1920s, for example, a woman known as Haruko-ma, working in a brothel and despairing over the life she leads, "confessed" to her diary that she was considering suicide. She discarded the thought, however, because she dreamed of avenging herself upon those who had debased her: "And I can't die without avenging myself on the broker, the proprietor and the men who have plunged me into this dark abyss. I can't die, after having been brutalized by these people, without doing battle against them."[1] The manner in which she prepares to battle against her enemies and against the former self who allowed her to become a victim is instructive.

> I must first kill my old self before I can do the work I must do here. I am now reborn.... As the first step on my road to vengeance, I shall keep this secret diary. This is my only consolation and it is also a declaration of my war of revenge against these people. Oh, diary! You are my friend, my master, my God! You shall keep my life pure and refined.[2]

In turning to the word to redeem her life, the prostitute Harukoma is adhering to a persistent tradition among Japanese women. She determines on a path of endurance and resistance and sees the power of the written word as capable of sustaining her. Many of the women of the Yoshiwara were too desperate or too uneducated to be able to make the same choice,[3] but to the extent that their story can survive and be seen as other than the charming vision of the "floating world" that we glimpse in the wood-block prints of the

---

[1] Mikiso Hane, *Peasants, Rebels and Outcasts: The Underside of Modern Japan* (New York: Pantheon Books, 1982), quoted on pp. 216–217.

[2] Ibid.

[3] Ibid., p. 215.

pleasure quarters then the images of centuries of Harukomas cannot be totally effaced.

Like the self whom Harukoma seeks to create in her "secret diary," the female protagonists in literature by Japanese women have more to do with strength and survival than with daintiness and fragility, more to do with history and social limitations than with fantasy. They contain more resistance to the extinction of the will than transparent yielding to ephemerality. The woman writer again and again returns to this theme of endurance, as though the largely silent struggle of Midori against the inevitabilities of life in the pleasure quarters, Hiroko against the economic deprivation and exploitation of the female factory worker, Riyo against loneliness and poverty, Tomo against the loss of her place in the family and of self-respect can find its easing only in the writers' own telling. That is why in "Otoko no hone" the "letter in Chise's blood" motivates the tale and symbolizes a bond between the experiences of women. That is why there is even a connection between Harukoma's diary and the equally vengeful tones of the narrative of "Natsu no owari"; the two works share an imperative to create a realm of negation in which language is used for the assertion of an aggressive will, in which it plots in secret and attempts to distance emotion in the name of gaining control over that anti-"world of words" which is all that is left to it.

Varied as the works of the Japanese women have been, this common theme indicates that even where an individual author's work can most effectively be appreciated by examining it within the literary context of its particular period, the reader can also glimpse a connection to a shared realm of experience that belongs most particularly to women. Japanese readers are, of course, well aware of this and recognize that, behind the cultural definitions that women writers may share with them, there is an emphasis upon a kind of inner toughness that such writers have tended to validate in their protagonists and that contrasts with the more symbolic representations of the feminine that many male writers prefer. Unlike the Western reader, the Japanese reader can hear both voices.

In spite of the reemergence of the woman writer in the century just past and especially of the abundance of women writing in the decades since the war, the Western reader is virtually unfamiliar with the tones and themes of the Japanese woman writer. Her creations seem in a perverse sense almost more "foreign" to Western eyes than is the vision of the exotic that seems to be so enticingly realized in projections of Japanese femininity by certain widely translated male writers. More drawn to the Eternal Woman or the transparent beauty of the moment by an implicit connection between the erotic and the exotic than to those writers who do not fit the formalizations that have grown up in the West about the Japanese woman, Western readers are at two further removes from their Japanese counterparts, for their appreciation of the power and complexity of the Japanese woman's approach to literature is obscured by visions, interpretations, and omissions that originate in their own culture.

Some of this shortsightedness, of course, has been prestructured by what is available in translation in the West. Only in very recent years have works by women made it past the barrier of language. The situation in criticism and analysis is much worse. Although Ichiyō's work has been the subject of a full-length study in English, the Taishō and Shōwa periods are virtually untouched, and even so obviously important a figure as the early feminist poet Yosano Akiko has not received the attention her work demands. We need not even agree with Hiratsuka Raicho's comparison of Ichiyō and Yosano to suspect in part that, even though, as we have seen, Ichiyō is not just telling one more story about "the sad fate of a weak woman," a kind of unconscious translation screen has been in operation. Many of Yosano's most feminist poems have not passed through that screen, while most of her translated poetry is more traditional in theme and form. Sata, in her turn, with an extensive oeuvre of short stories and novels, has suffered the fate until very recently also accorded Hirabayashi Taiko and Miyamoto Yuriko—the fate of being largely ignored as a subject for translation. Since she has strong leftist sympathies, translators in a culture with a definite suspicion of the left and an estimation that proletarian literature is, at the very best, merely dull but worthy, may deem her work ideologically unacceptable. We can, then, find possible reasons for the scarcity of works by women in translation, but that scarcity itself suggests that the first barrier may lie in unconscious assumptions underlying the choices made until very recent years.

Of course, we can only speculate as to why this should be so, since each translator's choice is both individual and personal. Perhaps the expectations of an academic discipline still largely masculine in its orientation have worked for the unconscious "selecting out" of those writers who did not fit the formalizations of the West, or who contradicted or defied cherished but tacit "values" that are part of the attraction the Japanese culture seems to exert upon the outside world. Moreover, perhaps the woman writer of Japan suffers from being lumped together with her Western counterparts in that outlying province called women's fiction. The woman writer has for so long been considered a "minor figure" in literature, especially in the United States, that works of women in other cultures, where they are and have been a more substantial and earlier literary presence, have automatically been discounted in advance. The last decade has seen attacks upon the American canon that call its gender distinctions into question, but the international repercussions of such labeling seem particularly cavalier in the case of Japan, where the classical age was built upon the prose writing of women. And, in fact, were more of the writing of modern Japanese women available in English, it is probable that the very different interactions between those who write and the contexts in which they write in Japan and the West could be especially illuminating to feminist criticism.

Western readers, however, are still at the mercy of a scarcity of materials. We have, consequently, been slow to perceive, let alone appreciate, the role that women writers have played in the twentieth-century literature of Japan. Full-length works by women have been especially rare in translation. Only very recently have a number of anthologies of short fiction by Japanese women been available in translation, and, not too surprisingly, all of the editors and translators of such anthologies have been women.[4] That is changing, radically, but we must ask ourselves why it has been so long in changing. We can and should still ask ourselves, moreover,

---

[4] Phyllis Birnbaum, ed. and tran., *Rabbits, Crabs, Etc.: Stories by Japanese Women* (Honolulu: University of Hawaii Press, 1982); Noriko Lippet and Kyoko Selden, eds. and trans., *Stories by Contemporary Japanese Women* (Armonk, N.Y.: M.E. Sharpe, 1982); Yukiko Tanaka and Elizabeth Hanson, eds. and trans., *This Kind of Woman: Ten Stories by Japanese Women Writers, 1960–1976* (Stanford: Stanford University Press, 1982).

why there has been such an imbalance in the messages we have long received from contemporary Japanese fiction. Like the weight of the Heian example, which became à frozen model of style and content that prevented women from adopting more current modes for centuries, the very "success" of the Japanese woman on one level of transcultural exchange may well have impeded recognition of her achievements on others. The very attractiveness of the Japanese woman as a cultural artifact or literary symbol of the exotic in the West has overshadowed, even obliterated, the achievements of the Japanese woman writer.

Pinkerton asks Sharpless, "Is't...maid or myth—I cannot tell you." (We suspect he hardly cares as he sketches in familiar outlines of his dream creature.) To him she appears "almost transparently fragile and slender, dainty in stature, quaint little figure"—a doll woman, in fact, deeply akin to Tanizaki's Koharu-Ohisa model in *Some Prefer Nettles*. The dynamic of aestheticization already inherent in "maid or myth" is intensified. She seemed "to have stepped down/Straight from a screen," unreal, that is, foreign (exotic). "But from her background of varnish and lacquer" she ultimately becomes metaphorically nonhuman: "she flutters, and like a butterfly, hovers and settles." Poor Butterfly—the dynamic is clearly predetermined. We have seen its like in the works of Kawabata. Innocence, delicacy, fragility—all more/less than human—are aesthetically destined for the death incumbent upon the breaking of "her frail wings."

Utterly devoted, loyal, and submissive, Butterfly could not survive the moment of her signifying loveliness as a metaphor. And she doesn't, of course, but comes instead to signify, in all the permutations that will adhere to her image, a Western and masculine dream of the submissive beauty, outside the protection of custom and tradition, who will literally self-destruct when her existence becomes inconvenient or embarrassing. Something of the same perennial appeal of the transparent, ephemeral object of love, desire, and yearning is evident in Kawabata's aestheticization of women, especially in those of his works that have appeared in translation. Thus, it is not surprising that his imagery seems almost to flash across the gap of culture as dream meets dream. Small wonder, then, that the fictional metaphors through which the Japanese woman writer conveys her own aesthetic perception of women's relationship to their society are of less immediate attraction to Western translators and readers than is the reinforcement of the delicate, yielding Madame Butterfly who has for so long been a part of the Western fantasy about the Japanese woman. In other words, in Western eyes the Japanese woman is more appealing as a sign than as a signifier.

Fortunately, when she did write, the Japanese woman writer has always recognized her particular importance as a signifier. Michitsuna no haha, writing at the brilliant height of women's literary achievement ("In the beginning, woman was the Sun"), knew this. Her *Kagerō nikki* would correct the lies of the "old romances" and present her world as she lived in it. Harukoma, writing in a harshly different time and place ("Now she has become the Moon"), thought to do much the same thing and believed equally in the power and rightness of her own turning to the page as an act of self-creation, of setting the record of experience straight. The act was very similar; only the world had changed. When the Japanese woman writer once more began to fashion her verbal constructs of the society that is Japan, she no longer spoke in the language of the court aristocrat, but in that of modern Japan and in the accents of varied classes. Even in fiction, however, her task is much the same as that of Harukoma—to free herself from the images that cling, to form her own image, and to end the long centuries of silenced metaphor. When her voice can be heard clearly, and in all its variations in tone even in the West, her function in the literature of her own nation will be understood and her place in the literature of the world assured.

TRANSLATIONS

The Inn of the Dancing Snow
(Yuki no mau yado)
SATA INEKO

As the three women rode from Hanamaki Station to Shidotaira Hot Springs, only Haruko constantly scanned the scene outside the taxi window, as though looking for old friends.

"There used to be a little train running over there. Isn't that so, driver?" She pointed to the mountains on the right as she spoke. "How long has it been gone, I wonder?" Resigned to a lack of response from her two companions, she addressed the driver instead. But he was too young to know for sure, and gave only a vague reply.

"I don't know, perhaps ten years."

"I suppose you're right. A train like that one couldn't still be here. Just the same, it had such character!"

As their guide on the trip, Haruko wanted to share her memories of a visit thirteen years earlier. She had even told her friends about the tiny matchbox train that had toiled up the mountainside, puffing away. But it was gone now; a bus had taken its place, and a broad highway stretched out before them. The north Honshu countryside, almost bare of snow, held no interest for Akiye and Shigeko. It was still February; yet the sun that had shone through the window of their train from Tokyo had been warm, almost springlike.

After his graduation from the university, Akiye's son had found a job, married, and moved into a home of his own. Her old friends, Shigeko and Haruko, planned this trip to celebrate. When Akiye mentioned a desire to see snow in the quiet of the mountains, Haruko remembered that thirteen years before, returning from a family gathering, she and her husband had come up to this hot spring for three days. The two of them climbed down from the little train, and while they were trudging to the inn, the deeply piled snow squeaked under the weight of their feet. The sound—like someone rubbing heavy silk—had penetrated her heart, and that memory prompted her to suggest visiting this place once more.

Even in the village in the northern mountains, however, there was hardly any snow this time. Arriving at Shidotaira, Haruko was also shocked to find a large, modern hotel standing there. She expressed mortification, remarking, "How can it be so changed that there isn't even any snow?" and appeared to feel it was her fault that her companions' hopes had been disappointed. According to the driver, however, the scant snowfall was very unusual. Other things, such as the inn's entranceway, were changed, too, but at least the quiet peace of the gorge in which the hot spring nestled was still the same; and when they were shown to a room facing on a swift mountain stream, the tree-covered slopes that met their eyes were white with snow, and long icicles hung down from the rocks.

After they returned to their room from the hot spring's bath, Akiye gazed out at the stream and commented, "Well, it is the north, after all. Even the air in the halls is cold." It was growing dark, and while they were at the bath a light, powdery snow had begun to fall. "Look, it's started to snow! Everything's going to be just fine."

"So it has. Up here it's like that—just when you think the sun is out, it clouds over and starts snowing. I hope it really piles up!" Haruko was determined to put her friends in the right mood, and Shigeko, too, caught her excitement. Sitting next to Akiye and gazing at the stream, she remarked, "Well, after all, we did spend nearly seven hours coming all this way because you wanted to see the snow. That certainly was a natural wish on your part; however, you must have felt that way because you are in a special mood right now."

"What do you mean by 'special'?" Akiye laughed self-consciously.

"Well, don't people say that a son's marriage makes his mother feel deserted?" Shigeko had to phrase it this way, since she herself was childless.

Akiye turned back to the *kotatsu*, smiling slightly at this. "Yes, people are always saying that. Still, I don't feel that way at all. Because everyone talks that way, though, I sometimes wonder if I'm cold-hearted. However, I know how much I care about my children, so I don't really think I'm callous. It's just that when my son got married I wasn't at all sad. Instead, I felt that my responsibilities were lighter now that there is someone else to look after him."

"You've said that before," said Haruko, "but that's because you have your work. When my turn comes, I know that I'll burst into tears just the same."

Glancing at her, Akiye remarked with a laugh, "You'll still have your husband around, you know."

"Yes, of course," was Haruko's response, meek and somewhat abashed because Akiye's situation was rather more difficult than that of her two friends. Her husband had died when their son was still in junior high school, and from that time she on struggled to bring up her three children alone. She became a certified public accountant after her husband's death and had been working ever since.

The powdery snow was still falling when the evening meal was brought to their room shortly thereafter. As they looked out into the darkness, the swirling snow spread a whiteness abroad, and when blown about by the wind, it looked almost like the wild dance of living things. Inspired by that dance, Akiye exclaimed, "My, it's really falling now; it seems to welcome us—we who have come here to pay a call on the snow."

"I'm so glad," said Haruko and held out the sake bottle. "Well, then, shall I pour? For Akiye first..."

Offering her cup, Akiye said, "How wonderful here at this snowy inn to feel the happiness of being alive."

"Yes, indeed," Shigeko put in quietly, sensing the complex feelings in Akiye's words. She realized that, for Akiye, even "the happiness of being alive" meant cherishing the memory of her late husband.

Outside, the flowing stream made the only sound. The large hotel itself was quiet. It was a weekday, and there were no guests in the adjoining rooms.

"I'm so glad we decided to come here, aren't you?" asked Haruko, and the others agreed readily. After having lived separate lives for so long, the three good friends were united now by a feeling of closeness. Her eyes softened by the sake, Haruko felt that she could not hide from them that, from the time they had resolved on coming to this inn, she had been recollecting her former visit.

"Really, you know, I have many fond memories of this place," she said with a hesitant smile.

"With the two of you here alone, it must have been a second honeymoon."

"Well... you don't just leave the children behind and go off on a trip for no reason at all, you know."

"Something had happened, then?" Shigeko inquired, but her tone suggested that she already guessed what that "something" was. Akiye seemed to feel the same way; she brought her cup to her lips in silent anticipation of what Haruko would say.

"I was seriously considering a separation from my husband at the time." Haruko spoke in a tone that was almost self-mocking.

"And yet you came up here together?"

"That's right. I was acting very strangely then."

As she said this, Haruko reflected that there had been far more of injured pride than love in the way she had felt, for only after it had already gone on for a year did she discover that her husband, Kawada, an architect, had been having an affair with a woman who owned a bar he had designed. Haruko now thought her reaction on learning of the affair from one of her husband's subordinates—a young man she used to invite for an occasional home-cooked meal who, because of her kindness, felt oppressed by his complicity in Kawada's affair—had been frenzied.

One day the young man came to see Haruko. His face tense and his shoulders squared, he burst out, "I can't keep hiding this from you. First of all, I must tell you that all this time Mr. Kawada has not been staying at my place playing *mahjong.*"

The revelation did not take Haruko completely by surprise. Her wifely intuition had told her that something had indeed been going on. Later, when she confronted Kawada with an accusing look and demanded, "What's been going on?" he answered with deceptive nonchalance, "Nothing at all, why?" Haruko felt as if she were lost in a dense fog, and her suffering was all the more intense. But when she first learned of the affair, she stood rooted to the spot, unable to control the trembling of her body.

"Thank you, I understand completely," she said, bowing to the young man. And then she murmured, "How embarrassing this is!" The faint smile that had touched her lips had vanished in a shudder. "I suppose it's that woman." Haruko blurted out the name of the woman who owned the bar as if deliberately inflaming her own wound.

"Do you know her?" asked the startled young man, but she had already lost the power to respond, and her body felt as if it were being pounded by violent waves. After what she learned that evening, Haruko lashed out madly, openly confronting her husband. Just at this time there happened to be a gathering of Haruko's family, and even as she was contemplating a divorce, Haruko insisted that her husband accompany her to her parents' home. Then, upon their return, she declared that she was going off alone to the hot spring. Awestruck and uneasy at his wife's behavior, Kawada finally went along with her.

When the story reached this point, the two listeners caught their breath. Akiye broke into the narrative. "You knew all along that your husband would come with you didn't you?"

"I was not so confident as that. But if he hadn't come I would have killed myself out of spite. I hated him. It wasn't a matter of love, but rather of pride."

"But doesn't that mean that you loved him?"

"Well, I don't know. In any case, at that time I simply could not behave like a dutiful wife, enduring it all silently." While she was saying this, Haruko's eyes flashed as if she were reexperiencing old feelings. It was Haruko's nature to be energetic, and the way she had lured her husband to the hot spring seemed characteristically assertive.

Akiye smiled at this. "Well, you certainly handled it well. And so, this became the place of reconciliation for the two of you?"

Haruko nodded at these words as if she were still reliving past emotions. Her listeners might regard her story as just a sentimental recollection, but she was too caught up in the recital for that to matter.

Shigeko nodded in understanding. "Of course. That's why the memories here are so precious for Haruko."

And Akiye broke in once more. "And to think we had been kept in the dark about all this until you brought us here!"

Haruko's thoughts returned at last to the present moment, and she let out an embarrassed laugh. "Oh, my! I'm sorry. But that's not why I made you come."

"I was just teasing you," said Akiye. "It's marvelous here. The snow ... I wonder if it's still falling." She went to the window, drew back the curtain, and peered out. The snow fell without a sound; and although under the cover of the darkness the scene outside was turning white, it was only in those areas illuminated by outside lanterns that the swirling dance of the snow could be seen. "This snow is piling up. It should be wonderful tomorrow."

"Well, then, at least one of my responsibilities will be discharged," said Haruko. Her laughter was easy and cheerful now.

The three women had trouble falling asleep after they went to bed that night. They had rarely traveled together, and all three were thinking of Haruko's confession. Later, when Haruko expressed some embarrassment about her story, Shigeko remarked that something similar had happened to her, but Akiye asked in a sleepy voice if they couldn't talk about it the next day.

"Let's do that," Shigeko answered gently, for she surmised that though such stories were painful, Akiye must have felt that such matters were the concern of women who had husbands.

By morning the snowfall had stopped. A pale sun had emerged, and the whole landscape was brightened by the snow piled up on the surrounding mountains. The trees in the forest were whitened by drifts on one side of their trunks, and from time to time the snow heaped on the branches would drop off. Between banks smothered in pure whiteness, only the rapidly flowing stream made any sound. When the three friends put their heads out of the window, the clear, crisp air stung their faces.

"Shall we take a walk later on?" asked Haruko.

"Why don't we just admire the scenery from the *kotatsu*?" Akiye replied. "We wouldn't want to slip and fall." Her suggestion startled her friends, since she was the one who had wanted to come and see the snow in the first place, but it was true that the paths through the snow seemed quite deep with drifts.

"Well, shall we have another women's conversation, while we sit at the *kotatsu* and watch the snow?" This time Akiye spoke with studied politeness, but without sarcasm, for she remembered Shigeko's words of the previous night.

Shigeko spoke to her frankly. "I'm afraid that would hurt your feelings."

"Not at all. That subject doesn't upset me anymore." Akiye's answer was candid and spontaneous, but there was a dryness in her tone that hinted at the great burden she carried, and even Haruko remained silent, having no desire to give a trivial response.

After a long bath, they walked casually around the spacious inn, selecting picture postcards and buying mandarin oranges at a small shop where everything from canned goods to cosmetics was displayed. When they returned to the room, a fine, powdery snow was whirling outside their window once again. But the fact that the pale sun was still visible through the swirling snow amazed Akiye, who was unfamiliar with the snow country.

"Why, even though the sun is out, the snow is falling!"

Haruko replied from behind her, "That's right. Just as I said before. When you think the sun is out, the snow starts falling."

"That's not what I mean. The snow is falling, but the sun is still out."

"It's only the wind blowing the falling snow around."

"I wonder if that's all it is."

More than wind blown, the snow was indeed falling, even as the pale sun shone on. And the mountains opposite gleamed with its reflected brilliance. In the air before the women, the snow was whirling thick and fast. Then, as they watched, the sun vanished abruptly, the snowfall became heavier, and the whole area was enclosed in a sheet of white, as though a thin silk curtain had been drawn across it.

Akiye remained standing by the window. She recalled the previous night's conversation about how, here in this inn, Haruko had engaged in a violent confrontation with her husband, and smiled to herself. The snow, which looked as though it was dancing lightly, was actually falling quite fast. It seemed to be hurrying with all its might to weave the figured cloth of silk, and gazing at it, she felt a soundless, exhilarating rhythm somewhere in her heart. She, too, thought that her desire to see the snow had been inspired. Not in the way Shigeko had meant, however. Rather, the words that she herself had spoken had acted as a kind of suggestion that she examine her own heart. The snow, while whirling round and round, was drifting down. Might her own life up to this time have been just that way? Would not her daughters, too, be going off on their own soon? Such thoughts flitted through Akiye's mind. Far from being sorrowful, the exhilaration evoked by the rhythm of the falling snow was bracing, refreshing.

"You'll catch cold, standing there after your bath," one of her companions sitting at the the *kotatsu* said.

"Yes, I'm certainly beginning to feel chilly." Obediently, Akiye joined the others in the warmth of the *kotatsu,* and they began to peel oranges in unison.

"Now Shigeko is going to tell her story," Haruko said.

"That's right. Last night we left it in reserve, didn't we?"

Saying, "Oh, really now, it isn't anything," Shigeko assumed a sober expression.

Noticing this, Haruko said, "I can't believe any such thing could have happened, since your husband is so very nice."

"You wouldn't think so," Shigeko agreed. Akiye understood what Haruko meant also, for Yoshizawa, Shigeko's husband, had a quiet, friendly nature, and the couple's warm relationship was beautiful to see. Since they had no children, they tried to keep one another company, and so whenever Akiye or Haruko went to Shigeko's home her husband joined them.

Shigeko herself agreed with the objective view that they were a devoted couple. "Now, he is a good, almost wonderful husband. I don't say that lightly. Just the same, there was a time when he did something that hurt me deeply. Once I had a pet cocker spaniel. I doted on it since it was a puppy, but I was shocked to find out that the puppy's mother belonged to a woman who had had a long affair with my husband."

When Yoshizawa first came home holding the puppy, Shigeko had exclaimed and taken it from her husband's arms and hugged it. Its broad ears were almost too much for its head to bear, and it wore a placid expression. Its soft, pale brown fur had a sweet smell, as if it had been sprinkled with lotion. When Shigeko eagerly asked where he had gotten it, her husband replied that an associate had given it to him. From the beginning, Shigeko was enslaved by the puppy's lovable ways, and she had no suspicions at all. From that time on, the puppy became the household's center of attention, and when her husband came home from work every day, Shigeko would report on the behavior of the puppy—which they had named Marie—before they talked of anything else. Noticing that the dog's long ears were a nuisance, flopping into her saucer, Shigeko tied them on top of her head with a ribbon. Whenever she was anxious about the dog, she would take her to the veterinarian. Marie was soon irreplaceably dear to Shigeko. Thinking that her husband felt the same way and chattering to him with cheerful affection about Marie's lovable and funny ways, she even felt she had found a new happiness.

And then one day everything became clear. "When I found that Marie was the puppy of one of the woman's dogs, I felt unspeakably bad. All that time when I had been thinking about how adorable she was, my husband had been looking on with an innocent expression. I was confused about my feelings toward Marie, and of course, a dog can't be expected to understand. But I couldn't control the way I felt, and ended up by making myself sick over it." There was pain on Shigeko's face as she remembered how she would pick Marie up to hug her, then let go of her with a surge of resentment, only to instantly regret her harshness and pick her up again.

To pursue the story a bit further, Haruko inquired, "What finally happened to the dog?"

"There was nothing we could do. We couldn't just give her away. After the truth came out, she lived with us for another five years before she got sick and died. Now my husband is fine, and I sometimes think it's all due to that experience. However, people are like that; even someone like him does cruel things sometimes."

"It was a good thing it was only a dog," said Haruko with a third party's detachment. "Oh, I'm sorry," she broke off abruptly, as the indignant glance Shigeko darted at her seemed like a strong rebuke, for certainly that wasn't the point of the story.

Akiye, too, thought the story sounded distressing. She felt she had to agree with Shigeko's remark about the way people are; yet, perhaps because she knew Yoshizawa, she could not bring herself to censure him. If her own husband, Tamiya, had still been alive, she, too, might have had a similar experience by now. Akiye did not reject the notion; she had no conviction that her family would have been any exception, for during this time Akiye had been searching her own heart and asking such questions of herself. Her own experience as a woman without a husband had made her capable of understanding the feelings of others. Her husband's death had been her turbulent time. Moreover, hidden away inside her was something the whole bitterness of which she alone knew. And she alone knew how incapable she was of coping with it.

But it had happened only in her imagination, she now decided, not without a certain melancholy. Looking at the experience more objectively, she could see that it had been a sentimental wavering of the heart. It might in fact be good to talk about it, but what would Shigeko or Haruko say if she were to mention it?

The maid inquired when they would like to have their evening meal, and they decided to spend the time until it came by soaking in the bath. Even now, the snow continued to fall; and whenever the wind rose, the snow swirled about confusedly, only to fall back down. Outdoors, in the gathering dusk, the landscape was engulfed in white.

They would be leaving the following morning. The three of them talked about the fact that they had come so far for such a short stay, but it had been worth it just to see the snow. For Haruko, moreover, it had been a place of deep associations, and Shigeko maintained that coming so far had freed her feelings and made it possible for her to reveal her personal secret. The experience had brought them all closer together. Therefore, Akiye felt that it was now her turn to speak.

For someone of Akiye's temperament such a thought would normally be troubling, but that was not so now, perhaps because of the snowy inn's beguiling atmosphere. Akiye began speaking, deliberately making the pretense that she had had too much to drink. "You two, what would you think if I told you that something had happened after Tamiya died?"

"That's what I was thinking," said Haruko, her face suddenly serious. Shigeko also seemed surprised, but Akiye thought it all mildly amusing.

"Never mind, there's really nothing to tell. Anyway I'm too much of a coward."

"Well, you had your children to take care of. It must have been hard, but you did very well in raising them. And that's quite an accomplishment."

"That may be so," continued Akiye, "but when we were talking this afternoon, Shigeko said 'people are like that,' and I agreed with her. It's strange. I could say that the whole thing proved there was something of the woman left in me, but even so, what I have to tell you is odd. For my moment of emotional weakness happened not just a while after my husband died, but right afterward."

The expressions on the faces of the two listeners showed that they did not fully grasp what Ayike meant.

As Akiye had said, her emotional crisis had occurred immediately after her husband's death. It was due to the vagaries of the human heart, for it happened when she still seemed to feel her husband's warmth clinging to her own skin. Tamiya had died in an accident at work. It had been a sudden and bitter loss for Akiye and her children; but in spite of this, because he had died on the job, Akiye had to conduct legal negotiations with her husband's firm. To do so, she consulted frequently with a young lawyer. Although the relationship involved nothing more than official business, Akiye began to enjoy meeting with him. She was thirty-three at that time, the lawyer perhaps a bit younger. And even while she was talking about her dead husband, Akiye's heart had begun softening toward her partner in these consultations. Having suddenly lost her husband, she found her spirit was foundering in a frightful helplessness rather than in grief, and she sought reassurance in the lawyer as an advisor. Even so, she had not forgotten her husband. One might say that Akiye, while bitterly longing for her late husband, was reaching out for the physical presence of a man.

"He, too, was aware of me in that way. You see, there was one day during the summer rains...We had gone for the umpteenth time to the company to negotiate, and on our way back we walked all the way along the palace moat from Hibiya clear to Kudan." Akiye said this, but it seemed as if she were speaking of someone else.

In her mind's eye Haruko could picture the figures of the two of them walking under the fresh green leaves of the willows on the embankment as the rain fell softly on them, and it made her own eyes shine. "My, how splendid. But what were you talking about?"

"I don't remember. I suppose it must have been the negotiations." Akiye evaded the question, but she was smilng to herself as she recollected the way in which her gently yielding form and expression had been overflowing with a woman's coquetry.

"If anything had happened, I would have been in a strange situation, you know, because it was right after my husband's death."

"Nothing came of it then?"

"Well, I doubt if my own self-control could have been counted on. But he was a gentleman. And thanks to that, there was nothing for me to apologize to my late husband's memory for. At any rate, this much is true. It was really my husband I loved."

"Human nature is really strange," responded Shigeko, showing by the way she was nodding her head that she understood very well. She went on to say, "It was a reflection of your love for the dead man," and this was probably quite true.

Smiling, Akiye spoke in a different tone. "Yes. Well, very recently I ran into him in Shibuya. We merely greeted one another with the usual commonplaces and then parted, but at the time I happened to be rather dressed up. And after we had gone our separate ways, I couldn't help thinking that it was a good thing that I had been looking my best that day. That's a woman's reaction for you. I still have these feelings." Akiye laughed, amused at herself. Outside there was the sound of wind. She got up, went to the window, and opened it. The cold air struck her face sharply. Looking out into the darkness she could see that the snow was still falling, and the landscape was covered by a pale whiteness.

Inwardly Akiye spoke the words "Dance, snow!" The next day they would return to Tokyo and to the frantic bustle of everyday affairs, but here she had found a steadying rhythm. Had coming all this way meant nothing at all? No, one couldn't say that. She consigned her reluctance to reveal herself completely to her friends to that snow, blown by the wind and swirling down, and once again murmured, "Dance, snow, dance!" in the depths of her heart.

The End of Summer
(Natsu no owari)
KURAHASHI YUMIKO

Our resolve had not changed. K must be transformed by our own hands into a heavy, dead lump. Just as we had jointly possessed K as a lover, my sister and I were completely united in this *idée* also. Since this affair had invaded our lives, it had been festering like the wound from a noxious cactus spine under the skin. We were confident that one day in the course of this summer we would cram K into the maw of death. We had only to decide upon the method and the time to seize our chance. My sister and I had so thoroughly gone over the fine points of our various schemes that we took great pleasure in savoring the nuances of each one on our tongues.

This summer I had reached my nineteenth birthday at our detached villa on a certain cape. The many summers previously spent here had been buried intact in my girlhood, completely closed buds that had never opened. Those had been rather satisfying childish summers. But on the day we arrived I had a premonition that this year would be different. I recall seeing the burgeoning image of some frightful thing when I looked down at the sea from the veranda. The glare of the sky above the ocean had yawned open like the crimson flesh inside of fruit. And I didn't know how it might be made to close. Shudders of horror and joy shook my body. The two of us were still as carefree as liberated children. Last summer mother had died at this villa. The dead could spread no protective wings above us. Thus this summer would belong to us alone.

The cape commanded the entrance to a bay. The inner side of this, a sandy beach, embraced the bay, describing a gentle arc. The seaward side was a rough shore of crags and cliffs. Since the villa stood on the brow of the cape we could climb down in barely five minutes either to the cheerful sandy beach or to the turbulent ocean shore. On the day we arrived, we told the caretaker to prepare a late lunch for us and immediately scrambled down to the bathing beach with feverish haste. Light green waves stroked the sand languidly.

Once we neared the sea, the pungent smell of saltwater invigorated us. The bare skin of the bathers refracted violent colors as if sprinkled with gleaming crystals. My sister wanted to have a beer. She was sixteen years old and very much like me. People thought of us as twins, and we made a habit of acting as if we were. The rest-house managed by S railroad company caught my eye. In its shop scantily clad men and women mingled. At our table, a young man was eating soft ice cream. Eyeing his wet hair, his down-covered chest, and his nicely shaped aristocratic calves, I felt expansive and giddy. I felt a stimulating sexual excitement. When he had completely devoured the soft ice cream with the thoroughness of a dog or a robot, I smiled unconsciously. My sister poked me in the thigh with her finger. He reacted to my smile with a startled frown, then asked me if he hadn't seen me somewhere. I yielded to this natural but clumsy overture. Perhaps he had. Since he and I were at the same university, though in different departments, it was entirely possible. Thus we engaged in desultory conversation, K drinking the beer we offered him and I leaning on both elbows and clasping and unclasping my now dry fingers. Then my sister and I stood up, smiled identical smiles, told K where we were staying, and left. We were hungry and, with our stomachs in knots, joined hands and scrambled up the cape through the rocks and pines, heading for the villa, where a meal of fresh fish and shellfish awaited us.

My sister asked what he had said his name was.

I answered with the initial K. This abbreviated, symbolic way of naming him amused my sister. I was rather pleased with it myself. We decided to go on referring to him that way. The caretaker talked about our mother and her death as he set the table, while we ate on intently behind a bright screen of indifference. The caretaker commented on how close the two of us were. Next he observed that this had not been particularly so when we were children. I casually agreed to the truth of this. My sister suddenly ran over to her suitcase and took out a Charlie Parker album. Soon a haze of mounting sound spiraled around us. When we had finished eating lunch, we went upstairs and complained about the caretaker. Although he looked young for his age, he was approaching sixty. My sister remarked that he seemed kind on the surface, but when you chewed on his remarks, they oozed like the insides of a snake.

No one knew any more about him than that he had resettled from a former colony, but he was probably a man who had seen something of the underworld in his younger days. My sister clapped her hands sharply and said that at some time or other he had lost the tip of his little finger. I said that it was past history and we shouldn't bother about him, and my sister agreed. Tired, we sat down in the rattan chairs, stretching out our legs and tickling one another's feet while we waited for the sea to lose its glare.

This K...my sister said. Will he really come tomorrow? He will, I said casually, but with no special basis for the prediction. Then I asked her if she would like to have him as a tutor. Fine, she said, if K agrees.

Early the next morning K came. Torn from our rest, we met him in the morning's glare. My sister complained that he had disturbed us, but soon we were all joking and laughing uncontrollably. While the two of us ate our breakfast, K smoked, enjoying a modern jazz L.P. that we had brought with us, and then drank some chilled apple cider. I felt strangely jealous of his beautiful profile. Soon this feeling was transformed into the desire to possess him in his present sharply defined form. We climbed down to the ocean shore where the sea had violently eaten notches in the rocks. I said that I wanted to go swimming. K remarked that he could swim but...He understood the waves were violent here and that there were a lot of stinging jellyfish. Large and small rocks appeared and disappeared in the surges like stepping stones, and a huge table rock poked out of the waves. I suggested we go out to it. Heading that way, we scrambled toward the big rock, which resembled a cockscomb, the slimy surfaces and churning, howling, waves tormenting us all the way; the perfect level and depth of the ocean stretched out before us as we went. The surface of the ocean undulated, pregnant with a deep blackness, and castles of metallic cumulonimbus clouds soared above the horizon. The sharp contrast these made to the overbright sun made me shiver. My sister's lips had lost their color; her toes gripped the rocks tightly, making her seem like a bird. I called out buoyantly, pointing to the outline of a ship rising and falling out on the open sea. With its thick, chocolate color, it looked like a child's toy that could be picked up and played with in the palm of the hand. When the thundering of the waves subsided, I asked K if he would take on the job of tutoring my sister. He replied that he would be happy to. When I suggested we negotiate about it, he said that since he didn't have the money to pay for a summer at the ocean, he would be grateful if we could put him up at our place. I answered that nothing could be simpler. And we gazed at the sea in silence. My sister said that she felt sick to her stomach. Holding hands, we began to retrace our steps over the treacherous rocks to the shore. Just then, a high shriek, like someone falling to her death, rang out. My sister had lost her footing. Caught between two rocks she was engulfed by the foam. The blood drained from her face. K caught her in his arms and carried her up to the gravelly beach out of reach of the waves. With a pale smile she said that the sea made her sick. I asked if she was hurt, but she said no. K told her to look up, and smoothed her hair back from her face, using his fingers as a comb. When he put his arm around her, I assured myself that she would feel warm with him holding her—I would feel that way if it were I being held in his arms. My sister had discovered the meaning of the word love from her first contact with K's arms, and I guess I did the same. We returned to the villa right away, K carrying my sister on his back and I in high spirits.

That afternoon my sister took a sedative and went to sleep. When the caretaker left to buy food at a fishing village two kilometers away, I decided to go swimming with K. In the room K took off his brick-colored polo shirt as if he were peeling a banana. Then I too changed my clothes. I realized then that I wanted to fall in love with K. I don't know whether it was for the sake of reconciling my existence with the world around me or for the sake of making a wound through which to drain away the disappointments of life. I suggested to K that we get completely undressed. His teeth showed in a smile of agreement. Leaving my polo shirt on, I took off my shorts and tossed them aside, and when K pinned me down from behind, deftly stripping off the rest of my clothes, I was naked. We fell on the bed and began caressing one another as wordlessly as if we were actually following a course of action planned in advance. The pain soon drifted away...We sat up on the bed again, nose to nose, so that we could gaze into one another's burning eyes for a while, and then we put on our swimsuits and ran to the beach. I ran chasing after K, laughter dripping from my eyes and mouth. I reached the surf, breathless, and held fast to K's shoulders. Telling him that his body looked as though if I were to bite him the sap of a rubber tree would come out, I nibbled at his skin. Arms linked, we staggered into the water, flinging our bodies against the ramparts of the advancing waves.

For a number of days after that K and I were absorbed in solidifying our love as if we were carving a totem pole. Without saying a word he would apply himself to the task. When we began to try to put our situation into words, they had the quality of the dialogue of a classical play and were attended by symbolic gestures in this mid-summer setting that reigned over the rocks and sun. K, the star performer, had no talent or taste for self-expression. K and I acted before my sister as a pair of lovers in joint possession of the image of love. She was still forbidden to swim because of her physical condition, and presumably for the same reason she would watch us languidly with only her eyes standing out from a weakly smiling mask. At night we sandwiched K between us and stretched out our listless bodies on the veranda. My sister would savor K's and my love like merchandise. On one particular day she turned to me, licking her lips with the tip of her tongue in an innocent way. Is K kind to you, she asked. Yes he is, I answered. How do you and K make love, she continued. What do you mean, how, K laughed, and she asked again in a completely toneless voice. I remarked that she shouldn't ask him that kind of thing (you had to ask K for yes or no answers. I was used to this), and stretching out my fingers I grasped K's arms. Then K and I performed our embraces and caresses. I was pleased that K responded not as an accomplice but as a well-trained co-actor. My sister said she wanted to have a turn. And when I moved, creating an empty space, she completely inserted herself with her arms and breast into the chair K was using. K's arms enfolded her as naturally as the branches of a carnivorous plant, and I watched them meet face to face, bringing their lips together. When my sister offered her lips to be sucked, she slightly exposed the moist, gleaming darkness inside her mouth. I looked at her thrown back head, with its closed eyes and teeth shining like knives inside her mouth. My attitude was tolerant even to serenity: It was my desire to achieve a balance between the external and internal aspects of the performance. And they too, as if ministering to my desires, succeeded in making flesh and feeling balance against each other—just as it was with K and me.

As she recovered her physical health, my sister appeared to free herself from her initial fear of the sea. The two of us passed the greater part of each day by the sea in K's company. Washed by the water, we played, our bare, slippery bodies resembling fish. One cloudy afternoon, after we had taken a motorboat out on the ocean, the wind rose, and we shut ourselves up in the villa. I dozed off, listening to the sound of the rain in the trees. When I opened my eyes again, the rain had veiled the ocean with white smoke. I went upstairs. My sister had said she would be studying trigonometry with K. Her room was quiet. All I could hear was the sound of rain. I knocked. A muffled voice told me to wait. I waited a rather long time. When I finally entered the room, I saw K and my sister stretched out together on the bed. My sister burst out laughing and said, I borrowed K. I also laughed at my sister's use of the initial K in front of him. Asking, how was he—K, I made it a threesome. I felt no jealousy. You might say that I couldn't discover any of its poisonous fangs or dangerous slivers lodged in my emotions. In place of these was the necessity for a slight alteration in the notion of possession. Not a monopoly, but a graceful joint ownership. When K got out of bed, he said that he was hungry. Giving him a kiss, I cheerfully invited the two of them for a snack. The rain came down even harder. As we sat at the round dining table, the three of us exchanged soft glances.

None of us were about to sully our triangular relationship with embarrassing innuendos and none of us descended to that level. I derived a pleasurable pain and a certain feeling of legitimacy from this relationship of mutual possession. You might even say that I and my sister, who was like me, were not susceptible to the corrupting influence of jealousy. In the night, after K had gone down to his room to sleep, we exchanged opinions about our joint possession of love, especially in its outward manifestations. We looked at the skin of the human being, ignoring the bowels and bodily fluids, failing to recognize the fragile, unstable union that made up the jointly owned being whom we called our love. That was because we were not possessed by the disease of self-absorption. If my eyes had been devouring my own insides, the relationship to another person that we call love would have been completely swallowed up by the emptiness within me in an instant. However, protected by our pliant flesh, we believed in the healthiness of our existence. Love must not have the quality of a gaping pit. Such was our love for K, who was a plaything in our hands. This was something that resembled sport. We talked together about performing all kinds of acts with K, made comparisons, and examined them. And either one of us, but sometimes both of us, tried out our theories on K. He became the subject of investigation, the chemistry of passion translated into the dynamics of the flesh. Since our close resemblance made us completely in union in physical appearance, we thought that the act of possessing K in turn could be mutually explored. We considered that this kind of relationship would become more desirable the more we got used to it.

One day in August the seas got higher in the afternoon, and the wind began chasing the bilious clouds. Father, who had arrived on the previous day, had gone fishing with the caretaker at dawn. They still had not returned. My sister and I had a premonition that put us in a playful mood. It delighted us when the world showed its cruel nails. On my sister's suggestion we decided to go see K, who was staying at the fishing village while father was with us. A heavy rain beat down, and it took us almost half an hour to reach the village. This sad and gloomy place was made up of low, straggling wooden buildings. In front of the S railway station we spied a tawdry, country-style bar with a sign shaped like a ship and went in. Inside were a number of tourists who had taken refuge from the rain. My sister suddenly said that she wanted to see a movie. Why didn't I go by myself to see K? Don't you want to go, I asked. Rubbing her lips with the rim of her glass my sister said, me—I don't feel like going. Then fixing my eyelashes and pursing my lips in a smile, I went off to the inn where K was staying. He was sprawled on the bed in a room facing the harbor. Your sister didn't come, he asked, and I nodded. He took me in his arms. It's dark in here, isn't it, I said, shaking him off. More than anything else, the lack of light showed K as a lazy, lethargic youth. Probably I'm the same way too. He told me he wanted to go outside for a walk. Where, I said in the ill-tempered tone of a lover. He said he would walk me back to the villa, and took my arm in his damp hand. The wind and rain, although intermittent, were getting ferocious. A typhoon was on its way. When I mentioned that I had promised my sister that we would return together, he shook his head coldly. When we reached the cape, we kissed atop the rocks. K was drenched. We passed through the pine grove that surrounded the villa, but K continued walking along, clutching my hand. I said again that my sister and I had to return together, whereupon K stopped in his tracks and looked me in the eye. I don't want to go back, he said. Then for the first time I realized that something resembling uneasiness had tumbled into my secure existence. I looked at him quivering. His skin had begun to peel all over. Under the peeled patches I saw the dark, pitted underskin. Dropping all pretenses, I almost felt hatred toward him as he stood there like an ugly clod of earth. However, laughing insanely, I hung around his neck and dug my chin into his shoulder. He spoke in a hoarse voice. When he slept with my sister she always demanded to know if it was she he loved and not me. K always replied that he loved us both, but then she asked with whom he made love more often. In a high, level voice I said that it had all been a meaningless game from the beginning. K said that it wasn't so—at least as far as he was concerned. With an odd laugh, K said it couldn't go on as it was. I felt threatened. K asked what we should do. Still, which of us do you really love, I asked. Of course, this question had no special significance. In a wary tone, K answered that it was me he loved. I realized that an unbridgeable gap had opened in our concept of joint ownership. At that instant, I knew that I had better leave K. Still, we pressed our water-logged bodies together. Come tomorrow, I said, after the storm. When I had said this, I left K and ran to the house.

My father and the caretaker had not yet come back. I don't recall what I did until dark. It was past eight o'clock when my father returned. This put me in a bad mood, as though he had returned from the dead. Where is your sister, my father asked in a grating voice. I answered that she had gone to the village to see a movie. Father's mood went from bad to worse. Then there was a blackout. My sister returned an hour later. K, who had brought her home, was standing in the doorway. He left, and father assumed a grim expression. I don't want you mixed up with that guy, he said. My sister murmured that this must be the caretaker's big mouth. Father came toward us, and we widened our eyes as if we were being persecuted. You two, my father shouted, you might as well have killed your mother. And he pronounced his verdict. All right, tomorrow you're leaving here with me. We were silent. We had agreed to be silent in such cases.

The following day the sky was a sparkling blue vault. My father, in a falsely good mood, laughed a lot and passed the morning with us at the beach. He left for Tokyo without us. After it was dark, K arrived, looking uneasy. I suggested to my sister that we draw lots to see who got to sleep with K. I drew up the lots. And my sister won.

My sister and I felt no strain on our relationship. Although a foreign body had intervened in the presence of our joint property, K, that did not change our relationship. You might say, to borrow K's words, that we had not lost the flawless symmetry of two casts from the same mold. And if it was I whom K loved—and I didn't entirely believe that—it was nothing more than sheer chance. It was true that at first K had loved only me. However, K had begun to break down. Therefore, in our love, which placed a premium on shared ownership, he had bit by bit begun to lose substance. One day while we were walking to the beach, we searched for the site of mother's death. We soon found the rock, and looking at it again made me feel that I was seeing the almost unbelievable thing that had happened last summer in slow-motion flashback. Mother had called out to us in a sudden panic and fallen off the rock. She never got up again. We had gazed at her endlessly, the waves lapping at our legs. Now this same rock was separated from the beach by high tide. We looked at one another and smiled. I believe that this was the moment that we hit upon the *idée* of death. Have you ever thought about K's dying, I said to my sister. Sometimes people try to assert total ownership by destroying their own property. However, K's death, the death of our love, rather than meaning destruction or loss, was the one transformation necessary to make our possession of him eternal. He would be changed into a tombstone on top of the sand, whereupon we would be able to have joint ownership of the then bleached bones of our love made into a fixed *objet* outside of ourselves. The two of us, arms wrapped around our knees, would discuss the thought of K in this new mode of joint possession. And now, under the midsummer sunshine, love truly resembled death.

August moved toward its end; while squandering its store of sunshine it relentlessly approached the death of our love like a brain draining of its blood. Even so, the game suddenly bore an inconvenient fruit. A love on the verge of death gave birth to life. When my period was a week late, I realized I was pregnant. Conception and pregnancy, these were inadmissible foreign substances to me; the image they called to mind was nothing more than a carcinoma or a cancerous cell. Humiliation was the only word to excise it, to defeat it. I did not at all feel like sharing this humiliation with my sister. One evening when my sister and I were with K, I inquired what they would think if I were pregnant. K laughed and shrugged his shoulders. My sister's fingers seemed to stiffen on her fork. However, I'm not sure of that. I'm just kidding, I said. That kind of problem—pregnancy and childbirth—was completely despicable, and the thought of marriage in this empire of sun-scorched sea and rock was more than anything else a tawdry comedy. Late that evening, K knocked on the door of my room. He demanded to know if I were really pregnant, and without waiting for an answer said that the child should be born and raised. Me give birth? Feeling that I had been pursued to the very jaws of a trap, I yelled, I'll never give birth to a child! I explained my feelings about pregnancy to K. As I talked, I felt ashamed of even discussing such a stupid thing. K restrained me, saying that he wanted to talk this over thoroughly later. I said that would be useless. If anybody got pregnant, it would be my sister, not me. Whereupon K declared that wasn't possible. He had taken precautions against pregnancy when making love to her. I said I didn't believe him. K went on with his explanation. The difference between his love for me and for my sister was the difference between the real thing and a copy. Well, even if that were so, I said that was no reason why I had to give birth to and raise K's child.

Even then the thought that inside my body a being that was not mine was eating up time and swelling ever larger filled me with nausea. The only idea that could counteract that nausea was that of K's death. The conviction I had had when I had first repudiated the world, that at least I was alive and healthy, had changed before I knew it into a dark, corrupt fruit within my vitals. I desired the caretaker's death, my father's death, and even my sister's death.

Only a great number of deaths were worthy of the sea, lapping at the sand like a mollusk.

After our usual late breakfast of prawns, crabs, and sea plants, the three of us sat around in idle silence. K oiled our arms and legs with the palms of his hand, and when we giggled, he, too, started to giggle like a child. It seemed as if the previous jointly shared love relationship that my sister and I had perfected was being revived. Nevertheless, what we were jointly sharing at this moment was the notion of K's death. While playing mahjong with the caretaker, we discussed murderers' strategems as though fired with a mania for detective fiction. Everyone was in a good mood. After that we listened to a Modern Jazz Quartet album. We sat around waiting for the end of summer, so that in enduring it something else could be consumed by the scorching winds of August. Suddenly my sister stood up. K and I got up, too, and the sun, which was already blocked by the shadow of the cape, sank down toward the beach. There were few people on the beach, and the waves seemed terribly cold. The ocean, however, was extremely calm. We swam for the open sea. When the sun's governing light had been withdrawn from the land, we could not help swimming toward it. Passing the break-water, we rounded the cape, and I could feel the cold tidal current. Then my sister and I, who were swimming abreast, exchanged glances, and I made up my mind with a sudden action. Grabbing K around the neck, I kissed him. My sister did, too. We laughed as we caught hold of K and bobbed in the water, but this playfulness was gradually infused with the features of death. Heavy layers of water on arms and legs, a funnel-shaped hole opening beneath him, and his heart pressing against his chest were the heralds of the approach of death. K's death in reality surpassed anything that I had imagined. I lost sight of K amid the foam. My sister, too, disappeared from view.

There's not much left to say. In order to survive, I rounded the cape and swam on and on; beyond was neither hope nor despair. People spent the night searching for my sister. I didn't mention K's death to anyone. Probably only the caretaker has his suspicions about what happened. The following day I found out that I was not pregnant. After a few days I left the coast.

Summer had ended. I now waited for my summer, which had strangled itself with its own hands, to turn into a stiffened corpse.

Victoria Vernon is Assistant Professor at Hamilton College in Clinton, New York, where she is a member of the Department of Comparative Literature and the Committee on Asian Studies. Ms. Vernon received her Ph.D. from the University of California, Berkeley, in 1981. She is the author of forthcoming articles on the image of modern Japanese women and on modern Japanese women writers.

Index

Fujiwara clan: marriage politics,
21; Fujiwara Shunzei, 25;
Fujiwara Teika, 25
Fukuzawa, Yukichi, 31
Futabatei, Shimei, 38, 42, 61

Genroku period (1688–1704),
29, 30, 37, 66, 144, 145
gesaku (popular prose fiction of
Edo period), 19, 26, 41, 64,
75
Gilbert, Sandra M. (*The Madwoman in the Attic: The
Woman Writer and the
Nineteenth-Century Literary
Imagination*), 8, 17n
giri (duty or responsibility), 145,
191, 200
Gubar, Susan (*The Madwoman
in the Attic: The Woman
Writer and the Nineteenth-
Century Literary Imagination*),
8, 17n

Haga, Noboru, 39
haikai (seventeen-syllable poetry
later termed *haiku*), 26, 29
Halliday, Jon (*A Political History
of Japanese Capitalism*), 72
Hane, Mikiso (*Peasants, Rebels
and Outcasts: The Underside
of Modern Japan*), 65, 144n,
209
Harper, Thomas (*Motoori
Norinaga's Criticism of the
Genji Monogatari*), 24
Harukoma, 209, 210, 214
Hasegawa, Hiroshi, 74

Hayama, Yoshio, 73
Hayashi, Fumiko, 13, 14, 73n,
138–141, 143, 144, 148–158,
168, 169, 171, 172, 208, 209;
"Bangiku" (Late
Chrysanthemum), 150,
154–156, 168, 169, 197, 198,
202; *Cha-iro no me*, 150, 151,
155–158; "Fubiki," 150, 151,
154; "Hōrōki," 148, 149;
"Inazuma," 149; "Shitama-
chi" (Tokyo), 150, 152, 201,
210; *Ukigumo*, 148, 150,
152–154, 194, 195; *Uzushio*,
150, 152, 154, 199
Heian women (prose writers
and their context), 5–7,
18–24, 30, 141, 195, 196,
202, 203, 207, 214
Heian-Kyō, 20, 21
Higuchi, Ichiyō, 10, 12, 14, 30,
31, 35–68, 69, 70, 71, 72,
74–77, 104, 107, 141, 143,
199, 201, 207, 211;
"Jūsan'ya," 65, 201;
"Nigorie," 42, 65, 201;
"Takekurabe," 12, 40–42,
44–66, 70, 74–77, 85, 86, 92,
143, 174, 194, 199, 201, 210
Hirabayashi, Taiko, 31, 73n,
149, 211
Hiratsuka, Raicho, 38–40,
42–44, 65–67, 74, 211. See
also *Seitō*
Hosoi, Wakizō, 73

ie (family or extended family
structure), 26–28, 65, 133,

INSTITUTE OF EAST ASIAN STUDIES PUBLICATIONS SERIES

CHINA RESEARCH MONOGRAPHS (CRM)

6. David D. Barrett. *Dixie Mission: The United States Army Observer Group in Yenan, 1944,* 1970 ($4.00)
15. Joyce K. Kallgren, Editor. *The People's Republic of China after Thirty Years: An Overview,* 1979 ($5.00)
16. Tong-eng Wang. *Economic Policies and Price Stability in China,* 1980 ($8.00)
17. Frederic Wakeman, Jr., Editor. *Ming and Qing Historical Studies in the People's Republic of China,* 1981 ($10.00)
18. Robert E. Bedeski. *State-Building in Modern China: The Kuomintang in the Prewar Period,* 1981 ($8.00)
21. James H. Cole. *The People Versus the Taipings: Bao Lisheng's "Righteous Army of Dongan,"* 1981 ($7.00)
22. Dan C. Sanford. *The Future Association of Taiwan with the People's Republic of China,* 1982 ($8.00)
23. A. James Gregor with Maria Hsia Chang and Andrew B. Zimmerman. *Ideology and Development: Sun Yat-sen and the Economic History of Taiwan,* 1982 ($8.00)
24. Pao-min Chang. *Beijing, Hanoi, and the Overseas Chinese,* 1982 ($7.00)
sp. Lucie Cheng, Charlotte Furth, and Hon-ming Yip, Editors. *Women in China: Bibliography of Available English Language Materials,* 1984 ($12.00)
27. John N. Hart. *The Making of an Army "Old China Hand": A Memoir of Colonel David D. Barrett,* 1985 ($12.00)
28. Steven A. Leibo. *Transferring Technology to China: Prosper Giquel and the Self-strengthening Movement,* 1985 ($15.00)
29. David Bachman. *Chen Yun and the Chinese Political System,* 1985 ($15.00)
30. Maria Hsia Chang. *The Chinese Blue Shirt Society: Fascism and Developmental Nationalism,* 1985 ($15.00)
31. Robert Y. Eng. *Economic Imperialism in China: Silk Production and Exports, 1861–1932,* 1986 ($15.00)
32. Judith M. Boltz. *A Survey of Taoist Literature, Tenth to Seventeenth Centuries,* 1987 ($20.00)

KOREA RESEARCH MONOGRAPHS (KRM)

5. William Shaw. *Legal Norms in a Confucian State,* 1981 ($10.00)
6. Youngil Lim. *Government Policy and Private Enterprise: Korean Experience in Industrialization,* 1982 ($8.00)
7. Q. Y. Kim. *The Fall of Syngman Rhee,* 1983 ($12.00)
8. Robert A. Scalapino and Jun-yop Kim, Editors. *North Korea Today: Strategic and Domestic Issues,* 1983 ($20.00)
9. Helen Hardacre. *The Religion of Japan's Korean Minority: The Preservation of Ethnic Identity,* 1985 ($12.00)
10. Fred C. Bohm and Robert R. Swartout, Jr., Editors. *Naval Surgeon in Yi Korea: The Journal of George W. Woods,* 1984 ($12.00)
11. Robert A. Scalapino and Hongkoo Lee, Editors. *North Korea in a Regional and Global Context,* 1986 ($20.00)
12. Laurel Kendall and Griffin Dix, Editors. *Religion and Ritual in Korean Society,* 1987 ($15.00)

JAPAN RESEARCH MONOGRAPHS (JRM)

2. James W. White. *Migration in Metropolitan Japan: Social Change and Political Behavior,* 1983 ($12.00)
3. James Cahill. *Sakaki Hyakusen and Early Nanga Painting,* 1983 ($10.00)
4. Steven D. Carter. *Three Poets at Yuyama,* 1983 ($12.00)
5. Robert A. Scalapino. *The Early Japanese Labor Movement: Labor and Politics in a Developing Society,* 1984 ($20.00)
6. Masumi Junnosuke. *Postwar Politics in Japan, 1945–1955,* 1985 ($25.00)
7. Teruo Gotoda. *The Local Politics of Kyoto,* 1985 ($15.00)